Catholic Social Te
Market Economy

Catholic Social Teaching and the Market Economy

PHILIP BOOTH

WITH CONTRIBUTIONS FROM

SAMUEL GREGG

ROBERT KENNEDY

DENIS O'BRIEN

DENNIS O'KEEFFE

ANTHONY PERCY

ROBERT A. SIRICO

THOMAS WOODS

ANDREW YUENGERT

The Institute of Economic Affairs

First published in Great Britain in 2007 by
The Institute of Economic Affairs
2 Lord North Street
Westminster
London SW1P 3LB
in association with Profile Books Ltd

The mission of the Institute of Economic Affairs is to improve public understanding of the fundamental institutions of a free society, by analysing and expounding the role of markets in solving economic and social problems.

A CIP catalogue record for this book is available from the British Library.

Paperback ISBN 978 0 255 36581 9
Hardback ISBN 978 0 255 36609 0

Many IEA publications are translated into languages other than English or are reprinted. Permission to translate or to reprint should be sought from the Director General at the address above.

Typeset in Stone by MacGuru Ltd
info@macguru.org.uk

Printed and bound in Great Britain by Hobbs the Printers

CONTENTS

PART THREE: SUBSIDIARITY AND SOLIDARITY – THE ROLE OF THE INDIVIDUAL, THE COMMUNITY AND THE STATE

THE AUTHORS

Philip Booth

Philip Booth is Editorial and Programme Director at the Institute of Economic Affairs and Professor of Insurance and Risk Management at the Sir John Cass Business School. He has an undergraduate degree in economics from the University of Durham and a PhD in Finance. He is a Fellow of the Institute of Actuaries and of the Royal Statistical Society. Previously, Philip Booth worked for the Bank of England as an adviser on financial stability issues. He has written widely, including a number of books, on investment, finance, social insurance and pensions, as well as on the relationship between Catholic Social Teaching and economics. He is editor of *Economic Affairs* and associate editor of the *Annals of Actuarial Science* and the *British Actuarial Journal*. Philip Booth is also a governor of his local Catholic secondary school, St Paul's Catholic College, Burgess Hill.

Samuel Gregg

Samuel Gregg has written and spoken extensively on moral questions in law, medicine and finance. He has a Doctor of Philosophy degree in moral philosophy from Oxford University and has authored several books, including *Morality, Law, and Public Policy* (2000), *On Ordered Liberty* (2003), *Ethics and Economics* (1999), *A Theory of Corruption* (2004), *Banking, Justice, and the Common Good* (2005), and *The Commercial Society* (2007). He also publishes in journals such as *Law and Investment Management, Oxford Analytica, Journal des Economistes et des Etudes*

Humaines, Economic Affairs, Evidence, Markets and Morality, and *Policy*, as well as newspapers including the *Wall Street Journal Europe*, the *Washington Times*, the *Australian Financial Review* and *Business Review Weekly*. He is Director of Research at the Acton Institute, an Adjunct Professor at the Pontifical Lateran University, a consultant for Oxford Analytica Ltd, and general editor of the Lexington Book Series *Studies in Ethics and Economics*. He was elected a Fellow of the Royal Historical Society in 2001, and a Member of the Mont Pèlerin Society in 2004.

Robert Kennedy

Robert Kennedy is a full professor and chair of the Department of Catholic Studies at the University of St Thomas (St Paul, Minnesota) and co-director of the University's Terrence J Murphy Institute for Catholic Thought, Law, and Public Policy. He also holds a joint appointment (as professor in the Department of Ethics and Business Law) in the College of Business, where he served as Chair of the Faculty in 2004/05. He received his PhD in medieval studies (with a concentration in philosophy and theology) from the University of Notre Dame, and also holds master's degrees in biblical criticism and business administration.

Denis O'Brien

D. P. O'Brien was educated at Douai School and University College, London. He was Professor of Economics at Durham from 1972 to 1997. Prior to that he taught at Queen's University, Belfast. His publications are mainly in the fields of industrial economics and the history of economic thought.

Dennis O'Keeffe

Dennis O'Keeffe was educated at St Benedict's School, Ealing, and at the universities of Durham and London. He is Professor of Social Science at the University of Buckingham and Senior Research Fellow in Education at the IEA. He has written widely in the area of education and social theory. He is also well known as a broadcaster and journalist. His latest work includes *Economy and Virtue*, a collection of essays for the IEA, and a translation for Liberty Fund of Benjamin Constant's *Principes de Politique*.

Anthony Percy

Father Anthony Percy is a priest of the Archdiocese of Canberra-Goulburn in Australia. He was ordained to the priesthood in 1990 and has served as an assistant priest, administrator and now parish priest in the archdiocese. He obtained his doctorate from the John Paul II Institute for Studies in Marriage and Family, in Washington, DC. He is author of *Theology of the Body Made Simple*. Father Percy also has a master's degree in Finance from the University of New South Wales.

Robert A. Sirico

Father Robert A. Sirico is president of the Acton Institute for the Study of Religion and Liberty. His writings on religious, political, economic and social matters are published in a variety of journals and he is often called upon by members of the broadcast media for statements regarding economics, civil rights and issues of religious concern. He is a member of the Mont Pèlerin Society, the American Academy of Religion and the Philadelphia Society. Father Sirico also served on the Michigan Civil Rights Commission from 1994 to 1998. He is also currently pastor of St Mary Catholic Church in Kalamazoo, Michigan. Father Sirico's pastoral ministry has included a chaplaincy to Aids patients at the National Institute of Health and the recent founding of a new community, St Philip Neri House, in Kalamazoo, Michigan.

Thomas Woods

Thomas E. Woods, Jr, is a senior fellow at the Ludwig von Mises Institute in Auburn, Alabama. His books include *How the Catholic Church Built Western Civilization, The Church Confronts Modernity* and *The Politically Incorrect Guide to American History*, a *New York Times* bestseller. He won first place in the 2006 Templeton Enterprise Awards for his book *The Church and the Market: A Catholic Defense of the Free Economy*.

Andrew Yuengert

Andrew Yuengert holds the John and Francis Duggan Chair of Business at Seaver College, Pepperdine University. Before coming to Pepperdine twelve years ago, he was a research economist at the Federal Reserve Bank of New York. He is the author of two recent books: *The Boundaries of Technique: Ordering Positive and Normative Concerns in Economic Research*, from Lexington Press, and *Inhabiting the Land: A Case for the Right to Migrate*, published by the Acton Institute.

FOREWORD:
CATHOLIC SOCIAL TEACHING – 'AS RADICAL AS
REALITY ITSELF'

Thirty years ago I was working on the remote East Coast of Sri Lanka in a joint Methodist–Jesuit project – perhaps the only one on the planet. One of our enterprises was to manufacture industrial starch. The Jesuits' secret formula meant that we beat the competition out of sight. But the government textile and paper manufacturers had their own cosy deals with other suppliers. So we had to rail-freight tonnes of our stuff across the country, and sell it to Muslim traders in the back streets of Colombo. We prospered, while the country suffered many of the ills associated with the suppression of the market. When the region was plunged into the horrors of race war, we went bust.

This book is a splendid attempt to bring the weight of Catholic Social Teaching to bear on this and many other harsh realities. It now seems obvious that an effective and competitive market contributes immeasurably to human well-being, especially for the world's poor. It was not always so. But that view, with many necessary qualifications, is the burden of the argument of *Centesimus annus*. It now seems clear that this epochal document is largely coherent with *Rerum novarum*. These are the great peaks of Catholic Social Teaching, and their shared vision appears ever more remarkable.

At the time of *Rerum novarum*, the Holy See found itself embattled by the modernism of the new great European States – Italy, Germany and the French Third Republic. Britain and America were no less problematic, but less pressing. Pope Leo kept his nerve, and answered the claims of modernity in its own language, but on the Church's own terms. Secular modernity gave us the catastrophic conflicts of the twentieth century, waged on the back of that unbridled state power against which *Rerum novarum* warned. That story needs to be retold, now that socialism has vanished and the world-wide significance of religion is daily more evident. A modern gloss on this extraordinary document might be that it is only in a free society that the Catholic Church can claim the space to be Herself.

Centesimus annus appeared in a world in which communism had collapsed and the shape of the future was unknown. Nearly two decades on, we find that the future which ensued bears remarkable resemblances to the past – a world of globalising prosperity, the erosion of Victorian values in the naughty nineties, when even the English decided to have fun – and a world armed to the teeth, both with weapons and with ideological prescriptions for their use.

Amongst its other contributions this book contains two modest proposals which will ruffle feathers in some places. The first of these is that Catholic education should be more ... well, *Catholic*. The second is that the busy scribblers of Eccleston Square should pay more attention to the fundamentals of Catholic Social Teaching when they formulate documents on today's vital topics, as for instance on taxation, the environment and the European Union. As a former busy scribbler of nearly twenty years' standing, I might say in our defence that it is sometimes difficult to resist the conventional wisdom of the day, especially when it comes in an authoritative package. The hardest thing is 'to be as radical as reality itself', as was remarked by Pope Leo's younger contemporary, V. I. Lenin. In that high calling these papers largely succeed.

One suggestion seems worthy of further study – that somehow the market cannot be held responsible for the ravening hedonism that is associated with it. Capitalism does come with its own culture. We once knew how to employ the moral disciplines of poverty in a world of scarcity. How do we now create the ethical framework that will serve a world of prosperity? Perhaps this is the question that arises most sharply from this volume, and makes it therefore doubly welcome.

REVEREND JOHN KENNEDY
Methodist minister, formerly Secretary for Church and Society at Churches Together in Britain and Ireland, and Secretary for Political Affairs of the Methodist Church

The views expressed in this monograph are, as in all IEA publications, those of the authors and not those of the Institute (which has no corporate view), its managing trustees, Academic Advisory Council Members or senior staff.

ACKNOWLEDGEMENTS

In the compilation of an edited book such as this one owes a great debt to many people, in particular to the authors. I would like to give special thanks to Dr Samuel Gregg of the Acton Institute, who has provided help and advice well beyond the call of duty as an author. I would also like to thank the anonymous referees who provided a number of helpful comments.

TABLES AND FIGURES

PREFACE

As Christianity spread across the Roman world, it was considered distinctive for its emphasis on compassion and on the dignity of human labour. After two thousand years, compassion and the dignity of human labour remain important to Catholic social thought.

Religious and lay Catholics continue to minister to peoples around the world. The twentieth century has, however, witnessed major new developments. One is the growth of the state in Western societies. The tendency of government to tax resources has made governments a favoured place to propose the expression of compassion. While there is continued private charity by ordinary individuals and by wealthier persons, there has been a redirection of means and ends in the political world.

Studies in the UK, Australia and the USA have described how the introduction of government unemployment and pension programmes earlier in the twentieth century contributed to the decline of the fraternal societies. The wide participation in the insurance programmes of the fraternal societies and associations represented a healthy level of member participation in administration and mutual aid. The government's introduction of universal coverage in order to aid a small minority not covered by fraternal insurance had the unintended consequence of devaluing important intermediate institutions and undermining subsidiarity. This consequence was warned against by the major Catholic fraternal and mutual organisations at that time.

In the USA, historical research has demonstrated the cohesion of the black family in the nineteenth and early twentieth centuries. Unemployment in the Great Depression was a strain on the black family. But legislation to relieve such strains sometimes had long-term negative effects. General minimum wage legislation meant there was no provision for lower rates for youths who did not have any work experience. The consequence was widespread youth unemployment, particularly in the black community, as young black people tended to have less education and thus commanded a lower wage than others. As the youth had no opportunity to gain work experience at an introductory wage rate, the black young men were condemned to general unemployment. This was an unintended consequence of a good intention.

Subsequent welfare legislation for women and children was dependent upon a man not being a member of the household. Since black men suffered unemployment owing to their not having gained introductory skills as youths, this attempt to assist women and children had the unintended consequence of undermining stable marriage. The exclusion due to legislation of black men from the dignity of labour has caused deep pathologies among the men and their families. The dignity of work for the disadvantaged has been a major casualty for them when legislation interferes with the improving process of the market economy.

Thus, many of the major advances in government social legislation have had the effect of unintentionally undermining the dignity of labour and of the family. It is a warning to us to be more careful in the application of compassion outside the decisions of individuals or intermediate groups in society. When the wealth and the power of government are applied the consequences, intended and unintended, can be heavy and ruinous. It can be the persons we most wish to help who can be injured by the compassion without intention.

The chapters in this book reflect this, and also reflect the insights of Pope John Paul II in the encyclical *Centesimus annus*[1] (Catechism, para. 2431):

---

[1] Papal encyclicals are named in Latin, with the name generally being based on an early expression in the document.

The activity of a market economy cannot be conducted in an institutional, juridical or political vacuum. On the contrary, it presupposes sure guarantees of individual freedom and private property, as well as a stable currency and efficient public services. Hence the principal task of the state is to guarantee this security, so that those who work and produce can enjoy the fruits of their labours and thus feel encouraged to work efficiently and honestly ...

Pope John Paul II's *Centesimus annus* was a celebration of the one hundredth anniversary of the encyclical of Pope Leo XIII, *Rerum novarum*. These two giants of the social doctrine of the Catholic Church deserve to be studied together.

The chapters in this book recognise the reality that the budgetary crises of the developed countries require the withdrawal of the state from many activities undertaken in the confusions of boundless expectations. The new realities mean a return to self-involvement of citizens in the affairs that affect their health, retirement, and so on. Of the many areas studied in this book, education may be the most important. It is the education of our children upon which the future of the economy and of the resources for the health and pensions of the older generation will depend. Yet the recognised shortcomings of the state education system, especially for the disadvantaged for whom it was especially introduced, seem the most difficult to resolve owing to entrenched structures.

Among the private initiatives in the 21st century will be increased attention to charity by the better off. In the USA there continues to be an expansion of charity. Those with middle as well as higher incomes and wealth observe the private institutions that are offering assistance and make their charitable judgements on the basis of their attention to these institutions. Many people are participating as volunteers in the assistance programmes. Some are dedicated to moving the disadvantaged from static welfare to the dynamic of self-help. The Christian is motivated by compassion to assist the disadvantaged to achieve the dignity of labour. This confirms one of the themes of a number of chapters of this book – where the state withdraws it gives room for voluntary, Christian initiative to 'breathe'. This is so not just in the spheres of welfare and charity, but in the cultural sphere too. Consumers and business people must respond to their Christian calling in all areas in which they are active.

This book makes an important contribution to our understanding of the dangers of conflating compassion with government action; it helps us understand the Christian case for a more limited role for government; and it helps us to see the true Christian vocation in the context of a smaller state that allows more room for private and voluntary-collective initiative in the economic, charitable and cultural areas of life.

PROFESSOR LEONARD P. LIGGIO

Executive Vice-President

Atlas Economic Research Foundation

**Catholic Social Teaching and the
Market Economy**

1 INTRODUCTION: UNDERSTANDING CATHOLIC SOCIAL TEACHING IN THE LIGHT OF ECONOMIC REASONING

Philip Booth

The authors of *Catholic Social Teaching and the Market Economy* were asked to achieve one or more of three objectives. The first objective was to apply economic theory, evidence and reasoning to the analysis of policy issues that are of particular concern to Christians. Thus, for example, there is a requirement for Christians who take an interest in public policy matters to be particularly sympathetic to the position of the poor, or to ensure that families can access education. Neither the Catholic Church, however, nor other Christian churches suggest specifically how these objectives should be achieved. Economic analysis must be one of the tools used to help inform the views of all Christians on such policy matters.

It might be thought that economic considerations should feature only in a minor way in a Christian analysis of policy. Moral, philosophical or theological considerations may be regarded as paramount. To think this way would be a serious mistake. Some Christians seem to wish to assume away certain economic laws when developing policies in areas such as the minimum wage or the provision of foreign aid. This is as sensible as assuming away the laws of gravity when considering the moral case for punishment by hanging. It is true that, if the demand for labour were not to decrease as wages increase, then a minimum wage might well help the poor. It is also true that, if the law of gravity did not exist, hanging might be regarded as a morally justified punishment by those opposed to the death penalty, because hanging would then lead only to inconvenience for the criminal rather than to death. But to proceed in such a way, by ignoring important economic laws when articulating the case for 'rights' in the economic sphere, is facile and ignores the fundamental nature of man as both a rational and an imperfect being.

We should also be careful before casually using words like 'moral' and 'just' to describe our favoured political policies. Those words have a powerful meaning and they should not be used without care. This is particularly so in the analysis of economic and political policies requiring compulsory redistribution of income or wealth through taxation. The issues are much more subtle than we may think. As the philosopher H. B. Acton put it, 'there is no morally defensible reason at all for forcing some individuals, irrespective of their incomes or circumstances, to give pecuniary help to beneficiaries whose incomes and circumstances have not been inquired into. In this way benefits are provided for people who may not need them by people who may not be in a position to afford them' (Acton, 1993: 81). This does not mean that the state should not provide for the poor. It also does not mean that policies to help the poor do not have a moral characteristic. We should be cautious, however, before using the words 'moral' or 'just' to describe such policies, not least because they always involve using coercion by taking the freely and properly acquired property of one individual in order to give it to another. We should also be cautious before we proceed to implement such policies lest we undermine the love and charity present when assistance is provided to those in need through an act of free will, uncoerced by the state, a process described so lucidly by Pope Benedict XVI in *Deus caritas est*.

Rigorous economic analysis of policy issues is a complex process. Even economists do not agree on the results of such analysis. As the Catholic French economist Frédéric Bastiat pointed out, however, without proper analysis there is always the temptation to take account of the 'seen' effects of economic actions and ignore the second-round or 'unseen' effects. The authors of this book try to address this particular problem. Notwithstanding this point, Christians should not necessarily feel that they need to be fully informed about economic issues. It is perfectly reasonable for Christians to reserve judgement on certain issues or to vote or speak according to their own experiences, without taking full account of the economic analysis that lies behind a proper appraisal of policy alternatives. We cannot all be experts in every field. It is not acceptable, however, for Christians to speak with absolute certainty, as if their perspective were the only perspective compatible with Christian belief, if they have not properly considered the economic principles that implicitly underpin their policy statements. One purpose of this book is to help Christians underpin their analysis of policy issues by a more rigorous understanding of the related economics and political economy.

Understanding policy issues in the light of Catholic Social Teaching

Our authors were also asked to examine Catholic Social Teaching to help us understand better how it can be applied to policy issues. There is always a danger when examining the social teaching of the Catholic Church in this way that aspects will be selectively chosen to fit an author's own line of argument. Thus, in the case of the authors of this book, criticisms of the market economy might be ignored and elements of Catholic Social Teaching promoting individual freedom, autonomy of the family and private property might be selected as being representative. I believe, however, that this problem has been avoided. In British writing important aspects of social teaching that favour the market economy are frequently ignored, or hidden under a bushel, and it is right that this text corrects that tendency. The authors have not been afraid, however, to engage Catholic Social Teaching and criticise it when they believe that it is wrong or that its application would undermine the very objectives it seeks to achieve. This is notable particularly in the chapters on foreign aid and on the just wage. Catholic Social Teaching is provisional and it is accepted that Catholics can agree to disagree about it. In disagreeing with teaching on economic and social matters the authors are not, in any sense, undermining the teaching authority of the Church in those areas of morals and theology where She claims special insights of truth.

Challenges to theologians and Christian politicians

Finally, our authors were asked to raise new questions or to take a fresh look at areas of policy that have both an economic and a moral aspect to them. The chapters on foreign aid, consumerism and the responsibility of business, for example, raise important moral questions for Christians and for the Church's social teaching. How should we proceed to help poor countries if the structures of government in those countries are such that development aid will bolster the bad governments that keep the poorest people poor? How should Christian consumers, and business people, respond to a materialistic climate that can develop in capitalist societies? Some of these questions are discussed briefly below and all are tackled fully in the main chapters.

The scope of Catholic Social Teaching and the market economy

This book does not pretend to look at all sides of the argument or consider all topics. Certain topics have been omitted. Free trade, provision of healthcare and stewardship of the environment are three important subject areas not covered in detail – though they are covered in the context of the analysis of wider issues. Also, while some authors do engage anti-free-market arguments, and some chapters are very balanced in their approach, other authors have analysed their subject area from a rigorous free-market perspective. There are important reasons for this. First, the book is intended to be relatively brief and succinct. There are other, more expansive, reference works that take in a broader range of subjects and lines of argument (see, for example, Charles, 1998). Also, rigorous economic analysis tends to lead in a pro-market direction: certainly the great debate between the opponents and proponents of central planning is now settled. Despite this, there is a relative dearth of literature that examines economic policy issues from a Christian perspective while taking proper account of free-market economics. On the other hand, Christian socialist perspectives on policy matters are abundant.

Nevertheless, the economic analysis of the issues presented here should be of value to people on all sides of political and economic debates. It should help Christians inclined to a free-market perspective to understand issues more clearly. It should also help Christians of a socialist perspective to understand better the obstacles that stand in the way of a socialist solution to problems such as poverty. The book may convert a few from that way of thinking; it may help others sharpen their arguments. The authors hope that it will, at least, cause them to pause for thought.

The authors were asked to limit their analysis to *Catholic* Social Teaching. Again, this was because we wanted incisive analysis of particular aspects of Christian theology and economic policy, rather than a broader text. But this book is intended to be useful for Catholics and non-Catholics alike – and indeed for non-Christians. The problems that are addressed should interest any person involved with public policy. The economics in the book is not Catholic economics! Furthermore, the problems considered are not only of concern to Catholics. Indeed, Catholic Social Teaching has seeped into the thinking on economic policy of most Christian churches. Catholic Social Teaching has also influenced the thinking on economic and political issues of non-Christians, just as non-Christian thinking on economic matters has influenced Catholic Social Teaching. Thus these new perspectives on Catholic Social Teaching are relevant to all who wrestle with the same policy problems and examine them from more or less the same moral perspective.

Like all IEA books, this text has been peer reviewed. Non-Catholic academics were involved in that process.

Fundamental messages

It is now generally accepted that the market economy is more efficient at producing and allocating economic resources than alternative forms of economic organisation. This argument is important: less efficient economic systems produce less while using more resources; people are poorer as a result; and the poor tend to be much poorer in socialist economic systems than in market-oriented ones. There are, however, deeper messages that the authors wish to convey in this book.

Community, society and government

One such deeper message of the authors is this: the fallacy that sees the provision of welfare by government as an extension of the charitable activity of the Christian community should be rejected once and for all. The main purpose of government is to protect individuals, families and communities, and their property, from harm. Government must also provide the legal framework that allows us to plan our economic and social life, allows us to provide for our welfare, and so on. If a government does not perform these functions then civilised and developed economic life is impossible, as we see in so much of the world today. In other words, government must provide the juridical and political framework within which human flourishing is possible. Even a government of a distinctly Christian character should not, however, take upon itself the duties of Christian communities to share goods, provide welfare and look after the aged and sick, except where efforts to provide these functions outside the government sector have failed. If a government goes beyond its remit in this respect, it undermines the free will, dignity and genuine love and charity of individuals within their communities: government action in these fields crowds out voluntary action and the innovation and personal response that are key characteristics of voluntary action motivated by true love.

The subtle but crucial distinctions between community, society and government can be better understood by thinking of the situation of many underdeveloped countries. It is often said, no doubt correctly, that in many African countries there is an important sense of community that has been lost in the West. That sense of community is, however, clearly distinct from the political structures that frequently exhibit the worst forms of corruption, violence and the abuse of power. Furthermore, attempts to generalise the sense of community that is apparent within and between families, within churches and so on, through the democratic control of economic resources via a socialistic political system have been catastrophic for African economies.

The democratic political process is absolutely necessary to resolve certain problems peacefully. But the whole point of the democratic process is that it is used to settle disputes between people whose views and interests are different. The losers in elections agree to abide by the result because they know that the winners would have done so had they lost. This tacit agreement holds if the government performs a limited range of functions. All the different communities, each made up of individuals and families, can then pursue their aims by working within the framework set by the democratically elected government.

Self-interest in the market and self-interest in the political system

The application of free-market economic principles is often criticised by Christian socialists because of the suspicion of the forces of self-interest that motivate decisions in free economic systems. Self-interest is often, incorrectly, regarded as synonymous with greed or selfishness. One counter-example is sufficient to show that this parallel drawn between greed and self-interest is fallacious. Every day I travel to work by train, rather than by car; and I cycle to the station rather than take a taxi. Both those decisions are motivated by self-interest, but it would be ludicrous to regard their motivation as manifestations of greed or selfishness. A market economy tends to put self-interest to good use because market transactions require agreement between transacting parties. It is in the self-interest of a shop to provide me with clean and reliable products. In other words, the shop provides for consumers by discovering what consumers wish to pay for while working in the self-interest of its own shareholders. This is an economic process wholly compatible with the natural human condition. In particular it is compatible with the Christian understanding of the human person as a being who lacks perfect knowledge and who is imperfectible. We lack the knowledge to plan centrally the allocation of economic resources effectively and, being imperfectible, it is important that our economic system ensures that the natural human desire for self-betterment is put to more general benefit.

On the other hand, greed and self-interest pursued through the political process can be destructive because government achieves its objectives by coercion. Christian socialists seem to assume away the forces of self-interest and greed when it comes to an analysis of the political process. Yet, if we allow the state to allocate economic resources, then voters, bureaucrats and politicians can still be motivated by the forces of self-interest that motivate individuals in a market economy. Voters, bureaucrats and politicians will generally, though not always, campaign for the redistribution of resources through the political system in their own interests. How often do we see a Member of Parliament campaigning for the closure of a hospital in his own constituency because it will release resources for other hospitals that may be in greater need? The allocation of economic resources through the political system can simply lead to resources being allocated to the politically powerful and the articulate. We should therefore, as Christians, seriously question a system in which nearly 50 per cent of the income of Christian families is taken from them to be spent by a secular state. Could we not do better with that money ourselves – both to provide for our own families, but also to aid the welfare of those who are less well off than ourselves?

The market allocates resources by agreement

It is worth dwelling further on the point that the market allocates resources through voluntary contract, yet the government allocates resources through the force of law. To a Christian, the former should be intrinsically attractive. Not only is the process of voluntary contracting most compatible with free will, it also ensures that economic resources are distributed by a process of peaceful voluntary cooperation and agreement. On the other hand, the governmental and political control of economic resources results in their being allocated though processes that can inherently lead to conflict, unless there is broad consensus in society. It is not a pretty sight to see protests by young people, farmers, the old and so on in France, all campaigning for more resources to be allocated to them through the political system. In the case of farmers, those resources come from the poorest people in the underdeveloped word as protectionism is used to bolster the incomes of EU farmers. Those who point to greed and materialism in the UK at the current time – and those are certainly moral issues that must be faced by all Christians – seem to forget the violent conflicts and strikes of the 1970s as groups competed for resources to be allocated to them through the political system.

Government intervention should take place when all else fails

It is also true that government has secondary functions, such as the provision of a minimum income for the poor or the protection of certain environmental resources that cannot effectively be owned privately or in common by voluntary communities. Catholic Social Teaching also frequently points out the dangers of unrestrained capitalism. These dangers must be taken seriously by all Christians, including by those who are unbridled supporters of a market economy.

There may be times in history when problems arise that appear to be the result of the free-market economy. Sometimes these problems arise because government is not performing its own legitimate functions properly. This occurs in many less developed countries, where exploitation of individuals or resources by multinational corporations can occur because governments do not fulfil their crucial roles of protecting and enforcing property rights and contracts.

But even where the outcomes of a market economy seem undesirable to a Christian, there are many possible responses. Sometimes Catholic teaching calls for moral restraint and the creation of a more Christian culture by those operating in the market. Such moral restraint and a Christian culture complements the market economy, it does not undermine it. We should be wary of the state having too much of a role in 'creating' our culture. If we have a predominantly Christian society, a Christian culture should develop. If we do not have a predominantly Christian society and we give the state too much of a role in developing society's culture then it is likely to be a culture that it is indifferent to or hostile to Christianity. Government needs to leave room for culture to evolve and to breathe. Christians would do well to spend more time influencing their culture rather than influencing government to influence their culture.

Where government intervention takes place, there are many options available to pursue a particular objective. If, for example, there is considerable poverty in a particular country, this could be addressed by governments providing a minimum income or by the imposition of a minimum wage, the latter being a policy that market economists would tend to reject. It is the role of Christian economists to evaluate which policy options will do least harm and most good and to evaluate whether any intervention, however well intentioned, will do more harm than good.

The market economy is not about 'getting and spending'

The authors of this book are also keen to stress the 'depth' of the market economy. We sometimes think of the market economy as a simple process of earning and then spending on consumer goods. This is unfortunate. Economics is not about consumption or about producing the maximum number of material goods at the minimum price. Economics seeks to explain how human action leads to the use of scarce resources to fulfil our needs and desires. The economic sphere is, of course, distinct from the religious sphere, but the former goes far deeper than the pursuit of material satisfaction. It is legitimate to use economics to seek to examine why South Korea is a producer of cars for export and New Zealand is a producer of lamb for export and why they may then trade with each other. But economics is also a subject that can be used to examine other forms of decision. The decisions to home-school rather than to work longer hours to earn money to pay school fees or to help out at the local Scout troop rather than going to watch horse-racing also have economic aspects to them. There may be a moral, charitable and altruistic dimension to such decisions too, but they are decisions about how we use our scarce resources in the pursuit of our legitimate ends.

Again, it was H. B. Acton who described how the market economy appears much shallower than it really is, or should be, because of the expansion of the remit of the state. For example, between one third and one half of the population have decisions about housing, pensions, unemployment and disability insurance and many other essential services taken for them by the state in the UK. For over 90 per cent of the population decisions in relation to healthcare and education are taken by the state. It is no wonder that, for so many people, a market economy looks like a process of earning money for conspicuous consumption: we are not allowed to take decisions about how we provide for less overtly material needs.

We should ask whether taking away responsibility from families for essential services such as education, healthcare, savings, insurances and housing actually undermines the development and flourishing of the human person. It certainly prevents the market economy from deepening and intertwining with the structures of voluntary communities to the extent that it could. This makes the market economy appear to be a much cruder institution than it really is and, arguably, limits the capacity of communities to provide for their most important needs. For the same reasons, as has been noted, it is important that the state does not try to supplant those good things that are provided by a sound culture in a developed society.

Nevertheless, debates between Christians on the appropriate scope of the market and the domain of the state in economic life are legitimate. The Catholic Church and scripture certainly do not exhibit a bias in favour of the use of socialised, political mechanisms to achieve the sorts of objectives (protection of the poor, provision of health and education, and so on) that Christian communities and others hold dear. Indeed, political mechanisms should be regarded as a last resort when other mechanisms have failed. In the words of the recently published *Compendium on Catholic Social Teaching*: 'Experience shows that the denial of subsidiarity, or its limitation in the name of an alleged democratization or equality of all members of society, limits and sometimes even destroys the spirit of freedom and initiative ... state action in the economic sphere should also be withdrawn when the special circumstances that necessitate it end' (Pontifical Council for Justice and Peace, 2005: paras 187 and 188). There is legitimate debate to be had on what those special circumstances are and when they have ended. The authors of this book make an important contribution to that debate.

The main themes

The book is divided into three main parts, though all the chapters are self-contained and can be read individually without reference to earlier or later chapters.

The first part is entitled 'Economic welfare and the role of the state'. It consists of chapters by Father Robert Sirico on welfare, Philip Booth on foreign aid, Thomas Woods on the just wage and Philip Booth on taxation and the role of the state. These chapters examine specific policy issues on which Christians often wish to speak from a moral perspective, informed by economics.

The just wage is an issue that has concerned Christians for many centuries. There are several aspects of this subject. Should businesses be forced *by law* to pay a minimum wage? Do businesses have a *moral obligation* to provide a living wage? If businesses do not pay a living wage, should income enhancements to the poor be given through income transfers via the state? Woods concludes that mandating a minimum wage simply harms the people it is intended to help. It might be desired by some to assume away the economic laws that lead to this being the case, but it is not within our power to do so. We should have more humility than that!

The second part is on 'Business, the consumer and culture in Christian life'. The ills of materialism surround us in very obvious ways and these are discussed by Andrew Yuengert in the first chapter in this section. Capitalism is very effective in providing material goods. This provides moral challenges to Christians as consumers because we can become materialistic in outlook. But it is simply shirking moral responsibility to resolve this problem by undermining the enterprise economy. Indeed, materialism is not specific to an enterprise economy. Socialist systems are explicitly materialistic as they attempt to raise the condition of the person through the provision of material goods. Those who allocate resources within socialist systems are not, of course, immune to the temptations of materialism. Thus, we have to think of materialism as being intrinsically a moral rather than a political problem. As such, the problem should be addressed by moral and cultural renewal rather than, in the first place, by recourse to the political system. It is important that the political sphere allows more space for the cultural sphere to assist us in making sound moral choices.

The second chapter in this section is a wider examination of the contributions and responsibilities of business by Robert Kennedy. Businesses, like entrepreneurs, are essential components of the economic system. They allow individuals to use their talents creatively to fulfil their own needs and the needs of others. We should recognise the immense contribution that business activity has made to economic and social well-being and not restrain it from performing its vital functions. Nevertheless, Christian business people have a particular moral calling which they should not ignore. They cannot allow materialistic motives to override their consciences.

Father Anthony Percy writes about entrepreneurship. We often think about the needs of workers in our prayers and when considering policy issues, but what about the needs of entrepreneurs? Just as some workers struggle to make ends meet, entrepreneurs struggle too. In addition, they take risks; they frequently cannot find unemployment insurance; and they rarely have their positions 'protected' by regulation. Entrepreneurs face the same moral dilemmas as workers – should I open the shop on a Sunday if much of my trade is at the weekend? Entrepreneurs, like other workers, have to decide whether to work harder and spend less time with their families. Presumably St Joseph was an entrepreneur. Entrepreneurs are, of course, workers too, but there are other aspects of their vocation that we should consider. We should pray for entrepreneurs; we should think about their needs in our church community and the special contribution they can make; and we should consider their needs when formulating economic policy. Entrepreneurship is, indeed, a noble vocation. On the whole, when entrepreneurs become rich, they have done so by taking risks and providing goods and services of value for the community. Of course, many entrepreneurs, having become rich by meeting the needs of consumers, then further help society by giving away their wealth to others.

Dennis O'Keeffe examines the role of the Catholic school in passing on the faith, including the way in which Catholic schools communicate the Church's teaching. He suggests that Catholic schools are not necessarily valued these days because they are Catholic but because they are successful in human terms – providing a good education, a safe environment, and so on. Catholic schools have an important role in shaping culture, however, which itself has been noted as being important in shaping the space in which business and the consumer operate. The teaching materials exist today to help Catholic schools to do a better job in shaping a vital Catholic culture, but Dennis O'Keeffe is not convinced that schools can do this given the current institutional framework within which they operate.

The final part of this book, 'Subsidiarity and solidarity: the role of the individual, the community and the state', discusses the basic principles that were important in analysing the specific issues covered in Part One and Part Two. In doing so, it acts as a conclusion to the book. Denis O'Brien's chapter on subsidiarity and solidarity makes several important points. The higher structures in society (local government, central government and, in the case of the UK, the European Union) do not exist to supplant the will of the lower structures (individuals, families, voluntary associations and communities), still less to pursue their own aims. The higher structures of government exist to serve the subsidiary structures in the pursuit of the latter's own legitimate aims. Thus, for example, governments should not provide education except, perhaps, as an absolute last resort. Rather, they should assist families, if it is necessary to do so, in obtaining education for their children. This is very different from the concept of subsidiarity that is supposed to operate within the European Union, where the higher governmental structures determine aims and then require the lower structures to pursue those aims. O'Brien also examines documents produced by the England and Wales Bishops' Conference and finds that they do not give the same emphasis to subsidiarity that is evident from papal encyclicals. Furthermore, the England and Wales hierarchy's understanding of solidarity often seems to bypass the most crucial vehicles of solidarity – the family, voluntary associations and the community – and jump straight to the state. It thus frequently recommends political action at the highest level of government, including the EU level, when sound economic analysis and the application of the principle of subsidiarity would recommend a different course. O'Brien has strong words to say about the public statements of the England and Wales Bishops' Conference. Not all will agree with those strong words. Nevertheless, an examination of documents produced by the Conference certainly suggests that more careful thinking on economic issues might lead to different policy prescriptions.

Finally, the chapter by Sam Gregg specifically deals with the question of the role of the state, the community and the individual as defined and discussed in Catholic Social Teaching. He stresses the crucial importance of the state keeping within its own legitimate space to prevent it from crushing the development of other instruments of socialisation. A large state will also prevent human flourishing. The state is an imperfect instrument, so a belief in God, argues Gregg, must lead us to believe that the power of the state should be limited because the 'infinite necessarily limits the finite'.

Overall, these contributions, by learned scholars from three continents, provide fresh thinking and challenge the paradigm within which so many of these issues are currently considered.

References

Acton, H. B. (1993), *The Morals of Markets and Related Essays*, Indianapolis, IN: Liberty Fund.

Charles, R. (1998), *Christian Social Witness and Teaching: The Catholic Tradition from Genesis to Centesimus Annus*, Leominster: Gracewing.

Pontifical Council for Justice and Peace (2005), *Compendium of the Social Doctrine of the Church*, London: Burns & Oates.

Annexe: a note on referencing

All the chapters in this book were written independently. All authors have used the same framework for referencing. Many of the references that are discussed by a number of authors cannot easily be referenced in a standard way, however. While the editor has tried to maintain consistency, he has not wished to stand in the way of an author expressing himself in his own style, and thus there are some minor inconsistencies in referencing. Major papal and Church documents are not listed in the references at the end of each chapter. They have been introduced within each chapter in which they are mentioned. Subsequent references to such documents within chapters are then generally made by the document's initials rather than the full title. References are given to the paragraph numbers of such major papal and other Church documents. In the Appendix on page 274 there is then a list of all the major papal and other related documents, with the date of publication and author (where appropriate), as well as a note of where they can be obtained free of charge. It was felt that this approach would allow the reader to have access to a list of all the major papal and related documents in one place within the text. Different authors have quoted from different versions of

Church documents, thus there will be slight differences in quotations. For example, some versions from which authors quote are in American rather than British English.

Part One
ECONOMIC WELFARE AND THE ROLE OF THE STATE

2   RETHINKING WELFARE, REVIVING CHARITY: A CATHOLIC ALTERNATIVE
Robert A. Sirico

Introduction

Let us consider the topic of welfare by analogy with religious practice. In the West today, a system of religious liberty properly understood, with no entanglement in religious sectarianism by the state, is considered the system most compatible with human flourishing and the one most likely to permit a flowering of faith in society. This is a hard-won lesson, one on which there has only recently emerged a consensus that what used to be dismissed as an 'American system' is the best all-round approach to the issue of religion in society. After all, the USA is one of the most religious societies in the world, and one reason is precisely because this sector of society was left to society to develop and grow, and not left to the state.

This is a counter-intuitive conclusion. Let us say that a person who knew nothing about the modern experience sought to design a pious society where everyone attended religious worship, where there was a church near every lightly populated neighbourhood, and where there were plenty of ministers to serve people's needs. One might suppose that the political apparatus needs to be deployed on behalf of the cause: building churches, putting ministers on the payroll and enforcing a moral code on everyone through legislation.[1] A laissez-faire policy would not be the first choice, mostly for the fear that one cannot know with certainty what the outcome of free decisions will be.

---

1   It is, however, clear that it would be very difficult for churches and religious communities to grow without a state that underpins basic constitutional and institutional elements, such as an independent judiciary and the rule of law, which are necessary for any society that does not want to lapse into anarchy.

This approach to religion was, after all, the historical choice that tended to prevail among Christians from the time of Constantine through the Reformation and all the way to the American experiment in religious pluralism. Who today would seriously suggest that it was theologically coherent for a Christian church to be headed, at least formally, by a head of a nation-state? Even today, remnants of the old world still survive in Europe, where there are state churches in many countries, where ministers and churches receive public subsidies, and where citizens are asked to declare their religious affiliation for the purposes of the tax rolls. Even as recently as the Second Vatican Council, the issue of religious liberty was a hotly debated topic within Catholicism.

Before the Council, much debate had been sparked by the publication of the American Catholic theologian John Courtney Murray's book *We Hold These Truths* (Murray, 1960). Murray, a Jesuit priest who devoted many years of study to the American founding, the place of natural law in that founding and the role undertaken by Catholics and other Christians in shaping the theological and philosophical underpinnings of that founding, is best known for articulating a classic Christian and natural law argument for limiting the state. As Murray puts it, 'the American thesis is that government is not juridically omnipotent. Its powers are limited, and one of the principles of limitation is the distinction between state and church, in their purposes, methods, and manner of organization' (ibid.: 68).

Murray served as a theological adviser to American bishops participating in the Second Vatican Council. American bishops, ranging from Cardinal Spellman in New York to Cardinal Meyer of Chicago, were determined to see the Council address the question of religious liberty, but without leaving the Church open to the charge of endorsing religious indifferentism or the notion that anything could be justified on grounds of religious liberty. Thus it was not surprising that certain aspects of Murray's idea were taken up and authoritatively elaborated upon in the Second Vatican Council's Pastoral Constitution on the Church in the Modern World, *Gaudium et spes*, which states: 'As for public authority, it is not its function to determine the character of civilization, but rather to establish the conditions and to establish the means which are capable of fostering the life of culture among all …' (GS 59). It also notes that 'Rulers must be careful not to hamper the development of family, social or cultural groups, nor that of intermediate bodies or organizations, and not to deprive them of opportunities for legitimate and constructive activity …' (GS 75).

Though Murray's treatise on religious liberty does not discuss economic questions at any length (aside from describing the basic institutional protections necessary for property inherent in a regime respecting the natural law), his book does contain an oblique endorsement of the free economy. 'The most obvious growing end of the free society has been its business system,' Murray states. 'Behind its enormous growth', he adds, 'has lain the pressure of the people's needs, wants, desires, dreams, passions, and illusions' (Murray, 1960: 99).[2] The Catholic Church in America, Murray wrote in 1960, 'has accepted this thing which is the American economy. Her life, the life of grace, is tied to it in multiple respects'. In particular, Catholic charities and public schools are wholly dependent on the productive energies of the free market. This market has created enormous wealth, and 'a wide distribution of wealth', without which the exercise of these Catholic virtues would be 'impossible' (ibid.: 180).[3] Murray further warns that alterations in the structure of the economy in the direction of 'state socialism' 'would

2   Murray adds, however, with characteristic humility, that he 'has no competence' to engage in economic theorising. He does so only briefly, but then with an uncharacteristic lack of clarity. He uses the language of 'power' to describe the role of corporations in society which 'direct' the activities of the 'economic-political system'. These passages could be understood on behalf of economic liberty if we construe these corporations as those that enjoy a privileged legal status from the state, and thereby do indeed exercise unwarranted power. But I make no claim that this is in fact what Murray meant to describe. If he meant to suggest the corporation itself exercises 'power' merely because it provides consumers goods and services they desire, and investors a return on their savings, then he is adequately answered by Novak (1982: 237–358).

3   As *Centesimus annus* says, 'not only is it wrong from the ethical point of view to disregard human nature, which is made for freedom, but in practice it is impossible to do so' (CA 25).

'subtly alter the relation of the Christian people to the institutions of the Church' (ibid.: 181).

Contrary to popular perception, Pope Benedict XVI is one who has always been thoroughly convinced of the necessity of religious liberty. Certainly the Catholic Church has always insisted that people should choose to order their freedom to the truth made known through faith and reason so that they might realise the ultimate freedom to which St Paul says all Christians are called. While Pope Benedict continues to emphasise this point to a world that commonly mistakes freedom for licence, he has also written of the 'real gift of freedom that Christian faith has brought into the world. It was the first to break the identification of state and religion and thus to remove from the state its claim to totality; by differentiating faith from the sphere of the state it gave man the right to keep secluded and reserved his or her own being with God ... Freedom of conscience is the core of all freedom' (Ratzinger, 1988: 202–3).

The welfare issue

At this point, we may consider an analogy between religious liberty and the welfare state. It is indisputable that the obligation to care for those in need is an integral part not only of the Christian faith but also of any modern notion of what it means to live in a good society. Whether the justification is based on a notion of secular justice or Christian love, hardly anyone is prepared to say that the poor ought not to be cared for, the disabled neglected, and the aged forgotten. Because of a notion of justice that seems innate to human nature, we want to live in societies where people who are victims of unfortunate circumstances are assured some modicum of care.

And yet the same points noted above about the religious sphere apply also to the welfare sphere. Many have come to believe that the only way to ensure a flourishing of such support is through an elaborate state apparatus. Throughout the West and especially in western Europe, we have created massive systems of social support for the aged, children, the disabled and many other groups perceived to be victims of society. The public is taxed heavily, bureaucracies are created, and political elections often turn on the management of these large systems of social insurance. Almost all economically advanced countries are in the throes of reforming these systems to make them less expensive and less easy to manipulate through electoral politics. But the question as to whether these systems ought to be rethought entirely is hardly ever raised.

We are at the first stages of considering a very radical question: whether the care of the poor ought to be treated in the same way that religion in society ought to be treated: that is, as something to be kept out of politics and immunised from political intervention, not because it is a lesser social priority but rather because it is of such high social priority that we dare not permit the state to dominate this area. Just as religion flourishes best when it is left to the free association of individuals and groups, so too perhaps the care of the less well off in society ought to be the first responsibility of society to manage on its own, and with the same counter-intuitive conviction that such an approach will yield more effective systems of support.

Within Catholicism, it was John Paul II who especially emphasised and clarified the importance of freedom in this sensitive area. He wrote the following strong words in his encyclical *Centesimus annus*:

> In recent years the range of such intervention has vastly expanded, to the point of creating a new type of state, the so-called 'Welfare State.' ... excesses and abuses, especially in recent years, have provoked very harsh criticisms of the Welfare State, dubbed the 'Social Assistance State.' Malfunctions and defects in the Social Assistance State are the result of an inadequate understanding of the tasks proper to the State. Here again the principle of subsidiarity must be respected: a community of a higher order should not interfere in the internal life of a community of a lower order, depriving the latter of its functions, but rather should support it in case of need and help to coordinate its activity with the activities of the rest of society, always with a view to the common good. (CA 48)

When the state becomes the primary and first caretaker of children, through well-intentioned laws designed to enhance their welfare, it tragically reduces the responsibility of parents and the value of children to parents. A particular problem occurs when the state subsidises behaviour that should be discouraged if we want to retain strong families. A good example is out-of-wedlock births, which have dramatically increased anywhere the state has chosen to give an excess of money to women in this position. When the state intervenes in this manner, it sends a signal to fathers that it is not necessary for them to stay in their roles as husbands and fathers, resulting in an increase in single parents (usually female).

Among the vulnerable in any society are the poor, whether in our own families or in the wider community. When this issue is usually discussed, the matter of inequality of wealth inevitably arises. But it is not the issue of inequality of wealth which should concern us primarily. After all, inequality can always be reduced by making everyone equally poor. The issue is poverty itself and the human suffering that accompanies it.

After several decades of an almost obsessive concern with issues of distribution, more and more Catholics have declined to remain locked in a 1960s approach to economics and have come to realise that the best solution to material poverty is wealth creation and a growing economy. It provides jobs, better pay, better working conditions, more opportunities, and growing opportunities for everyone to achieve. A growing economy requires that the market economy be allowed to function without the kind of excessive interruption, regulation and intervention that diminishes overall wealth.

Of course, there are cases when even a growing economy, and all its requisite institutions, leaves some people out. The causes can be many, ranging from personal misfortune to lack of initiative. A note of caution, however, should be recorded: so long as trade is voluntary, the state remains limited, and people can freely contract with each other, the cause of poverty cannot be the wealth of others, as Marxism would have us believe. That is why the temptation towards a policy of mere redistribution in the name of charity should be avoided. No benefit accrues from this policy to anyone but the radical egalitarian, whose impulses should not be allowed to drive public policy in a good and just society. Instead, we should strive to continue to expand the pie rather than fight over the various ways in which the pie can be sliced up.

Bureaucracy does not help the poor

In thinking about ways to help the poor, the virtue of prudence suggests that we must consider the costs and benefits of various strategies. If we turn to the government as a response of first resort, particular dangers arise. Government policies can create impersonal bureaucratic institutions with which the poor will be forced to deal, which can be demeaning (Niskanen, 1973). In addition, bureaucracies have a tendency to expand their own payrolls and, as Max Weber famously detailed, pursue their own agendas of self-preservation and expansion instead of focusing on serving others. Instead of staying within fiscal constraints, they invariably take a greater and greater share of private wealth. This means that the benefits of state aid to a specific group might well be outweighed by indirect and longer-term costs to the whole community.

State bureaucracies have demonstrated a lack of ability to fully understand the nature of the problem of poverty. Bureaucracy tends to be notoriously imprecise in targeting assistance to those in need. Public agencies cannot make the necessary distinctions between legitimate need and illegitimate demands. And they tend to impose heavy burdens of debt on future generations, which are best avoided. As John Paul II explains:

> By intervening directly and depriving society of its responsibility, the Social Assistance State leads to a loss of human energies and an inordinate increase of public agencies, which are dominated more by bureaucratic ways of thinking than by concern for serving their clients, and which are accompanied by an enormous increase in spending. (CA 48)

Even the worker in the bureaucracy himself is given attention by Pope John Paul II in his first social encyclical, *Laborem exercens*:

> [Dignity is] extinguished within him in a system of excessive bureaucratic centralization, which makes the worker feel that he is just a cog in a huge machine moved from above, that he is for more reasons than one a mere production instrument rather than a true subject of work with an initiative of his own. (LE 71)

Long-term poverty is more than a condition of lacking material goods; it is a condition that involves deeper and more structural problems that require personal attention. This kind of attention is best given by individuals, families and churches rather than by agents of the state, which have all too often proved not to be the friend of the poor. That is why the assertion of rights – to a job, to healthcare, to a good living – is such a serious business. Special care should be taken to prevent open conflicts between rights. Stating that everyone has a right to a job may implicitly oblige those in a position to hire to act in a way that violates their right to economic liberty as well as the stability of their enterprise, by which others are employed.

Jesus commands his followers to be charitable. It must be exercised in accordance with his will, and nowhere does he suggest this obligation can be passed on to public employees. Nor can the obligation be discharged by lobbying the government to take on new social welfare functions. Although it may tempt some, the existence of the welfare state and various forms of social regulation is not the fulfilment of Christ's commandment to care for the poor. Indeed, forms of charity that keep people in an unnecessary dependency relationship to the state actually do more harm than good. In this case, a person following the Gospel of Christ might have an obligation to speak out against the system or programme that is the source of the problem.

Historically, the most charitable societies in the world have been the wealthiest, and the wealthiest societies have also been the most free. When people have more disposable income, they can invest more in charitable causes. Only a free economy can generate this kind of wealth. Prosperity permits people to spend more time in leisure rather than work, which allows them to spend more time volunteering for community activities and service to the poor. A free economy allows for growing levels of voluntary free time to make this possible.

Daniel M. Hungerman of Duke University provides some very revealing data to back up this intuition. Before the Great Depression and the advent of the New Deal social assistance state, the US charitable sector was immense, spending up to six times as much money on charitable services as government spent. During and after the New Deal, church benevolence fell dramatically.

> We find strong evidence that the rise in New Deal spending led to a fall in church charitable activity. Our central estimate suggests that each dollar of government relief spending in a state led to three cents less church spending. This is a small level of crowd out in dollar terms, but it is large in proportional terms, since church spending at the start of this period amounted to only 10 per cent of the ultimate size of the New Deal. Relative to this baseline, there was a crowd out of at least 30 per cent, which can explain the time series decline in church benevolence over this period. (Gruber and Hungerman, 2005)

This study covers only one period of history, even if a decisive one that took place during the advent of the modern welfare state. How big might the charitable sector have grown in the absence of state intervention? How much wealth has not been voluntarily redistributed owing to the imposition of forced redistribution? And how much more efficiently, and with greater personal care, might all this have been done? These are the unseen effects that cannot be measured.

We should also remember that even the most competent helper of the poor does not discharge his whole duty to God because the poor are made better off. The 'preferential option for the poor' is not to be understood exclusively. This, John Paul II wrote in *Ecclesia in America*, is 'in part because of an approach to the pastoral care of the poor marked by a certain exclusiveness that the pastoral care for the leading sectors of society has been neglected and many people have thus been estranged from the Church' (EA 67). The preferential option for the poor, moreover, may never be construed as a legal preference for one class over another (Leviticus 19:15). In understanding assertions regarding the supposed inherent moral superiority of one class, we must remember the call to universal salvation issued by the same Gospel. As believers, love and service of God should always be our primary focus, and the obligation to others flows from that. When charity and concern for others become secularised and taken over by the state, they thereby become less of an instrument in the service of God.

True Christian charity

In many ways, John Paul II's writings on this topic can be seen as a development of Leo XIII, who wrote in *Rerum novarum* in 1891 that 'No human devices can ever be found to supplant Christian charity' (RN 30). That remains true today, though we are more confused than ever about what constitutes genuine charity. Some believe that paying taxes suffices to discharge our duties to our neighbours, because the state has undertaken so many activities to care for the well-being of those in need. Others think that charity comes from voting for political parties that support redistribution.

Benedict XVI is fully aware of this confusion, which is why his encyclical *Deus caritas est* sought to clarify the Christian teaching on charity by calling for a new civilisation of love – not one based on a superficial secularist understanding but one rooted in classical Catholic theology. The state cannot be the source by which this love is realised.

> There is no ordering of the State so just that it can eliminate the need for a service of love. … There will always be suffering which cries out for consolation and help. There will always be loneliness. There will always be situations of material need where help in the form of concrete love of neighbour is indispensable.

> The State which would provide everything, absorbing
> everything into itself, would ultimately become a mere bureaucracy
> incapable of guaranteeing the very thing which the suffering
> person – every person – needs: namely, loving personal concern.
> We do not need a State which regulates and controls everything,
> but a State which, in accordance with the principle of subsidiarity,
> generously acknowledges and supports initiatives arising from the
> different social forces and combines spontaneity with closeness to
> those in need …
> This love does not simply offer people material help, but
> refreshment and care for their souls, something which often is even
> more necessary than material support. (DCE 28)

There are a number of important insights here. The Pope engages in a *reductio ad absurdum*, speaking of the state that absorbs everything into itself, because this is precisely the tendency of the state that purports to care for the poor, the weak, the elderly and the sick. It becomes the cradle-to-grave state that knows no limits and for which no aspect of social management is off limits. The state's activities in this regard tend to crowd out the need for Christian charity in three senses: they bind the recipient to a dependency relationship to the state, one that tends to be more materially generous than private charity (and thus providing a moral hazard to the recipient); second, they encourage an attitude among potential charitable workers and donors that their charity is not needed – 'I gave at the office'; third, the sheer expense of the welfare state is paid out of the reserve capital of a country's wealth, which might otherwise go towards building up a robust charitable sector.

Even in the case of such a crowding out, Benedict XVI reminds us in *Deus caritas est* that the Church has a positive obligation that it can never forgo:

> The Church can never be exempted from practising charity as an
> organized activity of believers, and on the other hand, there will
> never be a situation where the charity of each individual Christian
> is unnecessary, because in addition to justice man needs, and will
> always need, love. (DCE 29)

Defining and dividing responsibilities: solidarity and subsidiarity

As for the tendency of the state to expand and encroach on aspects of the Church's obligation, consider that the whole of society is made of spheres, which are both distinct and intertwined. The state is distinct from society, society from locality, locality from community, community from church, church from family, and family from individual. Each is essential. Each has a function to fulfil. The function is most efficaciously accomplished when each sphere stays within its own domain as much as possible. We should not want the state, for example, to assume the task of facilitating spiritual renewal: that is the task of the Church. Correspondingly, we should not want the Church to assume the task of secular law enforcement, for this is the state's responsibility.

We do well to consider, then, which social functions are best addressed by which sphere and to establish protections for the resulting domains. This is not to say that the spheres cannot overlap. Business, for example, is the place for enterprise, but a family business can be among the most efficient. The community can engage in charitable work that complements the work of the Church. But we err if we forget that each institution has a primary function often exclusive of others.

Thus the state's primary purpose is the enforcement of the rule of law and the administration of justice. With regard to other social and individual human problems, we should not regard the government as the problem solver of first resort. Establishing that a moral obligation exists – to help the poor, for example – does not also establish that government should become the normative agency to fulfil that obligation. Allowing for the encroachment of one function on another should be carefully thought out, but a special danger exists when the state is made to interfere with functions that are not its own. 'Power tends to corrupt' (Acton, 1988: 519) precisely because the state has a legal monopoly in its use of coercion.

Just as the social functions should be distinguished among institutions, the principle of subsidiarity must be brought to bear for the common good of the community. This principle says that social issues are best addressed by those closest to the problem, and that higher orders should be enlisted only in cases of obvious failure. The care of the aged and poor, for example, is best left to the lower order of the family, church and community, and not the higher orders of the nation and state. Subsidiarity also warns the higher orders against intervening unnecessarily in the affairs of the lower order. Indeed, as the *Catechism of the Catholic Church* states, 'the principle of subsidiarity is opposed to all forms of collectivism. It sets limits for state intervention. It aims at harmonizing the relationships between individuals and societies' (Catholic Church, 1994, para. 1885).

The principle itself is not satisfied unless the lower orders themselves take care to address the needs that most closely and directly fall within their purview. The unfortunate temptation raised by the existence of centralised state welfare provision is that these responsibilities may be shoved aside by lower-order groups. The principle also establishes an ordering of responsibilities, so that we understand our primary responsibilities are to God, our families (immediate and extended) and to our community of faith.

This manner of approaching social issues ensures that governments consider carefully what powers legitimately belong to them and whether their exercise would increase or reduce the capacity for responsible decision-making at lower levels. Governments, and those who advise them, need to recognise the considerable limits of governments in addressing human problems. Government can be effective as an instrument of coercion, but not usually as a force for compassion.

Here we ought to recall that the principle of solidarity is not intended as a countervailing force to that of subsidiarity, but rather its complement. If subsidiarity helps us to identify the respective responsibilities of each individual and social group vis-à-vis others, solidarity represents the interdependence of all of society's individuals and institutions. 'Today perhaps more than in the past,' Pope John Paul II wrote in his second encyclical, *Sollicitudo rei socialis,* people are realizing that they are linked together by a common destiny, which is to be constructed together, if catastrophe for all is to be avoided. From the depth of anguish, fear and escapist phenomena like drugs, typical of the contemporary world, the idea is slowly emerging that the good to which we are all called and the happiness to which we aspire cannot be obtained without an effort and commitment on the part of all, nobody excluded, and the consequent renouncing of personal selfishness. (SRS 26)

Interestingly, some Christians fail to see that the free economy promotes the formation of cooperative associations, business firms, mutually beneficial exchange, charitable actions and institutions, families and civic associations, and also encourages everyone's participation in shaping political institutions consistent with the dignity of the human person. Solidarity, then, presupposes freedom of association, opportunities for exchange and enterprise, and material abundance to ensure that intermediating forces between the individual and the state can form and thrive.

Thus in the USA, which has one of the world's freest economies, 89 per cent of households give to charity, with the average household giving $1,620 or 3.1 per cent of income. Some 42 per cent of households report doing voluntary work with no remuneration on top of this, for a total of 15.5 billion hours at a value of $239.2 billion. Among those who volunteer, charitable giving is even higher, up to $2,295 per year.[4] The largest motivation for giving is religious, with the rich giving far more than anyone else. The total size of the private charitable sector in the USA, including foundations and labour time, approaches half a trillion dollars per year (Brooks, 2006).[5]

Can the private sector replace the public sector in terms of total dollars spent? It is doubtful; nor is it necessarily desirable. Public sector provision

---

4   See *Giving and Volunteering in the United States*, The Independent Sector, Washington, DC, 2001.

5   Among many findings herein reported is that people who attend worship services are far more giving than those who do not.

can be too generous in some areas and not so generous in other areas. The main problem, however, is that those resources too often go towards bureaucracy, not to true human assistance. Private sector charity is more efficiently employed towards desirable ends. It can better discern the needs of the poor, avoid the problem of dependency and be accountable to the donor base. Thus private charity simply does not need the same resources as public sector welfare provision to achieve the desired results.

There is nothing inherent in the mechanism of the free economy that somehow causes people to extend a hand of charity to the less fortunate. The impulse to do this stems from religious and cultural motivation that can exist or not exist within any system of economics. The advantage of the market economy lies precisely in its ability to generate the vast wealth necessary to create the means to live out moral obligations and ideals. It is precisely the market economy which provides the means that allow people to carry out charitable activity in a way that other economic systems cannot.

Ultimately the source of an authentic social conscience must come from outside the market. It is from a personal knowledge of our Creator – mediated, Catholics believe as a matter of faith and reason, through the Catholic Church established by Christ – that we gain those virtues that enable a productive economy to thrive and assist all the members of the community. Only then is it possible to recapture an integrated and settled sense of the reality of man's origin, dignity and ultimate destiny.

Conclusion

There is probably no one in the Catholic Church who does not know the story of the Good Samaritan. This is invariably drawn upon as a model of Christian charity. But what does it say about the specific option of public versus private aid? The following fact is unavoidable: the Samaritan was not an agent of the state. He was a private individual. He helped of his own volition. This is his virtue, along with the fact that he transcended ethnic boundaries. He was not acting as a public servant. He used his own money. It was a sacrifice of the Samaritan's own time and resources. His actions were not only good for the poor suffering soul on the street; they also contributed to his moral flourishing.

'When I return,' said the Samaritan, 'I will reimburse you for any extra expense you may have.' This is generosity. This is charity. It is exercised by individuals acting on their own impulses as informed by ethics and good morals. There is no substitute for that. This is one of the many wonderful lessons of this beautiful parable, and points to a true model of charity in a free and virtuous society.

A final objection: how can we know for sure that the poor will be cared for in the absence of a welfare state? I would like to substitute the following rhetorical question as a way of refocusing the debate: how can we know for sure that people will be religious in the absence of a state-imposed religion? Let us trust in freedom – that 'product of the Christian environment' (Ratzinger, 1988: 162).

References

Acton, J. (1988), *Essays in Religion, Politics, and Morality*, Indianapolis, IN: Liberty Classics.

Brooks, A. (2006), *Who Cares*, New York: Basic Books.

Catholic Church (1994), *Catechism of the Catholic Church*, London: Geoffrey Chapman.

Gruber, J. and D. Hungerman (2005), 'Faith-based charity and crowd out during the Great Depression', Working paper, Meetings of the Association for the Study of Religion, Economics, and Culture, 6 November, www.religionomics.com/.

Murray, S. J., J. C. (1960), *We Hold These Truths: Catholic Reflections on the American Proposition*, New York: Sheed and Ward.

Niskanen, W. A. (1973), *Bureaucracy: Servant or Master?*, Hobart Paperback 5, London: Institute of Economic Affairs.

Novak, M. (1982), *The Spirit of Democratic Capitalism*, Washington, DC: American Enterprise Institute.

Ratzinger, J. (1988), *Church, Ecumenism, and Politics*, New York: Crossroad.

3   AID, GOVERNANCE AND DEVELOPMENT
     Philip Booth

Introduction

Throughout mid to late twentieth-century Catholic Social Teaching there
was a consistent articulation of the position that the developed world
should transfer economic resources to the developing world through
government-to-government aid financed by the tax system. The tenor of
the teaching has been unambiguous, though at certain times a different
emphasis has been put on the role of charity and the role of transfers
through taxation.

It is easy to see why there might be an inclination towards this
position. Certainly the parable of the Good Samaritan implies that
charity should not respect national boundaries; similarly, it could be
argued, the use of government aid, financed by taxation, to provide for
those in great need or to assist the process of development should not
respect national boundaries. The argument is less clear, however, with
regard to government aid than with regard to charity. If the notion of
national sovereignty is to be respected, it may, in practice, be impossible for one country to ensure that the conditions for development are
nurtured in another country – in other words, it may be impossible to
ensure that aid benefits its intended recipients. When examining appropriate policies in relation to government aid, it is important to have an
understanding of what does and does not work, underpinned by theoretical and empirical economic examination.

In this chapter we will subject Catholic teaching on aid to scrutiny
from an economic and political economy perspective. Important
questions are raised for Catholic Social Teaching. For example, if the

provision of aid makes the economic situations of countries worse, if it increases the power of corrupt governments, or if it centralises power and economic resources rather than disperses power and resources among those in need, how should developed countries respond?

Catholic Social Teaching stresses the importance of 'good governance'. But how should we proceed if the structures of governance in an aid-recipient country are such that poor government may be bolstered by the provision of aid? In other words, if the systems of justice in a recipient country are failing, how does a potential donor country meet its obligations in social justice, as they are described in Catholic Social Teaching? It is not possible to answer this question in detail in this brief chapter. It will be raised, however, as a fundamental question that Catholic economists and political theorists should attempt to answer if they are to make a meaningful contribution to raising the condition of the poor through aid.

This chapter will begin by examining some statements in Catholic teaching on the economic position of developing countries. These will then be contrasted with teaching on the fundamental structures that are necessary for a market economy to prosper and for justice to be administered. The economics and political economy of the case for aid will then be analysed. The focus is on development aid and not on disaster or famine relief.

Catholic exhortations to the developed world to finance 'aid'
A false premise

We will see from our discussion of taxation (see Chapter 5) that the Church does not regard property rights as sacrosanct in situations where some individuals do not have the means for basic living. It is therefore not surprising that the Church exhorts better-off nations to help poorer nations by taxing its own citizens to help those of other countries. Before discussing these issues, it is worth noting that Church teaching on these matters is, to some extent at least, based on a false premise that seems to go unchallenged within its teaching documents. This false premise is articulated, for example, in Pontifical Council for Justice and Peace (2005):[1] 'In fact, there are indications aplenty that point to a trend of *increasing inequalities*, both between advanced countries and developing countries, and within industrialized countries. The growing economic wealth made possible by the processes [of globalization] described above is accompanied by an increase in relative poverty' (para. 362, italics in original). In *Populorum progressio*[2] it is stated that 'the poor nations remain ever poorer while the rich ones become still richer' (PP 57). *Sollicitudo rei socialis*[3] speaks of 'hopes for development, at that time[4] so lively, today appear very far from being realised' (SRS 12) and '… the first negative observation to make is the persistence and often widening of the gap between the areas of the so-called developed North and the developing South'.

These statements are, at best, superficial. It is true that there are certain countries, sometimes described as 'failed states',[5] that have not shared in the economic growth arising from globalisation because they have not participated in the process of globalisation. As other countries have grown richer, partly as a result of globalisation, people in failed states whose incomes have only grown slowly, or have perhaps shrunk, become relatively poorer. But this arises because of the failure of such states to participate in globalisation, not because of inherent faults in the process of globalisation. This point is certainly not recognised in the *Compendium*, which, quoting from the encyclicals of John Paul II, explicitly talks about countries being left behind *as a result of* globalisation.

It is also worth noting that the *Compendium* focuses in the statement above on *relative* poverty. The emphasis on relative poverty in the *Compendium* is out of place. Catholic Social Teaching has gener-

---

1   That is, in the *Compendium of the Social Doctrine of the Church*, also referred to as the *Compendium* below.

2   Published by Pope Paul VI in 1967.

3   Published by Pope John Paul II in 1987.

4   That is, at the time of the publication of *Populorum progressio*.

5   See Wolf (2004).

ally emphasised meeting basic needs as the motivation for charity and government intervention. Though relative poverty was a theme of Pope John XXIII's encyclical *Pacem in terris*, the reduction of relative poverty would appear to be a misplaced aim for many reasons. First, it is inherently materialistic. If some communities wished to carry on meeting basic needs, but go no farther, whilst the rest of the world becomes richer, relative poverty will increase.[6] But why should we be concerned? Perhaps those who focus on material goals become worse off in other respects as a result. Second, if a large part of the world's population were able to meet basic needs as a result of globalisation, whereas they could not do so before, but, at the same time, other countries become richer still, it is possible for relative poverty to increase. But why should this be a concern? Individuals should not be encouraged to measure their living standards by comparison with others as that can foster envy and materialism.

As it happens, relative poverty has decreased during the process of globalisation and absolute poverty has decreased dramatically. In particular, the gap between countries that have only recently seen rapid growth and those countries that have been relatively well off for many decades has narrowed significantly. Stylised facts do not prove the point but they provide sufficient information to seriously question the premise that globalisation is leaving the poor behind. In China, 300 million people have been pulled out of 'dollar-a-day' poverty in the last decade. It is inconceivable that this would have happened without China's participation in the process of globalisation. The same could well happen in India in the next decade if the country continues to liberalise its economy and allows trade to develop – indeed absolute poverty has already begun to fall sharply. The income of poor countries has not, in general, grown more slowly than that of rich countries during the recent

---

6   I refer here to a situation of voluntary choice of individuals and groups of individuals. People in religious orders are, of course, the most obvious example. There may, however, be communities whose members freely choose a more simple way of life, uncoerced by government.

episode of globalisation. For example, India, Sri Lanka, China, Chile and Pakistan have all grown faster than the world average over the last ten years, whereas each of the six biggest economies in the world ten years ago has grown more slowly than the world average. Today the average Indian is twice as well off as ten years ago while the average Japanese or German is barely better off at all. China's GDP has more than doubled relative to that of the USA in the last 25 years. Taking a longer period, the growth rates of the poorest fifth of countries[7] from 1950 to 2001 were not significantly different from those of the other 80 per cent of countries (Easterly, 2005).

In making strong statements about the widening disparity between rich and poor an important subtlety is being missed. It is possible for the gap between the richest and poorest to become greater while the number of poor shrinks, perhaps dramatically. Indeed, this is what has happened. In the last 50 years, many previously poor countries have become much better off. In more recent years, many people in some formerly very poor countries containing around one third of the world's population have become better off.

Nevertheless, there are some parts of the world, particularly countries in Africa, that have not grown at all – and where in some cases incomes have shrunk. We will focus on those countries that are still very poor in absolute terms in this chapter.[8] If we understand that the underdeveloped world is getting smaller because many previously poor countries have grown richer, it allows us to understand better the conditions for successful development. It is a better starting point for constructive analysis than the false presumption that income disparities are widening.[9]

---

7   That is, the poorest quintile.
8   That is not to say that there are not serious problems, including significant income differences, within countries in Asia and South America which do not suffer from the absolute poverty of Africa. They are not, however, the subject of our discussion.
9   Indeed, it has been recognised in more recent encyclicals that development should be aimed at aiding other countries to develop rather than transferring income from rich to poor. This, implicitly at least, should lead us to focus on the inhibitions to development,

Catholic Social Teaching: making the case for aid

The Church has taught clearly that development assistance and responses to extreme poverty should be given not only through voluntary sacrifice or charity but through government action too. For example, *Sollicitudo rei socialis* states: 'The obligation to commit oneself to the development of peoples is not just an individual duty, and still less an individualistic one, as if it were possible to achieve this development through the isolated efforts of each individual. It is an imperative which obliges each and every man and woman, as well as societies and nations' (SRS 32). The absolute requirement that solidarity should not recognise international borders is also made clear (para. 39). This international vision of the principle of solidarity is rooted in the parable of the Good Samaritan – though this is a parable about charity, of course, not of international political and economic relationships between governments.

The Vatican II document *Gaudium et spes*, following on from Pope John's encyclicals *Mater et magistra* and *Pacem in terris*, emphasised the need to see 'solidarity' in global terms. Concern was expressed about inequalities in economic outcomes: 'For excessive economic and social differences between the members of one human family or population groups cause scandal and militate against social justice …' (GS 29); this theme then continues at the beginning of Chapter III of the document. Chapter I finishes with the statement that 'solidarity must be constantly increased until that day on which it will be brought to perfection'. While there is a case made for aid in *Gaudium et spes*, the background for 'home grown' development is also made clear: 'technical progress, an inventive spirit, an eagerness to create and to expand enterprises … all the elements of development must be promoted' (GS 64). The collective organisation of production was also criticised (GS 65). Nevertheless, paragraph 69 makes it clear that both individuals and governments should share their goods to relieve suffering and to help peoples develop themselves. In paragraph 84, the importance of international organisa-

---

many of which lie in the policies of underdeveloped countries themselves.

tions in fostering development was stressed. The document then went on to be critical of political systems that did not foster private property and sound money and promote the virtues of what today would be called 'good governance'.

Populorum progressio expanded the analysis of *Rerum novarum* to apply it to world problems – particularly those of development. As in *Gaudium et spes*, conditions of good governance and the conditions for development are spelled out. The importance of private property and free competition is emphasised. Planned and collectivised economies are criticised. The aid agenda is made explicit, however – and it is promoted as an agenda for governments rather than just an activity of charity. Nations as well as individuals are told they most partake in the process of building solidarity. People are told that they must accept higher taxes to finance distributions to poorer countries. An increased role for international institutions, particularly the United Nations, was proposed. Development is described as a 'right' that imposes a duty on all nations, both developed and underdeveloped.

Overall, in *Gaudium et spes*, there is a mature discussion of the problem of the poorest in underdeveloped countries. The conditions for indigenous growth are understood; the responsibility of Christian groups is made clear; it is made clear that development is primarily the responsibility of peoples themselves; and the conditions necessary for long-term development are understood and effectively articulated. However, *Populorum progressio* was to a much greater degree influenced by the fashions of interventionist development economists in the 1960s. Nevertheless, in both documents there is a responsibility put on the governments of developed countries and on international organisations (generally financed by developed countries) to finance aid both for relief and development. It is not asked whether development aid granted to countries in which the conditions of good governance do not exist could actually do harm. This observation is interesting given the context of *Populorum progressio*. It was strongly influenced by a visit by Pope Paul VI to India (Charles, 1998). India is possibly one of the best examples

of a country that failed to develop because of policies of poor governance and of central planning. It is reasonable for a Christian to suggest
that aid should be granted to countries even in such circumstances if
the aid benefits the poorest, or even if it does no harm. But the question
remains, what should Christians do if government-to-government aid,
of the type proposed by *Populorum progressio*, actually acts to strengthen
the institutions that have brought about the failure to develop in the first
place?

The *Catechism* (Catholic Church, 1994) makes a distinction between
the provision of aid to address particular problems and assistance given
for development. 'Direct aid is an appropriate response to immediate,
extraordinary needs caused by natural catastrophes, epidemics, and the
like. But it does not suffice to repair the grave damage resulting from
destitution or to provide a lasting solution to a country's needs' (para.
2440). To achieve the latter, argues the *Catechism*, requires reform of
institutions. The *Catechism* states that 'Rich nations have a grave moral
responsibility towards those which are *unable* to ensure the means of
their development by themselves or have been prevented from doing
so by tragic historical events' (para. 2439, my italics). Of course, this
may include those who are prevented from prospering as a result of the
policies of their own governments, but the *Catechism* emphasises the
importance of personal responsibility for development, where individuals are allowed to take such responsibility.

*Catholic Social Teaching: the relationship between aid and
governance*

Interestingly, comment by local Church leaders on issues such as foreign
aid almost never links aid with governance. One of many examples of
this problem is Cardinal Keith O'Brien's comments at the 'Make Poverty
History' rally in Scotland in 2006, together with his associated press
articles. In the *Scotsman* (1 July 2006) he said: 'They came from all over
Britain and further afield to ask for more and better aid for the world's

poorest countries, cancellation of their unpayable debts and trade rules that will help their economies grow. Acts not of charity, but of justice [*sic*].' This raises two questions. First, which should come first, charity or justice?[10] And, second, what precisely does justice mean in this context if the mechanisms for achieving the 'just' result are not within the control of those desiring to deliver justice? If the transfer of resources from government to government either does no good or actually does harm for reasons discussed below, how should a potential donor nation respond? It may not be within the power of the donor nation to achieve the aim of justice as defined by Cardinal O'Brien. To describe aid, in such circumstances, as an essential part of justice is therefore meaningless and unhelpful. Indeed, if the political institutions in recipient countries follow the forms laid down by Catholic Social Teaching, the need for aid may well disappear.[11]

The problem of providing aid where there are imperfect political structures is mentioned in social encyclicals, though the implications are not drawn out. The problems of imperfect political and economic structures are regarded as important issues in aid-dependent countries. For example, in *Sollicitudo rei socialis* it is stated that extreme poverty in underdeveloped countries happens, 'not through the fault of the needy people, and even less through a sort of inevitability dependent on natural conditions or circumstances as a whole' (SRS 9). More specifically John Paul II then refers to 'grave instances of omissions on the part

---

10 We will not discuss this further – there is more discussion of this issue in Chapters 1, 2 and 5. I think, however, it would have been more appropriate to say 'relieving the needs of the poor is a duty of justice if charity fails'.

11 Not only is there no reference to issues of governance in Cardinal O'Brien's articles and speeches, quite the opposite is the case. He strongly opposes promotion of policies by donors that can encourage economic growth and good governance, such as sound fiscal polices and privatisation. Clearly it is a matter of opinion whether such policies are beneficial, but to dismiss them out of hand as the Cardinal does is wholly inappropriate, particularly given the disastrous environmental consequences of state ownership and subsidisation of energy and water supplies. The Cardinal also suggests that budget cuts mean that poor countries have less to spend on healthcare and education – but if such services are paid for only by deficit financing the consequences are generally catastrophic for poor countries – particularly for following generations.

of developing nations themselves, and especially on the part of those holding economic and political power' as being responsible for the deterioration in the position of underdeveloped countries (SRS 16). Furthermore, John Paul then goes on to mention the problem of aid being misused: '... investments and aid for development are often diverted from their proper purpose and used to sustain conflicts'. The accent here, however, is not on misuse due to internal decisions but as a result of directions from donors – particularly in the context of the 'cold war'.

Pope John Paul then further examines the background in which development assistance is given. He comments on the structures of social sin, rooted in individual sin, that cause underdevelopment. Again, however, many of the problems identified relate to donor communities rather than the political systems of recipient countries – still reflecting the cold war period when aid was often used as a tool to obtain political influence. Responsibility is, however, thrust upon the leaders and peoples of developing countries: 'Development demands above all a spirit of initiative on the part of the countries which need it' (SRS 44); 'Other nations need to reform certain unjust structures, and in particular their political institutions, in order to replace corrupt, dictatorial and authoritarian forms of government by democratic and participatory ones' (SRS 44). Underdeveloped countries are then exhorted to open their trade to other underdeveloped countries. There is a clear emphasis here on creating the economic conditions to allow growth and development to take place.

The importance of the wider institutional background necessary for economic development and prosperity is stated clearly in the *Catechism*, which reaffirms the message of *Centesimus annus* (Catechism, para. 2431):

> The activity of a market economy cannot be conducted in an institutional, juridical or political vacuum. On the contrary, it presupposes sure guarantees of individual freedom and private property, as well as a stable currency and efficient public services. Hence the principal task of the state is to guarantee this security,

so that those who work and produce can enjoy the fruits of their labours and thus feel encouraged to work efficiently and honestly
...

Thus it is clear that the Church has not ignored the institutional and political requirements that are necessary for economic development and prosperity. Indeed, *Centesimus annus* goes further in making clear that those countries that *have* developed are those that have participated in 'international economic activities' (i.e. trade in goods, services and capital). This is an important move forward and change of emphasis from the encyclicals of the 1960s, which tended to emphasise income transfers; perhaps the later encyclicals responded to the better understanding of the economics of development and the economics of institutions that was prevalent by the time *Centesimus annus* was published.

This analysis still leaves open, however, the issue of how we should respond if the political, legal and economic environment is not only hostile to economic development but also such that aid will be wasted and may be used to centralise power within corrupt political systems. The existence of this possibility should at least make us hesitate before calling automatically for increased aid either to promote development or to help those on low incomes in underdeveloped countries.

The Bauer critique of papal encyclicals

Peter Bauer was severely critical of the teaching of the Catholic Church on issues such as the concentration of wealth and development aid in the 1960s and 1970s (see the essay 'Ecclesiastical economics: envy legitimized', presented to the American Enterprise Institute, published in Bauer, 2000). From *Populorum progressio* (published in 1967), for example, Bauer quotes sections, such as 'God intended the earth and all that it contains for the use of all human beings and peoples' (PP 22) and 'You are not making a gift of your possessions to the poor person. You are handing over to him what is his. For what has been given in common for the use of all, you have arrogated to yourself. The world is given to all, and not only to the rich'[12] (PP 23). On government planning, he cites *Populorum progressio* (PP 33): 'It pertains to the public authorities to choose, even to lay down, the objectives to be pursued in economic development, the ends to be achieved, and the means of attaining them, and it is for them to stimulate all the forces engaged in this common activity.' Bauer then quotes *Octogesima adveniens* (published by Pope Paul VI in 1971) as stating that there is a major problem as a result of 'the fairness in the exchange of goods and in the division of wealth between countries'.

Bauer raises some important issues. In particular, it is certainly possible that the tone of *Populorum progressio* and *Octogesima adveniens* have aided the arguments of many leading figures in the Christian community who have proposed wholesale reform of capitalist economies, international trade, financial institutions, aid policies and so on as the solution to problems of poverty. Bauer also argues that the encyclicals have given succour to those who argue that the rich become rich at the expense of the poor.

Charles (1998), in turn, criticises Bauer's analysis. Charles points out that Catholic teaching does emphasise that the burden of development belongs with underdeveloped nations themselves. He then suggests that Bauer's critique is inappropriate because he is unable to provide a fully argued case showing how underdeveloped nations can achieve development themselves without help from the outside. He thus suggests that Bauer effectively argued why the Popes, and the experts on whom they relied, were wrong, but never articulated 'the right' (pp. 455–6). But this leaves an open question. If a country is poor because its basic economic, legal and political structures do not allow economic and political freedom to give rise to human flourishing, might it be possible that little can be done through political systems external to the country concerned

---

12   Originally from St Ambrose.

to rectify this situation? It is perfectly reasonable for academics to point out that proposed solutions to particular problems will do more harm than good while still being unable, themselves, to resolve the problems. *Populorum progressio* argued that in good conscience we must support policies of higher taxes to finance aid – a notion strongly criticised by Bauer. *Sollicitudo rei socialis*, however, put it rather differently. This document suggested that *if we know how* to alleviate poverty and choose not to do so this is a moral failing.[13] Bauer believed that the developed world does not have it in its power to resolve the problems of the underdeveloped world, and this view would not contradict this sentiment of *Sollicitudo rei socialis*.

Aid in theory and practice

If we are to accept the case for development aid as articulated in papal encyclicals and other Catholic Social Teaching, then those making the case must be able to demonstrate that, on balance, it is effective in promoting development. The arguments and evidence will not be discussed in detail here but a prima facie case will be made that development aid can be harmful and that the case for development aid is weak. Those making the case for development aid need to challenge this argument or come up with methods of distributing development aid that will circumvent the problems discussed here. The problems with development aid presented here have been discussed at greater length by Bauer, Lal, Erixon and others.[14]

Aid and government

The provision of development aid is, by nature, a top-down process. At a fundamental level, therefore, aid rewards the governing elites in those countries where those elites keep their people poor. Aid also makes

---

13   I am grateful to Father de Souza, Kingston, Ontario, Canada, for this insight.
14   See, for example, Lal (2002), Bauer (2000), Erixon (2003) and Erixon (2005).

it more likely that incompetent, corrupt or brutal government will survive because aid provides the resources for governing elites to alleviate some of the internal problems caused by poor or unjust government. Frequently, such governments have, of course, pursued policies that have included the persecution or expulsion of the most productive ethnic groups in society. The availability of aid also provides incentives for governments to pursue policies that will attract more aid.[15]

Aid also changes lines of accountability in government. Governments become accountable to those from whom they receive aid – either other governments or international institutions – and not to their own people. Erixon (2003) describes how in 2001 Tanzania had to produce 2,400 reports and studies on different aspects of present and future aid. A former minister of finance of Kenya estimated he had to spend 75 per cent of his time in discussions with donors.

As Bauer has pointed out, development aid leads a country's political and economic structures to orient themselves inappropriately. In many African countries aid is a significant proportion of national income.[16] Talented and entrepreneurial people within a country that receives large amounts of aid have a strong incentive to direct their efforts upwards, towards government, to become beneficiaries of aid-financed projects, instead of attempting to raise their material position through business and entrepreneurship. Thus, aid encourages rent-seeking. This whole process strengthens the hold of government on economic life, which is generally one of the most serious problems in underdeveloped countries. On a wider scale, the greater the proportion of national income and wealth that is controlled by government, the greater is the incentive for ethnic groups to engage in conflict to try to control government: if freedom of contract, exchange and private property rights are the main

15 I.e. policies that lead to high levels of absolute poverty and policies that promote government consumption and not investment – thus giving the impression that money is not available for investment, health and education.
16 In Tanzania and Kenya, for example, it reached 30 per cent of national income in the mid-1990s.

vehicles for transferring and upholding the control of property, fruitful economic activity rather than political activity and conflict are more likely to produce increases in income and wealth for individuals and communities.

The negative relationship between economic growth and natural resources is now well established – the so-called 'natural resource curse'.[17] In economic terms, aid is very much like natural resources – it is an 'endowment' that empowers governments and makes it more worthwhile investing economic resources or even using military means to control the machinery of government. Aid can therefore nurture bad government, which is the very problem that entrenches poverty in the first place: Djankov et al. (2006) find a strongly negative relationship between the receipt of aid and the extent of democracy.

There is a tendency for aid not to be used for its intended purpose, such as health and education, but, instead, to be used to meet the aims of governing elites (often personal betterment). Erixon describes aid as being 'fungible'. The specific aid money intended for investment or health and education spending may be used for the intended purposes, in order to provide evidence for donors. But it displaces investment that otherwise would have taken place in such sectors, including private sector investment. The additional resources are then, in effect, used for government consumption. This reinforces the problems identified above – the government becomes more dominant in economic life and the source of economic betterment. The increased resources enhance the ability of government to pursue active industrial policies with the usual detrimental effects that such policies have. Increased resources also find their way into the hands of the governing elites and their supporters. In summary, aid entrenches the position of those who are rich and powerful and makes it more necessary for individuals who wish to improve their economic position to do so by developing relationships with those responsible for the spending of aid.

---

17   See Sachs and Warner (2001).

All these problems encourage corruption in public life. If development aid receipts are significant, the influence of government is greater, bad government is encouraged and is less accountable to the people, and the resources available to government are greater. Government functionaries and ministers have relatively more power and economic resources which they can use for economic preferment. Government officials and politicians are in a position where they control the allocation of substantial economic resources and therefore become more susceptible to corruption – particularly where legal systems are inadequate or are themselves corrupt.[18]

In an ideal world, the provision of aid might simply work to raise the income of all poor people in a country by an equal amount. People living at subsistence levels would then have more money to save, invest and provide education and healthcare for their families. Aid does not work like this, however, partly because it comes from governments of donor countries and is spent through governments of recipient countries, leading to the effects described above. But it is also not symmetrical in its effect on different economic sectors, particularly, paradoxically, if spent wisely. For example, if aid is spent on investment projects, it can lower the marginal rate of return from investment projects financed by private saving and thus reduce private saving and investment. In any event, it will raise the real rate of exchange in a country, thus reducing the competitiveness of export sectors.[19] Other non-export-oriented

---

18   This should not be thought a patronising remark about the governments of underdeveloped countries (see Senior, 2006). In any country where government officials have control of vast economic resources and significant discretion, fraud and corruption are likely to result (note the EU Common Agricultural Policy). If, however, countries are already poor because of bad governance, providing development aid can simply feed the system that keeps the country poor. It is also worth noting that vested interests are created within donor countries (government departments, consultants and those charities that receive large amounts of project support from governments) which have strong incentives to campaign for aid-financed solutions to poverty in underdeveloped countries.

19   This may seem like an esoteric point but a recent paper published by the NBER (Rajan and Subramanian, 2006) suggests that it can be of fundamental importance, particularly if aid flows are considerable in a country that has had little development. Gupta et al. (2006) provide a good discussion of these issues. They note that trade liberalisation

sectors may benefit, of course, but any structural adjustment caused by significant changes in aid flows may cause economic problems for particular sectors.

Both supporters and opponents of aid are agreed that policies to tie aid to economic reform have not succeeded where economic reform is initiated by the funding body (again, see Erixon, 2005, and the references therein). There are many reasons for this. It is too easy for countries to demonstrate, at the time that grants or loans tied to structural adjustment are being renewed, that progress has been made – even though progress is more apparent than real. Also, lenders and donors find it very difficult to not renew loans or grants if a country has become poorer because economic reform policies have not been followed.

Aid and development

A strong economic case for aid rests on two hypotheses. The first is that the preconditions for economic development and growth relate to a shortage of savings, problems caused by declining terms of trade, lack of education and so on that can be resolved by income transfers from rich to poor countries. The second is that, in practice, aid transfers can be managed by benign governments to resolve these problems. We have dealt with the second issue above. What about the first?

It is, in fact, hard to find a positive relationship between aid and growth; indeed, there appears to be a negative relationship. It does not follow that a negative relationship between aid and economic growth implies cause and effect, but it should, at least, lead us to reconsider whether we should regard aid as a moral imperative. After the late 1970s, aid to Africa grew rapidly yet GDP growth collapsed and was close to zero or negative for over a decade from 1984 (see Erixon, 2005). GDP growth in Africa did not start to pick up again until aid fell in the early to

---

should coincide with increases in aid to reduce the impact of the 'real exchange rate effect'. Pattillo et al. (2006) note that this effect can be most detrimental to the poor, though they also suggest that it can be avoided through good policy choices in other areas.

mid-1990s. In East Asia, South Asia and the Pacific, one finds a similar trend. As aid was reduced in these regions from the early 1990s, national income increased rapidly. Erixon cites a number of detailed country studies that find no benefits from aid whatsoever across a range of periods and a large number of countries. In total, in the 30 years from 1970 Africa received $400 billion of aid, under different regimes, tied to different forms of economic policy and reform, yet there is no evidence of a single country developing because of aid.[20]

If we take 1950 as a starting point, it is clear that many countries that were then poor have become relatively wealthy while others have remained poor. It is impossible to find evidence that aid was successful in helping those countries that have become rich to do so. Botswana, for example, increased its income per head thirteenfold from 1950 to 2001, while much of Africa had a zero or negative growth rate (Easterly, 2005). Botswana is regarded as having many of the important features of good governance – certainly differences in aid do not distinguish Botswana from other African countries. Easterly notes that around 40 per cent of the poorest one fifth of countries in 1985 were not in the poorest one fifth of countries in 1950. From these observations, three facts are clear: poor countries can develop without aid; countries that receive aid do not tend to develop; and countries that are relatively rich can become poor again. This is troubling for the 'aid overcomes lack of capital and promotes development' hypothesis.

Growth and governance

It is becoming increasingly clear both from studying countries that have developed (for example in Asia) and those that have not that the problems identified by aid proponents are not the crucial ones for development. The basic precondition for development is good govern-

---

20 There are a few exceptions to the general rule of lack of development in Africa, such as Botswana, but it is very difficult to find evidence linking the development of this small number of countries to the receipt of aid.

ance, including the enforcement of private property rights, freedom of contract, enforcement of contracts, the rule of law, the authority of law and the absence of corruption. This list is not exhaustive, of course.[21] It appears that, if these preconditions are present, development and growth will generally follow. This is not surprising. Economic activity, employment, saving and capital accumulation will not take place unless there is freedom of contract and enforcement of property rights.

The problem of the absence of formalisation and security of property rights is discussed in great detail by De Soto (2000). He argues that in underdeveloped countries much capital is 'dead capital' that is not recognised by the legal system. The absence of both secure and formal property rights prevents proper business contracts developing, leads to reduced opportunities for entrepreneurship, prevents capital secured on property from being invested within businesses, leads to corrupt legal and governmental systems and to 'private law enforcement' or 'mafia gangs' becoming dominant. In such a situation, issues such as land reform, the provision of capital through aid and so on become irrelevant to development. Unless legal systems are reformed to properly recognise freely acquired property, capital investment and land endowments for the poor will have no meaning and will not contribute to development.

Exchange relationships are clearly necessary for an economy to develop beyond subsistence level. If contracts are not enforceable in the courts or recognised by legal systems, or if corruption or violence leads them to be enforced perversely, then exchange relationships cannot develop. Similarly, if property rights are not enforced justly or are not recognised, only very limited capital investment can take place.[22]

The problems in developing exchange relationships, small businesses and entrepreneurship are well illustrated both by De Soto's

---

21 One could add fiscal prudence and sound money, for example.
22 It is sometimes difficult for people in the West to understand the importance of this point. If contracts that one makes as a consumer, employee, business person or employer are not enforceable (including contracts for borrowing and saving) business life simply cannot take place. Similarly, if one cannot enforce property rights in one's house, land or business premises capital investment will just grind to a halt.

findings and from regular reports by the World Bank and Economist Intelligence Unit. For example, De Soto shows how on average 15 per cent of turnover in Peruvian manufacturing businesses are paid out in bribes. For a business to become legal and register its property in Lima it takes over three hundred working days at a cost of 32 times the monthly minimum wage. A person living in a housing settlement where title was not formally registered would have to go through 728 individual bureaucratic steps to register title with the city of Lima authority alone.

India has similar problems, though liberalisation has brought some recent benefits to that country. *The Economist* reports that Delhi's 250,000 bicycle rickshaw pullers collectively pay bribes of 20–25 million rupees a month for the privilege of being allowed to pursue their trade. The World Bank and International Finance Corporation *Doing Business* report points out that of the 30 countries with the greatest legal obstacles to business, 23 are in sub-Saharan Africa.

Gwartney and Lawson (2004) show the relationship between economic freedom and growth. One particular statistic is compelling. One hundred countries were studied from 1980 to 2000 and their legal systems rated according to the criteria established by the Fraser Institute's Economic Freedom of the World index. The top 24 countries had an average GDP per capita of $25,716 at the end of the period and average economic growth of 2.5 per cent. The bottom 21 countries had an average income of $3,094 per capita and average economic growth of 0.33 per cent. The criteria used to rank legal systems were: consistency of legal structure, protection of property rights, enforcement of contracts, independence of judiciary and rule of law principles. This suggests that development is impossible without the basic legal structures necessary for free economic activity.

There are important subtleties in this debate which are discussed by Ogus (2005). For example, it could be argued that legal systems are less effective at enforcing property rights and contracts in poor countries because such countries lack the resources to develop effective legal systems. This argument may have some validity but is problematic as a generalisation because it raises the question of how any country manages to develop. Also, it would seem that this argument should not apply to resource-rich, underdeveloped countries, of which there are many in Africa.

An interesting study by Pattillo et al. (2006) examined the economic factors that explained sustained changes in growth in African countries. The macroeconomic environment (inflation, government borrowing and so on) was important – and many of the countries with improved macroeconomic environments were part of IMF programmes. Economic and political liberalisation were important too, as was trade liberalisation. Aid and debt concessions helped long-term growth when combined with an otherwise healthy policy environment. These results are helpful for economists in analysing combinations of factors that can aid growth but they do not help political economists answer key questions such as 'Should countries give aid when recipient countries are not undergoing internal reform?' or 'Can internal reform be driven from outside?'

The discussion in this section is neither conclusive nor comprehensive. It provides, however, a prima facie case against development aid. Those who make the case for development aid need to demonstrate how the problems discussed here can be overcome or are irrelevant. Furthermore, those who promote government development aid in the name of Church teaching should be cautious when implying that the teaching has moral backing. If development aid is damaging to the very people it is meant to help, it is difficult to see how its provision can be a moral good.

Catholic Social Teaching tempered by realism – is there a way forward?

Insofar as there was a consensus among economists in the 1960s behind the theories that underpinned *Populorum progressio*, that consensus is now broken. Aid has not been successful in achieving its goals and it has now become clear why this is so. Economists still disagree on policies relating to the appropriate extent of government intervention in any developing country and they will always do so. It has become clear, however, that development without good governance is impossible. Furthermore, if the basics of good governance exist, countries will tend to escape from poverty without aid.

The mix of charity and political action that is appropriate is not something the Church generally lays down and proponents of aid should be careful about drawing conclusions that ignore this tenet, when using Catholic teaching to justify their position: 'For the Church does not propose economic and political systems or programmes, nor does she show preference for one or the other, provided that human dignity is properly respected and promoted, and provided she herself is allowed the room she needs to exercise her ministry in the world' (SRS 41).

It is very difficult to justify or ascribe any meaning to statements such as that by Cardinal O'Brien (see above). In an abstract sense, he could be regarded as being correct: there is something lacking 'in justice' if people do not have the basic needs to live. But the statement was made with a practical policy implication. If it is not within the power of a donor government to put in place the processes of good governance that could allow aid to meet basic needs, then how can the developed world give effect to 'justice' through increasing aid? On the other hand, if it were within the power of potential donor governments to create systems of good governance, aid might well not be needed to nurture development. It is certainly a moral failing if we know how to alleviate poverty and do not do so. It cannot be a moral failing, however, to reject a particular approach based on an honest interpretation of the evidence and theory.

It may be possible to develop ways to better distribute aid so that the problems described above do not arise. Erixon (2005) suggests that aid can complement an internal reform programme that is already developing within a country – though aid tied to a reform programme imposed from outside does not seem to be effective. Others have suggested that aid could be given if there were an *established* record of reform: as the study by Pattillo et al (2006) suggests, this might well be effective.[23] Ogus's study (2005) might be regarded as implying that aid could be useful to help develop appropriate legal frameworks that nurture economic development. Ogus also points out, however, the difficulty of transplanting particular model legal systems into other cultures. The precise form of legal systems, norms for enforcing contracts, recognition of property rights, etc., will often be culture-specific.

The recent report of the Commission for Africa (2005) assimilates some of the points made above and makes clear the importance of governance and trade for growth. It suggests that aid should be a complement to internal policies to promote growth and to trade liberalisation by the West. In a sense it follows recent Catholic Social Teaching on development. Whether it is possible to deliver aid while guaranteeing that other reforms will take place, however, and while not giving incentives for the adoption of bad internal policies, is a subjective and pragmatic question. The history of promoting growth by 'blueprint' and 'planning' from outside is not a happy one, and it is difficult to be confident that the Commission's agenda will achieve the desired results.

Bottom-up-style approaches to providing development assistance are being attempted through the US-led African Development Foundation (ADF). The ADF appraises projects and has strict selection criteria. Thus it may have more hope of success. Of course, the conclusions drawn from any success by the ADF could not be generalised to the majority of potential aid recipients that cannot meet the strict conditions imposed by the ADF. At the time of writing there is little independent assessment of its success. If it is successful, it will have practical lessons for policymakers but few general lessons for theologians.

Without the conditions described by Erixon being applied to the granting of aid, it is at least possible that aid does little good and that it may do much harm. Indeed, as Bauer (2000) has suggested, if aid does

---

23   It is to be hoped that initiatives that encourage reform, such as the African peer review mechanism NEPAD, might be helpful. The record to date does not, however, lead to much hope. It may be the case that reform of a few countries within Africa, combined with the NEPAD mechanism, might promote beneficial reforms in other African countries.

do the damage its opponents suggest (by entrenching the power of bad government and undermining bottom-up development) the harm that it does is serious. If, however, aid has the benefits that its proponents suggest, the evidence indicates that, at best, those benefits are marginal.

Many of these issues are clearly understood and implicit in the generality of Catholic Social Teaching. Their acceptance, however, has implications for the specific exhortations that have been made in social encyclicals on the issue of development. Paragraph 47 of *Populorum progressio* suggested that individuals in good conscience should not just support projects to help the needy at their own expense but should also support the raising of taxes so that public authorities could expand their work in this area. It is difficult to justify such statements given the empirical and theoretical knowledge we now have on the record of development aid. Some Catholics in good conscience might support increased taxpayer support for aid. Others, equally in good conscience, might not. Given that experience of successful development strategies imposed or even nurtured from outside a given country is relatively limited, the specific guidance that it would be reasonable for the Church to give ought to be correspondingly cautious, perhaps along the following lines:

> Extreme poverty is an extremely serious matter: Christians should try to find and promote policies that they believe, in good conscience, and in a spirit of prudence, will genuinely help the promotion of development. They should also expend both time and money to assist charities promoting development. Christian politicians should expend time and energy seeking appropriate ways to aid development and to develop international bodies that may assist development and good governance more effectively than those that exist today.

In the Catholic Church's teaching, wider problems that prevent development and which might even make aid work against the interests of the people of developing countries have been recognised. Many of the points that have been made in this regard relate to the cold war age. Others relate to the international financial and trading systems with respect to which Christians are engaged in vigorous debate on different sides of the argument. These messages are well taken and well understood. But the importance of trying to nurture good governance is also understood in Catholic Social Teaching. This leads to particular geopolitical issues that cannot be addressed in this chapter but which are clearly very important for Christian social scientists wishing to make a positive contribution in this area. What should be the response of governments of developed countries when human rights, property rights, basic freedoms and basic principles of justice are absent in poor countries? In what way, if any, should intervention take place in order to create conditions that are conducive to development and the productive use of both charity and government aid? It is certainly reasonable for the Church to encourage Christians to try to understand these issues better and develop policy that will genuinely aid victims of bad governance and underdevelopment.

Charity and relief

Some of the problems that we have described with regard to aid also exist when government-to-government relief is given in times of particular need owing to famine and other disasters. Despite this, the arguments favouring caution and non-intervention in such circumstances are less strong. First, if there is an immediate need to be met then we should not necessarily think about the long-term consequences before deciding to meet it. Second, it is easier for the government to provide disaster relief using non-government agencies in the recipient country – thus, to an extent, avoiding the problem of the aid process entrenching bad governance.

Our main focus has been on *government* aid to underdeveloped countries. Charity, provided through bodies that are genuinely independent of political systems in both donor and recipient countries, is less likely to cause harm and may well do much good, even when administered in countries with corrupt and unjust regimes. Many of the problems with government-to-government aid do not apply to charity administered through voluntary agencies, particularly where those voluntary agencies administer assistance through well-established structures in recipient countries which provide not just money but personal ministering to the poor. It is important to point out that we should not wait for a just ordering of the world or good governance in recipient countries before supporting such organisations. A number of statements made in Pope Benedict XVI's first encyclical, *Deus caritas est*, stress the importance of charitable action by Christians, *regardless of the underlying causes of the need they are trying to meet*. Pope Benedict stresses that whether a just society exists here and now is irrelevant to our mission of charity: 'There is no ordering of the state so just that it can eliminate the need for a service of love' (DCE 28).[24] He also stresses that the exercise of charity is fundamental to the lives of Christians. It is then made clear that Christian charitable activity must be independent of parties and ideologies – it is an extension of the Christian mission of love not to be put at the service of political goals.[25]

Thus the duty of Christians to help those in immediate need is clear. This duty is not conditional on the political order, the reason why help is needed or whether the help leads to some long-run benefit. Some Christians may wish to apply this reasoning to development aid provided by the state. Aid provided by the state, however, is fundamentally of a different character to that provided by charity – both morally and economically speaking. On the basis of our knowledge of the theory and evidence it is difficult to argue that, with regard to the political agenda, the Church can go further than to stress the importance of lay faithful taking the issue of how to facilitate development very seriously and that

---

24   This can be considered from two perspectives. First, regardless of the political order, there will always be people in need who are deserving of charity. Second, as is made clear by Pope Benedict elsewhere in the encyclical, charity satisfies a deep human need that government bureaucracies distributing financial and material help cannot meet.

25   This is emphasised twice in paras. 31 and 33. In para. 33 it is stated that those involved in charity 'must not be inspired by ideologies aimed at improving the world, but should rather be guided by the faith which works through love'.

it is an issue where Christians are free to differ about the means by which desirable ends can be achieved. To go further would be to risk promoting policies that, on the balance of evidence, have clearly done little good and may well have done much harm.

References

Bauer, P. (2000), *From Subsistence to Exchange and Other Essays*, Princeton, NJ: Princeton University Press.

Catholic Church (1994), *Catechism of the Catholic Church*, London: Geoffrey Chapman.

Charles, R. (1998), *Christian Social Witness and Teaching: The Catholic Tradition from Genesis to Centesimus Annus*, Leominster: Gracewing.

Commission for Africa (2005), *Our Common Interest: Report of the Commission for Africa*, London: Commission for Africa.

De Soto, H. (2000), *The Mystery of Capital: Why capitalism triumphs in the West and fails everywhere else*, London: Black Swan.

Djankov, S., J. G. Montalvo and M. Reynal-Querol (2006), 'Does foreign aid help?', *Cato Journal*, 26(1): 1–28.

Easterly, W. (2005), *Reliving the '50s: The Big Push, Poverty Traps and Takeoffs in Economic Development*, Working Paper no. 65, Centre for Global Development.

Erixon, F. (2003), 'Poverty and recovery: the history of aid and development in East Africa', *Economic Affairs*, 23(4): 27–33.

Erixon, F. (2005), *Aid and Development: Will it work this time?*, London: International Policy Network.

Gupta, S., R. Powell and Y. Yang (2006), *Macroeconomic Challenges of Scaling Up Aid to Africa*, Washington, DC: International Monetary Fund.

Gwartney, J. and R. Lawson (2004), 'What have we learned from the measurement of economic freedom?', in M. A. Wynne, H. Rosenblum and R. L. Formaini (eds), *The Legacy of Milton and Rose*

Friedman's 'Free to Choose': Economic liberalism at the turn of the 21st century, Dallas, TX: Federal Reserve Bank of Dallas.

Lal, D. (2002), *The Poverty of Development Economics*, Hobart Paper 144, London: Institute of Economic Affairs.

Ogus, A. (2005), *Towards Appropriate Institutional Arrangements for Regulation in Less Developed Countries*, Paper no. 119, Centre for Regulation and Competition, Manchester: University of Manchester.

Pattillo, C., S. Gupta and K. Carey (2006), *Sustaining and Accelerating Pro-Poor Growth in Africa*, Washington, DC: International Monetary Fund.

Pontifical Council for Justice and Peace (2005), *Compendium of the Social Doctrine of the Church*, London: Burnes & Oates.

Rajan, R. and A. Subramanian (2006), *What Undermines Aid's Impact on Growth*, NBER Working Paper no. 11657, Cambridge, MA: National Bureau of Economic Research.

Sachs, J. D. and A. M. Warner (2001), 'The curse of natural resources', *European Economic Review*, 45: 827–38.

Senior, I. (2006), *Corruption – the World's Big C: Cases, Causes, Consequences, Cures*, Research Monograph 61, London: Institute of Economic Affairs.

Wolf, M. (2004), *Why Globalization Works*, New Haven, CT: Yale University Press.

4   THE UNANSWERED QUESTIONS OF THE JUST WAGE

Thomas E. Woods, Jr

The limits of the Church's teaching authority

The question of the 'just wage', the level of remuneration that an employer must award his workers if he is to satisfy the demands of justice, became an especially important one in the Catholic world following the publication of Pope Leo XIII's *Rerum novarum* (1891). There the Pope condemned socialism, but he also agreed with the conventional thinking of his time that, first, capitalist greed had forced the working class into their miserable state, and, second, that wage rates reached by means of the voluntary agreement of both parties might be unjust, particularly since the workers lacked the bargaining power necessary in order to win for themselves the wages they needed and deserved.[1] Thus the document criticised the notion of wages as 'regulated by free consent, and [that] therefore the employer, when he pays what was agreed upon, has done his part and seemingly is not called upon to do anything beyond'. Workers and employers may enter into agreements pertaining to wages, but

> there underlies a dictate of natural justice more imperious and
> ancient than any bargain between man and man, namely, that
> wages ought not to be insufficient to support a frugal and well-
> behaved wage-earner. If through necessity or fear of a worse evil
> the workman accept harder conditions because an employer or
> contractor will afford him no better, he is made the victim of force
> and injustice. (RN 45)

---

1   Although the Pope does not use the modern term 'bargaining power', this point is strongly implied in *Rerum novarum* (RN 1, 3, 36, 37). The US bishops expressed the argument in modern terms in 1984: see Block (1985: 151). For a critique of the idea that workers lack 'bargaining power', see Woods (2004).

Pope Leo later spoke of the need to pay wages 'sufficient to enable [the labourer] comfortably to support himself, his wife, and his children' (RN 46).

It has not been easy to carry on a fruitful, critical study of this issue, since supporters of the just wage so often attempt to stifle rational debate through a simple appeal to authority: the Popes, they say, have spoken. The teaching, however, is in fact quite recent, is not consistent over time, and is based on superficially plausible but dubious economic presuppositions (labour's supposedly unequal bargaining power being among those dubious presuppositions) that would appear to be debatable matters of fact rather than statements of faith and morals. The sixteenth-century Spanish Scholastics adopted a generally laissez-faire position regarding wages, arguing that no wage to which a labourer gave his consent could be unjust. If he was unhappy with the compensation he was being offered, he could terminate his employment. No one at the time reacted in horror, or declared it to be radically at odds with Catholic tradition.[2]

Catholic supporters of the free labour market, it is sometimes alleged, are no different from Catholics who dissent from the Church's official teachings on controversial topics such as abortion, medical ethics and human sexuality. This charge is completely without merit: the free-market Catholic typically objects only to instrumental rather than substantive features of the social teaching. In other words, the Catholic supporter of the free market wants to see the same good outcomes that the Popes seek, but fears that the means sometimes suggested to bring about those ends will not succeed. A similar point can be made about papal teaching on development aid (see Chapter 3). While the Pope has every right to declare abortion to be a moral evil, for instance, he cannot

---

2   It should not be thought that, at that time, there was a consensus of feeling among scholars and the ruling classes in favour of freedom of contract. Indeed, the reverse is the case. While it was recognised that the Spanish Scholastics spoke with reason, the prejudice in favour of administered, rather than market-determined, wages was probably stronger then than it is today.

by his *ipse dixit* make *A* cause *B* if in the nature of things course of action *A* in fact inhibits *B*. The leftist is dissenting from papal teaching on an issue involving substantial moral goods; the Catholic supporter of the free labour market is concerned simply that the Pope's recommended course of action to help the less fortunate will – contrary to the Pope's own true intention – either do no such thing or make the situation worse.

Archbishop John J. Myers recently made what should be the elementary distinction between means and ends that we are making here. While with abortion 'there can be no legitimate diversity of opinion', the same is not true of economic issues, where the best approach to take in concrete circumstances is a matter of informed judgement and individual conscience:

> For example, our preferential option for the poor is a fundamental aspect of this teaching. But, there are legitimate disagreements about the best way or ways truly to help the poor in our society. No Catholic can legitimately say, 'I do not care about the poor.' If he or she did so this person would not be objectively in communion with Christ and His Church. But, both those who propose welfare increases and those who propose tax cuts to stimulate the economy may in all sincerity believe that their way is the best method really to help the poor. This is a matter of prudential judgment made by those entrusted with the care of the common good. It is a matter of conscience in the proper sense. (Myers, 2004)

Our position in no way involves the claim that the social or hard sciences are exempt from moral evaluation. They are, however, exempt from *technical critiques* on the part of the Church, since churchmen may speak only as informed individuals on such questions and not for the Church as a whole. Thus if a certain medicine could be produced only by ripping the hearts out of living human beings, the Church should condemn such a thing no matter how many doctors were in favour of producing the medicine. But if two kinds of medicines are suggested to treat a particular ailment, and no moral objection can be raised to either one, then in such an area the Church must defer to those who are schooled in that specialised science.

Another claim is that Catholic supporters of the free market have defined the sphere of faith and morals too narrowly, and that the Popes' statements about the economy are a perfectly legitimate subset of those areas of life over which they have been given divine authority to instruct the faithful. The Popes, this argument goes, have every right to speak out on economic matters since economic affairs are not utterly distinct or removed from moral concerns.

This argument, too, misfires. No one denies that economic activity carries a moral dimension. The Pope is obviously well within his rights to condemn theft or fraud, or to instruct the faithful on the need to be generous with their wealth. He may likewise condemn government policies that involve oppression and injustice, such as burdensome taxation or inflation of the money supply. No one in this debate contests any of this.

The real issue at stake, which is obscured by these straw-man objections, is this. Suppose a Church document recommends a particular economic policy as being morally necessary because its drafters believe it will make the poor better off. Suppose further that they consider it so obvious that this policy will improve the lot of the poor that they do not consider the possibility that it could have any other effect, that there could be any good reason for opposing it, or even simply that a trade-off exists between the good outcome they hope for and unfortunate, unintended side effects of the given policy. And now suppose that the policy will, in fact, not only *not* improve the position of the poor, but may also make it even worse. What are economically astute members of the faithful to do? Are they forbidden to observe that not even the Pope himself can make reality otherwise than it is?

The question is not whether the Pope may instruct us on our responsibilities as moral actors in the marketplace (see Chapters 6 and 7). The question, instead, is whether the Pope's infallibility reaches to his empirical and theoretical statements about how the economy works. For instance, the Pope may certainly say that all morally licit means should be employed in order to improve the material well-being of families, since they are the building blocks of society and the little platoons (to borrow a phrase from Edmund Burke) from which its future members will one day emerge. But in his capacity as Pope, with the power to bind all Catholics on pain of mortal sin, may he go on to say what, from a purely pragmatic point of view, would be the best or most effective way to bring about this outcome? No orthodox definition of papal authority includes infallibility regarding such matters, and it would be rank superstition for a Catholic to hold otherwise.

A good example of this difficulty involves Pope Paul VI's 1967 encyclical *Populorum progressio* (see Chapter 3). There the Pope called for the very kind of Western-funded Third World development programmes that have proved so disastrous in practice. These programmes – as scholars like Peter Bauer pointed out in vain at the time – served to prop up some of the most brutal regimes in the world, and shielded dictators from the full consequences of their destructive economic policies. They delayed necessary reforms, enlarged the state sector at the expense of the productive economy, and created often violent ethnic and racial tension as competing groups scrambled to gain control of the state apparatus in order to control Western grant money. The encyclical was filled with the standard criticisms of the free market, yet it was the most market-oriented of the less developed nations that wound up prospering the most, and where the lot of the poor improved most dramatically (Woods, 2005a: ch. 4).

Thus Paul VI called for the implementation of policies that few informed and responsible people, looking at their horrific and lethal record, would continue to promote or defend today. There were people at the time who predicted exactly what would happen, but who were ignored in favour of the chorus of fashionable opinion that called for massive Western funding of state-led development programmes in the Third World. Now Pope Paul VI could certainly have instructed the faithful on the moral issues at stake, urging them to be generous towards their impoverished brethren. That is what a teacher of faith and morals is expected to do. But, by any standard, whether (for example) free trade or a system of protective tariffs is more effective for a developing country – obviously a matter of legitimate disagreement among Catholics – or whether state-led development programmes are a good economic idea are not issues on which the Pope may appear to make morally binding judgements. Not only are specific policy proposals all too fallible, but when enjoying the prestige of an encyclical they can unnecessarily trouble the consciences of good Catholics, whose disagreements are based not on any perverse desire to oppose the Holy See but on specialised secular knowledge they happen to possess. That is why Pope Leo XIII once said, 'If I were to pronounce on any single matter of a prevailing economic problem, I should be interfering with the freedom of men to work out their own affairs. Certain cases must be solved in the domain of facts, case by case as they occur. ... [M]en must realize in deeds those things, the principles of which have been placed beyond dispute. ... [T]hese things one must leave to the solution of time and experience' (Burton, 1962: 171).

The minimum wage, the plight of the poor and Catholic conscience

Paul VI, like many at the time, was sure the policies he recommended would benefit the least fortunate. It is clear from the context in which wages are discussed in the encyclicals that the Popes likewise take for granted that interfering with wage rates reached voluntarily on the free market, either through legally imposed wage floors or by means of moral exhortation, can make labour in the aggregate better off. Monsignor John A. Ryan, perhaps the twentieth century's most prolific American Catholic proponent of the concept of a just wage as something distinct from the freely agreed wage, wrote his books and articles on the living wage *because he thought these proposals would make labour better off*. It is difficult to imagine an official Church document arguing that forcing wages beyond the level they attain on the free market is an end in itself, *even if it makes heads of households materially worse off* by pricing some workers out of the market. No such document exists, of course, and it is safe to assume that none will ever be issued. But this is the very crux of the matter: how is a Catholic to respond to a teaching whose stated intent is to improve the well-being of struggling workers when he knows it will do no such thing?

While it is true that the Popes do not directly call for legally mandated minimum wages, the logic of their arguments leads in that direction. Since the overwhelming majority of people who have written on the social teaching, from ordinary laymen all the way to bishops' conferences, have in fact justified minimum wages and minimum-wage increases on the basis of that teaching and have never been corrected or rebuked by the Vatican, it must be safe to assume that such a position is at least a legitimate development of the teaching, and is certainly not excluded by it.

In a certain sense, though, whether or not the social encyclicals call for a *legally* mandated minimum wage or whether they simply declare the employer to be *morally* bound to provide one is largely immaterial. To a Catholic employer who believes the Catholic Church is of divine institution, there may be little practical difference between a minimum wage that is imposed legally and one that is imposed on his conscience by the official teaching of a national bishops' conference.

Of the measures we might propose in order to improve the lot of the poor, the minimum 'living wage' is very likely to be the worst of all.[3] By making unskilled workers more expensive to hire, it privileges those who are the most prosperous and skilled. This is why labour unions, which in practice tend to represent those who are semi-skilled or skilled, consistently favour minimum-wage and living-wage legislation even though their own workers earn much more than these minima and would seem

---

3   There are other measures such as welfare safety nets and social insurance that can be debated on their merits, but both of these are less likely to be damaging than the imposition of a minimum wage.

to be unaffected by them. By making their low-skilled counterparts relatively more expensive, they enrich themselves at the expense of the most vulnerable workers of all. And when the living-wage measure is introduced and the job losses inevitably come, it is once again the least skilled and most vulnerable who are the first to suffer.

The 'market power' argument

A common argument in favour of state coercion on behalf of the worker involves the issue of labour monopsony – cases in which workers cannot choose between potential employers but for whatever reason must sell their labour to a particular firm. It is often suggested that labour monopsonies were common at the time the first social encyclical was written. Labour economist Morgan Reynolds has raised a number of substantial objections to this alleged problem, all of which are relevant to the economies of the UK and the USA in the nineteenth century. If monopsony had been so serious and pervasive in the nineteenth century as is commonly assumed, it seems difficult to explain why wages rose for most of the century, how there could have been so much job-switching, or why large firms – more likely to hold monopsony power – paid higher wages than small firms (Reynolds, 1995: 12–13).

The major obstacles to a labour monopsony involve the tendency of new firms to enter an industry over time, attracted by the low wages offered by the monopsonist and the tendency of workers simply to move away and settle somewhere that has a friendlier economic climate and a greater diversity of employers. These incentives 'make widespread, sustained monopsony impossible in an economy like that of the United States' (ibid.: 247). The widespread availability of inexpensive transportation has now essentially buried the argument from monopsony once and for all, since workers are now able to canvass employers across a radius of at least several dozen miles.

Living or minimum wages are typically demanded on the grounds that the people who will receive them need such wages in order to support their families. That, indeed, is the very heart of the just-wage position. But suppose we argued as follows in the case of individuals supporting their families from business activity: the selling prices for most used cars are too low for the sellers of these cars to support their families. The poor in particular, since they tend to have the worst-quality cars to sell, suffer the most. Therefore, it will be illegal from now on for any used car to sell for a price below £12,000. That way, sellers of these cars will earn enough to support their families.[4]

Now, of course, what will really happen is that a great many used cars, valued in the common estimation of the market at less than £12,000, will simply not sell at all. The owners of those cars will not be able to support their families *at all*, and are much worse off than they would have been if they had been able to sell their cars for at least some amount of money (naturally, too, purchasers of cars will be harmed as well). In other words, it does not follow from the mere fact that someone needs something that it would be sensible to impose his desire by law. This is what minimum wages seek to do in the case of employed people. There is no difference in principle between the government mandating a minimum wage for employed people and mandating minimum prices for the goods that somebody who is self-employed tries to sell. If the product of the worker has a market value less than the mandated price or wage the individual will not be able to obtain employment.

Finally, it is morally relevant that there exists on the free market a natural tendency for real wages to rise over time. In a relatively unhampered market, business is free to invest its profits in machinery and other capital equipment that makes labour more productive. One person can then produce far more than he once could, and at lower cost. The economy can now produce in much greater abundance. These cost cuts are passed on to consumers in the form of lower prices.[5] These

---

4   I owe this example to Don Boudreaux of George Mason University: http://cafehayek. typepad.com/hayek/2006/06/testing_the_log.html.

5   In an economy with a rapidly expanding money supply, these price cuts are not always apparent. The point is that prices are lower than they otherwise would have been; another

increases in the productivity of labour, by increasing the overall amount of output and thereby increasing the ratio of consumers' goods to the supply of labour, make prices lower relative to wage rates and thereby raise real wages (Reisman, 1996: 603–72; Woods 2005a: 59–67). Leo XIII was therefore more right than he knew when he made the anti-Marxist observation in *Rerum novarum* that capital and labour were natural allies rather than antagonists. Here is the proof: both labour and the owners of capital should want the same economic policies – low or non-existent taxation, and no government discouragement of business investment – since both benefit from investment in capital equipment and the resulting increase in overall wealth.

We cannot assume away the fact that it is the poor who will suffer from a minimum wage ...

The teaching of the Church on what constitutes a just war includes the proviso that violence must be resorted to only as a last resort, when all other options have failed. The same logic might be extended to domestic issues as well (see also the chapters by Sirico on welfare and charity, Gregg on the role of government and O'Brien on subsidiarity and solidarity). Before resorting to coercion we should consider all possible alternative ways of achieving economic objectives. Indeed, according to our argument above, coercion is both unnecessary and counterproductive.

Peter Kwasniewski, a critic of the free market, is unmoved by this argument. In Kwasniewski's version of things, we can solve the problem of insufficiently high wages here and now. We want everyone to earn a decent wage? Then we can simply legislate one into existence! According to Kwasniewski, if someone claims

> that he agrees with what the Popes want (*e.g.*, a living wage) but
> he thinks he knows better how to get those results, he is dodging
> the problems that we are facing *here and now*. Let us pretend that

point is that wages increase more rapidly than prices, since the ratio of consumers' goods to the supply of labour has increased.

the magic of the free market will work things out to everyone's advantage ... *someday*. How long from now? Ten years? Twenty? Fifty? Meanwhile, do we let wage agreements contrary to the moral law simply stand unchecked, because the lives of some poor people have to be, as it were, manure to fertilize the ground for more prosperous days? It seems to me the Church is saying: The worker has to be given such and such, *here and now*. If not, mortal sin is being committed and the common good damaged. If this means inefficiency, okay; if it means a lower gross national product, okay; if it means the rich have to live more frugally, that's even better. (Kwasniewski, 2004)

Kwasniewski has dodged the entire question. He simply assumes that the poor can be made better off, with no side effects that he considers morally relevant (or, at least, no side effects, such as unemployment, that are worth mentioning as *no* potentially harmful side effects are discussed or even raised), through state coercion and mandating of a minimum wage. He assumes the very point that is to be proved. In fact, *the poor themselves* would be worse off, since his recommendation would make them less employable and, by making it more expensive and less profitable to do business in the first place, would discourage the very capital accumulation that alone can improve the lot of the poor across the board.

Had Kwasniewski lived during the Industrial Revolution we can only imagine his complaints.[6] We need 2,000 square feet per family here and now. We need the eight-hour day. We need modern amenities for all. Let us impose them through law, rather than wait for economic progress to provide these things as the miserly Thomas Woods and other believers in the market economy would have us do. In that capital-starved economy these regulations would have made just about everyone unemployable, and would have brought the inevitable (if gradual) improvement in everyone's standard of living to a grinding halt – the same effect such

6   On the Industrial Revolution and the increase in the standard of living of the overwhelming majority of people, see Woods (2005a: 169–74).

regulations would have today. If we wanted to be sure that the Third World never emerges from poverty, we should give them this kind of advice today. It isn't that Kwasniewski has considered what economics has to say about such policies and decided that the benefits outweigh the costs to the poor. As far as Kwasniewski is concerned, there are no costs to the poor from the pursuit of such policies. He will concede that the economy may be poorer overall – though he evidently assumes that this overall impoverishment will not appreciably hurt the poor – or that the rich may be poorer. He is willing to live with these costs, he assures us. But are there any costs for the poor? Not a word, other than an implicit assumption of 'no'.

Economist George Reisman suggests what would have happened if nineteenth-century poverty had been addressed by forcing the rich to live more frugally, as Kwasniewski suggests is possible. The problem is that

> there was virtually nothing to redistribute. The workers of the early nineteenth century did not lack automobiles and television sets because the capitalists were keeping the whole supply to themselves. There simply were no automobiles or television sets – for anyone. Nor did the workers of those days lack sufficient housing, clothing, and meat because the capitalists had too much of these goods. Very little of such goods could be produced when they had to be produced almost entirely by hand. If the limited supplies of such goods that the capitalists had could have been redistributed, the improvement in the conditions of the workers would hardly have been noticeable. If one person in a thousand, say, is a wealthy capitalist, and eats twice as much and has twenty times the clothing and furniture as an average person, hardly any noticeable improvement for the average person could come from dividing the capitalists' greater-than-average consumption by 999 and redistributing it. At the very best, a redistribution of wealth or income would have been useless as a means of alleviating the poverty of the past. (Reisman, 1996: 653)

Not only would it have been useless, but it would also have been positively harmful. If businessmen wish to stay in business, they must reinvest the vast bulk of their profits in still further additions to their capital stock – which in turn further increase the productivity of labour, thereby increasing the supply of goods that the economy is capable of producing. These increases in the productivity of labour, by increasing the overall amount of output and thereby increasing the ratio of consumers' goods to the supply of labour, make prices lower relative to wage rates and thereby raise real wages. Kwasniewski's plan to increase the lot of the working class would sacrifice the investment in capital equipment that business must now forgo, and would lower the incentive to engage in such investment in the future, since the business community now knows the fruits of such investment will be taken away (ibid.: 653).

Providing a living wage ... as soon as possible

In light of our discussion of wages and how they are increased, we are in a better position to evaluate Pius XI's statement in *Quadragesimo anno* that all men must be paid a wage sufficient to support their families in reasonable comfort, and that where this is not possible 'social justice demands that changes be introduced as soon as possible whereby such a wage will be assured to every adult workingman'. According to what we have just argued, when *Quadragesimo anno* urges us to introduce changes in order to make a living wage available to working men, a good way to comply with that instruction would be to remove as many obstacles to investment as possible, and to eliminate taxes on capital, 'excess profits' and the like. Unfortunately, certain ecclesiastical documents seem to call for just the opposite: practically every single recommendation set forth in the American bishops' famous 1984 statement on the economy would have made workers and the poor worse off (Block, 1985: 125–60). That document, among others, is an object lesson in the need for sound economic reasoning to inform our moral conclusions. 'What was wrong with Catholic social thought in the nineteenth century,' writes Father James Sadowsky, SJ, of Fordham University, 'was not so much its ethics as its lack of understanding of how the free market can work. The concern for the worker was entirely legitimate, but concern can accomplish little unless we know the causes and the cures for the disease' (Sadowsky, 1983: 125).

Non-economic arguments and the just wage

The matter of the just wage raises additional concerns beyond the merely economic. Imagine a case in which the authorities have somehow managed to pinpoint the 'just wage' as £5 per hour – and assume that the requirement is not statutory but is regarded as a moral obligation by some Christian employers. Then consider employee John, and firms A and B. Firm A, not considering John's labour worth the decreed wage, passes him over for employment. Firm B, however, willing to incur the criticisms of the wage authorities, employs John at the mutually agreed-upon wage of £4 per hour.

Consider how the 'just wage' proponent would apportion moral approval and censure in this case. Firm A chooses not to employ John at all. Firm B employs him at £4 per hour, which is £4 per hour more than John receives from Firm A. Yet in the 'just wage' framework, it is Firm B that merits condemnation, even though Firm A did not even hire John in the first place. Indeed, Firm A's action (or inaction) will not even be known about. Firm B makes the man at least somewhat better off than he had been before, while Firm A contributes nothing at all to his well-being. Is it morally preferable for someone not to be hired at all rather than to be hired at a wage that is somewhat below whatever has been decreed as the 'just wage'?

Roman law, in its treatment of prices, held that a thing was worth what it could generally be sold for. In the absence of any better offer for the man's labour, it is not clear on what grounds his current wage can be considered unjust. James Sadowsky poses the natural question: in the case of a worker in dire need, while 'certainly from a Christian point of view we ought to help him meet his needs, the question that *ought* to arise is this: "Why, however, should it be precisely the *employer* on whom this obligation falls, if in fact the employer is not worsening but bettering the condition of his employee?'" (ibid.: 124). If no one else can find any use for the man's labour at a price higher than or equal to what his current employer is offering, why is his current employer the only party to be morally censured? Isn't his employer doing more than literally anyone else on earth to improve his well-being? If this teaching makes the man unemployable by closing off this one employment opportunity, he is unlikely to be consoled by the assurance that at least justice has been served.

Rerum novarum bases some of its argument for intervention against employers and on behalf of labourers on the notion of the primacy of labour in the overall scheme of production. In the provision of commodities that the community needs, the document explains,

> the labour of the working class – the exercise of their skill, and the
> employment of their strength, in the cultivation of the land, and
> in the workshops of trade – is especially responsible and quite
> indispensable. Indeed, their co-operation is in this respect so
> important that it may be truly said that it is only by the labour of
> working men that States grow rich. Justice, therefore, demands that
> the interests of the working classes should be carefully watched
> over by the administration, so that they who contribute so largely
> to the advantage of the community may themselves share in the
> benefits which they create – that being housed, clothed, and bodily
> fit, they may find their life less hard and more endurable. (RN 34)

Leo XIII concludes by declaring it 'good for the commonwealth to shield from misery those on whom it so largely depends for the things that it needs'.

To be sure, *Rerum novarum* is correct to note the complementarity of capital and labour, since each of course needs the other. But it seems dubious to exalt the contribution of labour to the point of suggesting that 'it is only by the labour of working men that States grow rich'. Just how much could a worker produce with his bare hands, without the aid of the machinery and other forms of capital that a firm provides for his use?

Let us briefly dispense with the facile objection that capital equipment, too, requires labour for its production, and that this fact once again demonstrates the primacy of labour.[7] What this argument overlooks is that brawn alone will never produce a steam shovel, a forklift or a Pentium processor. Only when informed by the knowledge of inventors and supplied with the capital saved by capitalists can the average labourer produce the tiniest fraction of what he is today accustomed to producing. There is, therefore, no sense in which the position of the ordinary labourer in the overall structure of production can give him a prior moral claim on the monies of his employer (for that reason, it seems that the Pope speaks better when he says elsewhere in *Rerum novarum*: 'Each needs the other: capital cannot do without labor, nor labor without capital' (RN 19)).

Indeed, if we are going to dismiss wage rates voluntarily arrived at as potentially 'unjust', and instead apportion monies on the basis of some theoretical reckoning of each component's contribution to the production process, the outcome will not please proponents of a 'just wage'. As we have seen, it is investment in capital equipment which increases the productivity of labour and thus increases real wages. In light of that, should workers be required to hand over a portion of their salary as a kickback to their employers to compensate them for the capital equipment (and the abstention from consumption that made investment in that capital equipment possible), none of which was in any way earned by the worker? Free consent as a basis for wage determination would appear preferable to wages determined on the basis of highly debatable philosophical propositions and counter-propositions.

Other intractable problems seem to plague the just-wage concept. George Stigler once observed that human beings could acquire a physiologically adequate diet for a mere $8 a month (in 1950 prices) by eating,

---

7   Christopher Ferrara advanced this argument in a lengthy series of articles in *The Remnant*, a traditional Catholic newspaper published in the United States, in 2004/05.

over the course of the year, nothing but 370 pounds of wheat flour, 57 cans of evaporated milk, 111 pounds of cabbage, 25 pounds of spinach and 285 pounds of dried navy beans (Stigler, 1952: 2). It is not clear how appeals to 'justice' in wage determination can resolve such practical questions on anything but an arbitrary basis. Such a diet as this would, almost certainly, be unbearably monotonous even if nutritionally satisfactory. But just how diversified a diet can we derive from justice in the abstract as morally obligatory for an employer to provide? That question, furthermore, neglects the enjoyment a worker derives from eating an occasional meal in a restaurant rather than at home, but here again justice does not disclose to us how many restaurant meals, if any, an employer bears the moral burden of providing.

We would likewise need to adjust for the widely varying circumstances in which people find themselves. Consider a father of eight compared with a celibate Opus Dei numerary. Leaving aside the virtual certainty that such a wage would render him unemployable, does the father deserve a wage eight times as high as the numerary? The numerary may be responsible for a sick relative. How would that consideration be factored in? Would the employer need to enquire into how many people live in the numerary's Opus Dei house, what their mutual obligations are, and what the needs of the house are?[8] Would he need to enquire into the father's budget for babysitters, the relative importance he places on entertainment, or the number of movie rentals he watches per month? Would movie rentals be considered a luxury or a component of a truly just wage? These questions are not meant to be facetious, but simply to illustrate the difficulties involved in calculating a just wage and of applying the concept of 'justice' to the determination of economic and material conditions.

---

8   I owe this point to Sam Bostaph of the University of Dallas.

Conclusion

A contemporary Catholic reviewer of Monsignor John Ryan's *A Living Wage*, writing in the *Catholic University Bulletin*, tried without success to point out to Ryan that a business is not a charitable foundation but an enterprise devoted to producing some good or service at the lowest cost to the consumer. Ryan's critic concluded: 'As an individual or as head of a family, the laborer produces the same amount of work; how then could the employer as such be obliged in strict justice to take into account a condition which is of no advantage to him?' (Sauvage, 1907: 474). These were the days of Pope St Pius X, and at that time the *Catholic University Bulletin* never published anything that called any solemn Church teaching into question. That the publication nevertheless considered this matter an essentially open question available for rational debate is not without significance.

Pope Pius XI made an important concession in his encyclical *Quadragesimo anno* (1931). He acknowledged that limits must exist to what the moral theologian may legitimately say within the economic sphere, since 'economics and moral science employs each its own principles in its own sphere'. It is true that the Pope then went on to deny that 'the economic and moral orders are so distinct from and alien to each other that the former depends in no way on the latter'. But once it has been conceded that economics is a bona fide science possessing an internal coherence of its own, problems immediately arise for those who would claim that Catholic Social Teaching definitively settles all major economic matters in an absolute and binding way. As A. M. C. Waterman points out, this concession by Pius XI 'throws doubt on the authoritative character of that very substantial part of Catholic (or at least papal) social teaching which consists not of theological and ethical pronouncements, but of empirical judgments about the economy' (Waterman, 1982: 112–13).

A great many unresolved issues remain in the area of the just wage. Those who raise them are not wicked men, perversely desirous of causing mischief in the Church. Most are serious Catholics who understand that this is an evolving teaching, and one that partly depends on means–ends connections that in the nature of things are obviously open to debate. Edward Grant tells us that in the medieval university 'reason was enthroned ... as the ultimate arbiter of most intellectual arguments and controversies. It was quite natural for scholars immersed in a university environment to employ reason to probe into subject areas that had not been explored before, as well as to discuss possibilities that had not previously been seriously entertained' (Woods, 2005b: 66). Likewise David Lindberg reports that although there were broad theological limits, the medieval professor 'had remarkable freedom of thought and expression; there was almost no doctrine, philosophical or theological, that was not submitted to minute scrutiny and criticism by scholars in the medieval university' (ibid.: 220). There is no reason that the same spirit cannot continue to animate Catholic discourse now. Let the discussion be carried on in a spirit of charity, reason and faith, and let us assume the best rather than the worst about those with whom we disagree.

References

Block, W. (1985), 'Neglect of the marketplace: the questionable economics of America's bishops', *Notre Dame Journal of Law, Ethics, & Public Policy*, 2: 125–60.

Burton, K. (1962), *Leo the Thirteenth: The First Modern Pope*, New York: David McKay Co.

Kwasniewski, P. (2004), 'This goes way beyond free markets: thoughts on the disagreement between Woods and Storck', 5 July, http://chroniclesmagazine.org/News/Kwasniewski/NewsPK070504.html.

Myers, Archbishop J. J. (2004), 'A time for honesty': a pastoral statement by The Most Reverend John J. Myers, Archbishop of Newark', 5 May, http://www.rcan.org/archbish/jjm_letters/ATimeforHonesty.htm.

Reisman, G. (1996), *Capitalism*, Ottawa, IL: Jameson Books.

Reynolds, M. (1995), *Economics of Labor*, Cincinnati, OH: South-Western College Publishing.

Sadowsky, J. A. (1983), 'Capitalism, ethics, and classical Catholic social doctrine', *This World*, 6: 115–25.

Sauvage, G. M. (1907), Review of *A Living Wage*, by John A. Ryan, *Catholic University Bulletin*, 13: 470–75.

Stigler, G. (1952), *The Theory of Price*, rev. edn, New York: Macmillan.

Waterman, A. M. C. (1982), 'Property rights in John Locke and in Christian social teaching', *Review of Social Economy*, 9: 97–115.

Woods, T. (2004), 'Forgotten facts of American labor history', Mises.org, 22 November, http://www.mises.org/fullstory. aspx?control=1685&id=74.

Woods, T. E., Jr (2005a), *The Church and the Market: A Catholic Defense of the Free Economy*, Lanham, MD: Lexington.

Woods, T. E., Jr (2005b), *How the Catholic Church Built Western Civilization*, Washington, DC: Regnery.

5   TAXATION AND THE SIZE OF THE STATE
Philip Booth

Introduction

This chapter begins with a discussion of Catholic teaching on the role of taxation. In the discussion of Catholic teaching we concentrate on the later teaching of the Church, starting with the publication of *Rerum novarum* in 1891. There was, of course, earlier authoritative comment by the Church and Her teachers on economic matters (see, for example, Charles, 1998, vol. 1: 209, 361–71 for some discussion of this early comment); also the late Scholastics warned against excessive taxation. The early Church's role in what could be described as 'social witness' rather than social teaching in the medieval period is important too: the Church, not the state, was the dominant provider of welfare in line with the principles of subsidiarity (see ibid., but also Bartholomew, 2004, for an account of the remarkable achievements of the Church in welfare provision in the UK). This earlier work and the early examples of social witness are important, but the post-1891 teaching of the Church made this earlier analysis explicit in the wider public domain and so it is on the post-1891 period that we shall focus. The documents that have been used to express Catholic Church teaching since 1891 are easily available.

An understanding of taxation must be set in the context of the principle of private property and that of the universal destination of goods. There is not space for a detailed discussion of this issue here, but some brief comments are worth making. With regard to the principle of the universal destination of goods, the Catholic Church teaches that the fruits of God's creation are for all to be enjoyed. It does not follow from this, however, that all should have access to all goods equally or that redistribution and common ownership in a socialist political system should be the vehicle for facilitating the universal destination of goods. With this in mind, the Church also teaches that private property is an important way in which the universal destination of goods can be achieved. The principle of private property is not inviolable, but it accords with economic efficiency, family autonomy and free will: there is an excellent discussion of these issues in the recently published *Compendium of the Social Doctrine of the Church* (paras 171–84)[1] and also in Spieker (2005). Taxation, of course, violates private property. In the context of the Church's teaching on the universal destination of goods and on private property it can be seen that, while taxation may be permitted, excessive taxation is likely to be problematic. As such, the precise level of taxation is clearly a matter for prudential judgement informed, at least in part, by economic reasoning. Therefore, the Church, in Her teaching, has limited Her statements to general principles and not made judgements about appropriate rates of taxation. That part of the laity involved in political debate and decision-making, however, will, of course, have to draw conclusions, informed by the Church's teaching and economic reasoning, on the appropriate level of taxation.

Modern Catholic teaching on taxation and the role of the state: taxation for redistribution and welfare
Rerum novarum

Pope Leo XIII's encyclical *Rerum novarum* was a landmark in that it began a stream of writing from the modern Popes on economic problems and political choices in industrial and post-industrial society. It is often described as the 'workers' encyclical', and it was critical of many aspects of behaviour by the owners of capital and businesses. Interestingly, however, it provides no basis for arguments proposing a substantial tax burden or for the state to take upon itself wide-ranging functions akin

---

1   Referred to as Pontifical Council for Justice and Peace (2005).

to those it undertakes today in most developed countries. Furthermore, *Rerum novarum* provides strong a priori arguments against excessive taxation and frequently recommends other mechanisms for the achievement of specific economic objectives. For example, paragraph five states, 'Socialists, therefore, by endeavouring to transfer the possessions of individuals to the community at large, strike at the interests of every wage earner, since they would deprive him of the liberty of disposing of his wages.' The state is to serve man, not the other way round: 'Man precedes the State, and possesses, prior to the formation of any State, the right of providing for the substance of his body' (RN 7). Paragraph 13 stresses the complete primacy of the family over the state and lays out the importance of the principle of inheritance to transmit productive property to children.

Rerum novarum sees no place for the pursuit of equality as an end in itself, nor for taxation for its own sake. Applying this to policy, this would appear to exclude systems of taxation that lead to greater equality but lead everyone, including the poor, to be poorer. In the words of *Rerum novarum*: 'The door would be thrown open to envy, to mutual invective, and to discord; the sources of wealth themselves would run dry, for no one would have any interest in exerting his talents or industry; and that ideal equality about which they [socialists] entertain pleasant dreams would be in reality the levelling down of all to a like condition of misery and degradation' (RN 15). Pope Leo then went on to express belief in the inviolability of private property[2] as the primary method of raising the condition of the poor, and suggested that inequality is far from disadvantageous to individuals or to the community. Pope Leo (for example, RN 22) lauds the principle of charity by which people should give to others that which they do not need for themselves. It is suggested that

---

2   Pope Leo stated exceptions to that inviolability. Later encyclicals tended not to use the phrase 'inviolable' and, indeed, suggest that, though rights to property are of great importance, they are not inviolable. This later emphasis is in accord with the teachings of St Thomas Aquinas.

giving alms is not a duty of justice,[3] except in extreme cases, but of Christian charity – 'a duty not enforced by human law'. Action by voluntary groups and associations and by the Church Herself are praised, and those who would replace voluntary action with a system of state relief are criticised.[4]

Pope Leo does not object to the principle of taxation, but even when proposing that taxation can be put to certain ends such as helping the poor it is suggested that the more in line with Christian principles are the general laws of a state, 'the less need will there be to seek for special means to relieve them [the poor]' (RN 32). Nevertheless, it is clear that providing citizens with a basic income (for food, clothing and shelter) is a potential role for taxation envisaged by Pope Leo. It might be added that *Rerum novarum* also suggested certain forms of regulation of wages to achieve the objectives of assisting workers.

Excessive taxation and taxation of the poor was certainly not favoured by Pope Leo. The poor, it is suggested, can only escape their condition through the ownership of property (as many people as possible should become owners: RN 46) – ownership should not be undermined by taxation as that would be to undermine the means to help the poor save.[5, 6]

---

3   A duty of justice might imply intervention by the state.

4   These sentiments also pervade Part II of Pope Benedict XVI's first encyclical, *Deus caritas est*, though they are expressed rather differently. *Deus caritas est* discusses how state action, however well directed and well intended, will always be incomplete. Welfare given from love and charity fulfils a deeper need.

5   It should be noted that the share of government spending in national income in the UK was about 10 per cent when *Rerum novarum* was written – about one fifth of today's level. This is also the case in almost all other European countries for which data exists (see Heath and Smith, 2006).

6   The *Compendium of the Social Doctrine of the Church* has only a brief section explicitly on taxation – stating it is necessary for the provision of certain services and functions in the name of the common good. Although many of the warnings about the welfare state, discussed below, are referred to in other sections of the *Compendium*, there is no mention of the points discussed above in relation to arguments for limiting taxation. This would appear to be an omission. Also worth noting is that, in the back cover text of the English-language edition of the *Compendium*, it is stated, 'Through landmark encyclicals issued by Popes since *Rerum novarum*, the Church has built up a wide-ranging body of teach-

Quadragesimo anno

Quadragesimo anno, by Pope Pius XI, has been criticised by free-market economists[7] for taking a position sympathetic to the economic models proposed by fascists in the 1920s and early 1930s.[8] These involved cooperative economic arrangements between workers' organisations and employers' organisations, together with a suppression of competition. Nevertheless, a significant role for taxation in redistribution is neither envisaged nor proposed by Pope Pius. Much of the burden of raising the condition of poor workers is allocated to corporations and to workers' and employers' organisations. Strong statements were made against taxation of the poor and the pursuit of equality for its own sake: 'Wherefore the wise Pontiff [Pope Leo] declared that it is grossly unjust for a State to exhaust private wealth through the weight of imposts and taxes' (QA 49). Strong statements are also made about the lack of resources of the poor, but charity is regarded as far more than the marginal activity that it has become today: 'the rich are bound by a very grave precept to practice almsgiving, beneficence, and munificence' (QA 50; see also QA 137, 'How completely deceived, therefore, are those rash reformers who ... in their pride reject the assistance of charity'). Ensuring that the poor can become property owners, and shareholders in the businesses for which they work, are regarded as important ways to raise the condition of the poor, help them to maintain a family and pass something to the following generation (see, for example, QA 61 and 65). Pope Pius does suggest that a wage sufficient for basic family needs (adjusted

---

ing on justice, equality and human rights.' There is no mention of family and personal autonomy, freedom and property rights in this back cover text. And Church teaching on equality, at least in the economic sphere, is not what people might expect given its bracketing with 'justice' and 'human rights' in that sentence.

7   See, for example, Rothbard (1960).

8   It should be noted that this does not, in any way, imply that there was sympathy with other policies of fascists; the economic policies of fascist movements are not materially different from the corporatist policies pursued by, say, Heath's Conservative government in the early 1970s and by many Christian Democrat and Social Democrat governments in continental Europe. There is a good discussion of the nuances of this debate in Hinze (2005).

according to family circumstances) should be *assured* (QA 71). While the taxation system and the state are not mentioned explicitly for this purpose one assumes that the state should be a possible last resort in providing for basic needs if they are to be *assured*. Pope Pius was really appealing, however, for a reorganisation of the economic system along more corporatist lines: the practical implications of such a reorganisation would transcend our discussion of taxation.

Vatican II and after

There is a change in tone in the Vatican II document *Gaudium et spes* (see also Chapter 10). It notes (GS 63) that the economy is marked by 'increased intervention by the state', but differences in income and wealth are also noted and strongly criticised. References to the inviolability of private property are more heavily qualified than in the encyclicals referred to above (for example, GS 71). The issue of whether income differences should be alleviated by charity or through state taxation systems is also left much more ambiguous than in the encyclicals: 'Thus, under the leadership of justice and in the company of charity, created goods should be in abundance for all in like manner' (GS 69). Nevertheless, governments are urged to support the development of voluntary associations (from family to larger voluntary groups) and individuals are urged not to attribute excessive power to political authority nor to make demands upon it in their own interests (GS 74)[9]. Remarkably, though, it suggests that 'the complex circumstances of our day make it necessary for public authority to intervene more often in social, economic and cultural matters' (GS 74).[10] These interventionist

---

9   In a sense this prefigures public choice economics: it asks people to show moral restraint in the 'political marketplace' just as they should in the economic marketplace.

10 This point reflects the intellectual trends of the time. It seems to be the case that it was only in the 1980s that intellectual opinion properly understood the implications of the 'calculation debate' of 50 years previously. The emphatic conclusion of that debate is that the more complex is economic life, the more important it is that individual economic agents have autonomy as they process and discover dispersed information so much more

sentiments reflect the thinking of Pope John XXIII's encyclical *Mater et magistra*.

Gaudium et spes helps provide a context for the discussion of later encyclicals. There appears to be a shift of emphasis with fewer cautions against socialism and the undermining of family autonomy, combined with less emphasis on charity. It is a document written by committee, however, and which had to be agreed upon by a wide constituency. It is looser in its wording than the encyclicals are. It is appropriate, perhaps, to try to interpret *Gaudium et spes* in the light of Church documents that were produced in the following four decades.

Sollicitudo rei socialis[11] mainly deals with the plight of those in the poorest countries. The main issues brought up in that encyclical have been discussed in Chapter 3.[12] There are, however, other general messages in *Sollicitudo rei socialis* relevant to our analysis. It gives more concrete expression to many of the issues raised in *Gaudium et spes*. It was particularly critical of the gap between incomes of the developed and developing world and, oddly, suggests that the gap is widening.[13] Like the earlier encyclicals it is, nevertheless, against enforced equality as something that would destroy initiative and lead to a levelling down (SRS 15). It also recognises charity as fundamental to a genuine expression of solidarity (SRS 40). The concept of the 'preferential option for the poor' is introduced in paragraph 42. It is stressed that this relates to decisions of individual charity as well as to 'social decisions'. It is implied by

---

effectively than centralised decision-making units such as governments. Hayek uses, for the purpose of criticism, an almost identical quote to this one from *Gaudium et spes* at the beginning of Chapter IV of *The Road to Serfdom* (Hayek, 1944) – the quote is from Mussolini.

11 Written by John Paul II in 1987.

12 *Populorum progressio*, published two years after *Gaudium et spes*, communicated similar points and was also dealt with in Chapter 3.

13 Of course, the gap between the developed and the developing world might be widening while the developing world becomes smaller! In other words, the income of the very poorest, often living in 'failed states', might not change but, as many poor states become better off and rich states continue to grow, the gap between the richest and the poorest grows wider while the number of poor people shrinks.

the later discussion of property rights and trade reform (SRS 43–4) that the preferential option for the poor also relates to political decisions. It seems reasonable to conclude that Pope John Paul is suggesting that the normal presumptions of inviolability of property rights, the right for a worker to control use of his wages and so on can be suspended for the purposes of the state aiding the poor.

Centesimus annus, in many respects, echoes faithfully the sentiments of *Rerum novarum*. There are many warnings about the power and size of the state. Nevertheless, John Paul II continues to support redistribution to provide for basic needs, although, once again, the main responsibility for ensuring adequate incomes is placed on private-sector bodies – employers and unions (CA 15).

A clear expression of the problem of providing for contingent needs (such as help in times of disability, old age, unemployment, etc.) is also provided in *Centesimus annus*. Quoting *Rerum novarum*, and reaffirming its relevance today, John Paul II notes that the mass of the poor, particularly wage earners, have no resources to fall back on and should be specially cared for and protected by the government. This statement would appear to be difficult to justify in the modern developed world and was certainly not true in the UK even in the nineteenth century (see, for example, Bartholomew, 2004, but also the impressive range of original sources and evidence quoted by that author). If it is the only justification for the state providing for the contingent needs of low-wage earners, it is a poor one. More specifically, *Centesimus annus* calls upon the government to provide unemployment insurance (CA 15) and strongly implies that the government should be involved in efforts to provide training to employees to improve their productive capacity.

As is the nature of encyclicals, these sentiments are not backed up with economic theory or empirical evidence that suggests that the finance of training, or its provision, is best undertaken by government or that lower earners are not able, if they are not overtaxed, to provide welfare benefits for contingent needs. Also, these statements must be set in the context of a general comment on the welfare state which speaks for itself:

In recent years the range of such intervention has vastly expanded, to the point of creating a new type of State, the so-called 'Welfare State'. This has happened in some countries in order to respond better to many needs and demands, by remedying forms of poverty and deprivation unworthy of the human person. However, excesses and abuses, especially in recent years, have provoked very harsh criticisms of the Welfare State, dubbed the 'Social Assistance State'. Malfunctions and defects in the Social Assistance State are the result of an inadequate understanding of the tasks proper to the State ... By intervening directly and depriving society of its responsibility, the Social Assistance State leads to a loss of human energies and an inordinate increase in public agencies, which are dominated more by bureaucratic ways of thinking ... and which are accompanied by an enormous increase in spending. (CA 48)

The paragraph goes on to explain how real needs are best answered by people who can provide fraternal love and support. Pontifical Council for Justice and Peace (2005) describes how solidarity without subsidiarity can '*degenerate* into a "Welfare State"' (CA 351, my emphasis).[14]

A right to various forms of insurance (health, sickness, old age and so on) is articulated in various post-Vatican II documents (see, for example, *Laborem exercens*), but, other than assistance being given to the unemployed, the state is not envisaged as the provider of such insurances. Indeed, in Pontifical Council for Justice and Peace (2005), quoting John Paul II, the onus is very much put on workers' associations to develop new ways of providing for income security against contingencies, as traditional models based on salaried workers in big business break down. The state is, nevertheless, regarded as 'the guarantor' of systems of social insurance (para. 355). But this role could take many forms without

---

14 Papal encyclicals choose words very carefully though they are, of course, translated from Latin. 'Degenerating' literally involves declining or deteriorating to a lower mental, moral or physical level, becoming debased, degraded or corrupt: it is a strong word to use. It should also be mentioned that the paragraph continues with cautions against 'subsidiarity without solidarity'. It is important to note, however, that solidarity does not necessarily imply political action: solidarity starts in the family, which is the smallest unit for welfare provision.

being intrusive and without requiring significant levels of taxation (for example, providing a minimum basic income in times of need or upon the failure of private and mutual systems of social security, compelling membership of private systems, making payments into private systems on behalf of the poor, or, perhaps most importantly, providing the legal framework in which private systems can operate).

Centesimus annus reiterates points made in many encyclicals that support should be given particularly to families to ensure that basic needs can be provided for. The family unit is regarded as including the elderly as well as children. Provision should be made so that women are not deterred from working within the home. Again, this has implications for the tax system – but perhaps more for the shape of the tax system rather than for the level of the tax burden. For example, tax allowances transferable between non-working and working members of the family may help achieve this particular objective (see below).

The right to an education is discussed in similar terms to the right to healthcare, to a basic income and so on. For example, in Pope Paul VI's encyclical *Gravissimum educationis*, published in 1965, it is stated (Section 1) that 'All men of every race, condition and age, since they enjoy the dignity of a human being, have an inalienable right to education.' This can be interpreted in a number of ways, and the duty to deliver education is put first on parents and the Church (see Sections 1 and 3). Nevertheless, in Section 3 it is made clear that, while the main role of the state is to protect the duties and rights of parents and teachers, providing those who cannot afford education with aid, financed by taxation, is also a duty of the state. In Section 6 it is made clear that such aid should facilitate parental choice and autonomy.[15]

Other Church documents confirm this interpretation. *Familiaris consortio*,[16] for example, suggests that the state should provide families

---

15 In Anglo-Saxon Western countries (and also in much of western Europe with exceptions such as the Netherlands and Sweden) the state has provided funds for education by a method that explicitly reduces parental autonomy.

16 Written by John Paul II, published in 1981.

with aid to meet their educational needs and that aid must be in proportion to the needs of the family. This would seem to suggest some form of means-tested assistance to help with the finance of education. The duty to provide education is clearly laid upon the family, the Church and other intermediate institutions. It is also worth noting that the Church goes as far as suggesting that it is an *injustice* for the state not to support attendance at non-state schools, that a state monopoly of education offends *justice* and that the state cannot *merely tolerate* private schools (Pontifical Council for Justice and Peace, 2005: para. 241). It is difficult to conclude other than that the Church is teaching that the state's role in *providing* education should be much more limited than it is in the UK today – even if the state were still to *finance* education. (See Chapter 9.)

Summary

Catholic Social Teaching sees a legitimate, but limited, role for the state in the area of income redistribution. Charity is more virtuous than redistribution through taxation because it is based on love and not coercion. Equality is not a goal that should be pursued for its own sake. Mechanisms of improving the condition of the poor by giving them access to property (widely defined) are regarded as desirable. The principle of subsidiarity demands that government and coercive measures are a last resort. 'Subsidiarity means that the family, not the State, not large organizations, must be given responsibility in managing and developing its own economy' (Rio Declaration on the Family: para. 3.12).

A very important role is seen for various non-state institutions (unions, professions, employers' organisations, insurance and mutual societies and so on) in providing fraternal help. While the Church has proposed a role for the state in financing education, the state must nurture private provision. Contingent welfare in times of need (health and disability benefits, etc.) is another *potential* area of state intervention, but how such benefits are best provided and financed is left as a matter for personal, prudential judgement. The Church also teaches that the *shape* of the tax system should not discourage family life.

Modern Catholic Social Teaching and the role of the state: the provision of legal institutions

Church teaching on the provision of institutions is explicit and only brief consideration is necessary. There are institutions that are fundamental to the role of the state and the Church has always supported their provision by government. In the *Catechism* (Catholic Church, 1994) it states:

> The activity of a market economy cannot be conducted in an institutional, juridical or political vacuum. On the contrary, it presupposes sure guarantees of individual freedom and private property, as well as a stable currency and efficient public services. Hence the principal task of the state is to guarantee this security, so that those who work and produce can enjoy the fruits of their labours and thus feel encouraged to work efficiently and honestly … (para. 2431).[17]

Arguably these institutions that Church teaching suggests must be provided by the state are essential for the functioning of a market economy and the delivery of justice. They thus provide the framework in which a free economy operates.

Even though government intervention is encouraged in these matters the principle of subsidiarity still applies. Lower levels of government are responsible before higher levels of government. Voluntary associations have the responsibility before any level of government. It is important to note that subsidiarity does not mean simply that higher levels of political authority do what cannot be done by lower levels of political authority.[18]

---

17   This is a direct quote in the Catechism from *Centesimus annus*, para. 48. The quote appears elsewhere in this text and its sentiments are referred to on other occasions. It is an important quote as it succinctly expresses both the role and limits of government in economic life.

18   This seems to be the approach to subsidiarity in the European Union and between central and local government within the UK. Higher levels of authority define the aims and those

Rather, subsidiarity is the process by which the state is used to help private and intermediate groups attain the latter's legitimate ends, never supplanting their initiative, only facilitating it.[19]

Modern Catholic Social Teaching and the role of the state: the distinction between charity and taxation

In a number of places, it has been noted that the Church prefers voluntary action to coercive taxation. It is worth exploring the important distinction between taxation and charity further. Many people today discuss taxation in the same terms as charity, as if taxation were simply an extension of charitable giving. Words such as 'generous' and 'compassionate', which can relate only to voluntary sacrifice, are often used to describe the actions of government to achieve particular ends through coercive taxation. Church teaching, however, makes clear the difference between charity and action through political structures.

Those differences are many. They include the fact that charitable giving is a genuine act of love whereas taxation is coercive – there is no choice exercised by the taxpayer and therefore no 'generosity' or 'compassion' is possible. Taxation is impersonal in that it cannot be used to meet the concerns of the taxpayer and the payer of taxes cannot develop a personal relationship between donor and recipient. The ends to which taxes are put are determined through preferences expressed in the political system. The people expressing preferences as to how tax revenues are used may be placing the burden of paying the cost on other groups: in other words acting in a self-interested manner. State redistribution through political structures is not an extension of charity but an alternative mechanism for the allocation of resources to that of the market and voluntary initiative.

These differences are well understood in Church teaching and it is

---

aims can be delegated to lower levels of authority: this is not true subsidiarity.

19   This principle is so pervasive that it is difficult to give one reference. There is a discussion in several places in Charles (1998), for example in vol. II, pp. 97 and 98.

therefore correct of Pope Leo to propose the use of coercive redistribution using political structures only after genuine acts of love, expressed through the charitable giving of money and time, have failed to make the necessary provision.

Pope Benedict XVI discusses some of these issues in *Deus caritas est*. He expresses the view that charity is a manifestation of love and a Christian duty that is inseparable from other aspects of the Church's mission. Charity involves an outpouring of love that combines material help with genuine personal concern. Pope Benedict confirms the message of *Centesimus annus* that a state that tried to provide for all material need would become a mere bureaucracy. He also notes that needs met by charities are not just material and that even in the most just state charity would be necessary – it meets needs in a way that is more fully human.

Charity can also be undermined by state action. This can happen in several ways. As the state undertakes functions that properly belong in the community or under the auspices of charity, its bureaucratic ways can prevent others helping those who are in need of charity. Furthermore state action crowds out charitable giving. If 50 pence of every pound earned is taken by the state (see below), it is harder for individuals to meet their own basic needs, to act for the good of themselves and their families and to contribute towards meeting the needs of others through charity. All this is not to deny a legitimate role for the state, but, in the Christian mind, that role should be subservient to solutions to need that involve the exercise of Christian love.

Informing Catholic Social Teaching with economic theory: the burden of taxation

Having summarised some of the Church's teaching on taxation, this section examines the economics of taxation. Catholic Social Teaching looks to the social sciences for illumination on technical issues. The economics of taxation is one such discipline that can help inform the application of Catholic Social Teaching in particular circumstances. We do not include any analysis of the relative merits of the government *providing* services (health, education and so on). This is because, in theory at least, the provision of such services can be separated from their finance. We are concerned with the tax burden implied by the government financing various aspects of economic activity and financing income redistribution. The purpose of this section is to provide an understanding of the basic economic principles of taxation that can be used to help us make judgements about tax policy in a Christian context.

Taxation, inefficiency and the work effort

The microeconomics of taxation suggests that tax leads to inefficiencies and disincentives to work. At high levels, taxation can impose costs on intended beneficiaries of the proceeds of taxation as well as on taxpayers.

Taxation on income drives a wedge between the product of a worker and his income and thus prevents a worker earning the full value of his product. A worker facing high tax rates may value the gross wage derived from an extra hour of work as worth the extra time spent working, but not undertake the extra work because the worker does not receive the full fruits of his labour. When considering the impact of taxes on efficiency one should include sales taxes too, as they are levied on products bought using a worker's net earnings.

Taxation at high rates also acts as an incentive to use labour that works outside the formal, taxed sector. Indeed, in some parts of the economy, work in the formal sector might be difficult to find once tax rates reach high levels. Heitger (2002), for example, shows that the high tax burden in the EU helps to explain the very high level of long-term unemployment. High tax rates can also reduce the incentives for training and education by reducing the net returns from such investment far below the gross returns.

There are situations where high tax rates can induce more work than a family would desire to undertake in the absence of tax.[20] High tax rates can therefore lead to a situation where more paid work than a family would desire in the absence of high rates of tax takes place. A current example of this phenomenon may be the increasing tendency for two parents to take on paid work because one parent cannot afford to stay at home as a result of the high taxes levied on the earnings of the primary earner.[21]

At high rates of tax the disincentives can become so severe, and people cut their work effort to such an extent, that overall tax revenue to the government is reduced if rates are increased further (or revenue is increased if rates are reduced). This is known as the 'Laffer curve effect'. It therefore makes no sense for the government to levy marginal tax rates on any group above this point, as nobody benefits. It is clear from our discussion of Catholic Social Teaching that taxation merely to create equality, but where everybody suffers, cannot be justified. Intuitively, this effect can easily be seen once tax rates are 100 per cent. At this level, few people will undertake work, without being forced to work, because they would earn no money from it. The tax yield will therefore be zero (just as if the tax rate were zero). A reduction in taxes from 100 per cent to 90 per cent will therefore yield an increase in tax revenues. Similarly, a reduction in tax rates from 90 per cent to 80 per cent will increase the total tax yield to the benefit of taxpayers and non-taxpayers alike, even if it induces only a 12 per cent increase in hours worked.[22]

---

20 This is as a result of the so-called 'income effect'. The substitution effect, arising from a worker's net pay being below his gross pay, will always lead people to work less hard. The income effect leads people to work harder to maintain a given net income in the face of high tax rates. Both effects are welfare reducing and they can apply in different ways to different groups of people. High marginal tax and benefit withdrawal rates typically apply at the bottom of the income scale (see below). Thus somebody who cannot command a high wage may find that the substitution effect leads to him not working at all. On the other hand, a family with a moderate-to-high income may suffer a high average rate of tax that leads it to try to maintain its net income by working even harder.

21 There are clearly other reasons for this trend, including the better education of women and also, in the UK, the high level of housing costs, caused largely by government regulation of the planning system.

22 This is, of course, declared hours worked – reductions in tax rates can raise yields simply

Estimates vary on how high tax rates have to be to lead to reductions in tax revenue from further increases in rates. Marginal tax rates on a person on average earnings in the EU vary between 40 per cent and 60 per cent (see Miles and Scott, 2002), though published figures frequently understate tax rates (see below). Those segments of the population that also face withdrawal of social security benefits as their income rises will face much higher marginal rates of tax and benefit withdrawal than those on average earnings. It is quite possible, therefore, that tax rates in many EU countries are at such levels that reductions in tax would lead to only small losses in revenue and might even raise revenue.

The Laffer curve also shows how redistribution to the poor can be undermined if the government uses tax to finance a wide range of government services. If the marginal tax rate on all groups in society is high because of government funding of services, further rises in the marginal tax rates on particular groups, to facilitate redistribution, may then induce a Laffer curve effect, reducing revenues. Thus, there is a tendency, when average tax rates are high, for the tax burden to be relatively even across all income groups in a country – because there is a limit to the tax burden that can successfully be imposed on only one group. Paradoxically, redistribution can be more effective when there are low general rates of tax.

Taxes on spending can affect efficiency in other ways. If some goods or activities are taxed and others are not, then consumers and producers will use goods that are not taxed to an extent that is inefficient. Most developed countries levy a sales tax[23] but have lower levels of this tax for transport, food and energy. This will encourage consumers to consume more energy, for example, than is efficient, because its relative price is lowered.

A further problem is that high taxes on labour can cause employers to substitute labour with capital, thus raising unemployment or lowering the take-home pay of workers.

---

by reducing the incentive to find ways (whether legal or illegal) of preventing earned income from being taxed.

23   Value Added Tax (VAT) in the case of the UK and other EU countries.

The concept of efficiency should not be dismissed by Christians as some dry economic, materialistic concept. Broadly, inefficiency means that resources of greater value are used to produce a given level of output than need to be used. Given that all resources are scarce and all needs will never be satiated, an inefficient use of resources leads to economic well-being being lower for a given value of inputs than if resources are used efficiently. The inefficient use of resources, in this respect, can include the inefficient use of environmental resources.[24] As man should act as a steward of nature's resources, their inefficient use is an issue that should be taken seriously.

The tax burden in practice

Thus, when looking at the tax burden in practice, we need to distinguish between two concepts: the marginal rate of tax on the next pound a worker earns and the average tax burden as a percentage of total income. A high marginal rate of tax is most likely to impair industry and effort in the group to which it applies, as suggested by Pope Leo, above. The average rate of tax shows the extent to which the government is financing activities that could be financed by subsidiary entities – including by families. It shows the extent to which the preferences of the state with regard to provision of education, health, pensions, insurances, such as for disability, and redistribution are being imposed on all, rather than families being able to make their own choices with regard to provision in these fields.

Average tax burdens today are very high throughout the developed world by historical standards, reflecting to a large degree the development of 'social assistance states' throughout the Western world (see Table 1).

---

24   In this respect it is particularly perverse that there is discrimination in almost all tax systems in favour of transport and domestic energy use.

Table 1 **Average government spending in selected countries, 2005**

Country	Government spending as a proportion of GDP (%)
Sweden	59.0
France	54.4
Belgium	49.7
Germany	49.4
Italy	48.5
The Netherlands	48.5
United Kingdom	42.8
Japan	38.3
USA	35.9
Ireland	35.2

Source: Data from Heath and Smith (2006).

The table above shows total government spending as a proportion of national income. This is a reasonable guide to the tax burden, necessary to finance government activity.[25] Assuming that income from capital, labour and land are taxed in roughly equal proportions, these figures mean that, on average, in the EU, for every £100 of value produced by a worker, approximately the same amount is spent on the worker's behalf by government as by the worker's family.

The marginal tax rate represents the number of pence paid to the government from each extra pound of gross income earned. Some attempt to illustrate the very complex picture for the UK is given in Figure 1. The level of explicit taxes on income, the most frequently quoted marginal tax rate, is the smallest bar for each income group (this is zero at very low levels of income): this rate includes employees' National Insurance contributions and income tax. This does not, however, illustrate the full impact of tax. National Insurance contributions are also paid by employers and, in a competitive labour market, the burden of this is borne by the employee.[26] The inclusion of employers' National Insurance contributions leads to marginal tax rates of between

---

25 In the short run, government spending can be met by borrowing, but this leaves a tax burden for future generations.

26 When calculating marginal tax rates the cost of this tax should also be added to gross wages as well as to the tax paid.

Figure 1   **UK marginal tax rates, 2005–06**

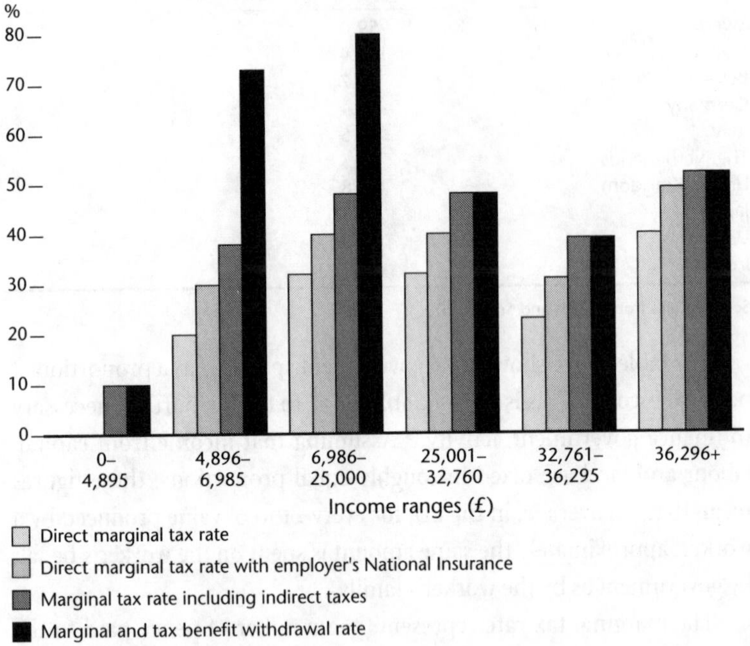

Income ranges (£)

- ☐ Direct marginal tax rate
- ☐ Direct marginal tax rate with employer's National Insurance
- ☐ Marginal tax rate including indirect taxes
- ■ Marginal and tax benefit withdrawal rate

30 and 45 per cent for all income groups, except the very lowest. Also frequently ignored is the impact of indirect taxes levied on spending from retained income.[27] This takes marginal rates up to about 40 per cent for all income groups, except the very lowest. This estimate would seem reasonable, given the overall fiscal burden of 44.9 per cent quoted above, and demonstrates the difficulty of achieving variation of tax rates with income once the overall tax burden has reached a high level.

In the UK, 'child tax credits' are paid to families with children. These

---

27   These have been assumed to be 10 per cent of net income made up of VAT on half the expenditure base plus various excise duties. Council tax, stamp duty and inheritance tax are excluded even though they relate to the purchase, ownership and sale of assets purchased from net income, thus making the marginal rates in the figure a conservative estimate.

are, in effect, means-tested social security benefits. They are withdrawn as the income of a family rises. For a recipient of tax credits, the marginal tax and tax-credit withdrawal rates combined are 80 per cent between the lowest levels of income and average income (approximately £25,000).[28] While tax credits are not taxes as such, and therefore not part of the tax burden, it is the rate of withdrawal of the credits combined with the rates of tax which determines the impact of decisions about whether to work and how much to work.

The tax system in the UK impacts on families in a particularly unfortunate way. Two examples are worth noting. If we take a family earning £25,000 with one earner and two children (for example, with the mother working in the home) the family would gain over £2,000 per annum of net income by having both family members going out to work with them each earning £12,500.[29] This arises because child tax credit is awarded on the basis of family income but income tax and National Insurance allowances are personalised. If the same couple split up and lived separately, the tax bill would be unaffected, but benefits would rise dramatically (by several thousand pounds). These illustrations are not dramatic examples of quirks; they are an integral part of the UK tax and benefits system (see Morgan, 2007).

These disincentives to self-sustaining family units and child-rearing within the home do not seem compatible with Catholic Social Teaching on tax and welfare matters. It is possible to design tax and benefits systems that do not give incentives for income splitting and household disintegration, even with high levels of tax. There are two obvious methods. The first is to 'personalise' benefits. This would involve taking family income assessment out of the benefits system, thereby giving benefits to individuals who do no paid work but who live in a family unit

---

28 This excludes the withdrawal of benefits such as housing benefit and council tax benefit. Tax credit can still be withdrawn at higher levels of income depending on precise family circumstances. The system is very complex.

29 In fact, this figure understates the difference by at least £1,000 as we have not included childcare tax credits or employers' National Insurance contributions.

with another earner: incentives for income and household splitting are thereby reduced. Alternatively, non-earning members of a household could be allowed to transfer their tax allowance to other members of a household who are earning.

Conclusion

The levels of tax we experience in the social assistance states of the West are surely not consistent either with the principle of subsidiarity or with efficient economic outcomes.

As we have noted, deviation from principles such as the right of a worker to earn his product can be justified by Catholic Social Teaching if it helps to promote a 'preferential option for the poor'. The poor can, however, experience the most deleterious effects of high taxes. Redistribution cannot be effective unless the overall tax burden is reasonably low. The poor in the UK pay both high average and high marginal rates of tax. The poor are also less able to rearrange their affairs in ways that avoid high rates of tax, and they are often caught in the most complex aspects of tax systems. If the services provided using the proceeds of taxation are not of a good quality, it is the least well off who are least able to find alternative provision.[30] Furthermore, long-term unemployment tends to be higher in countries with a higher tax burden. The poor can be particularly affected by high long-term unemployment and are also affected by a general reduction in economic growth caused by high levels of taxes – we should therefore not be surprised if the condition of the poor were worse in high-tax countries.

Evidence on this point is not unequivocal. One can certainly reject the hypothesis that the poor are necessarily better off in high-tax countries,

---

30 Perhaps this is most obvious with regard to schooling in the UK, where better-off families can purchase houses in the catchment areas of good schools (see Leech and Campos, 2003) and very well-off families can buy private education. Less well-off families have their net income reduced by taxation and have no means to escape inadequate state education.

however. Comparing high-tax Sweden with the lower-tax USA is instructive, for example (see Woods, 2005). At the turn of the 21st century, not only were median incomes in the USA 50 per cent greater than those in Sweden, the median income of US blacks (the lowest income group in the USA) was greater than median income across the whole of Sweden. Similarly, the income of the poorest 20 per cent of US citizens is higher than that for German citizens.

Informing Catholic Social Teaching with economic theory: public goods and externalities

There are certain 'public goods' that economists often argue are more efficiently provided by the state than by the private sector. Public goods are goods that other individuals cannot be prevented from consuming if they are provided for one individual.[31] Public goods will not necessarily be efficiently provided in the private sector because consumers have an incentive not to reveal their preferences for them so that they can 'free ride' on the provision made by others. It does not follow, however, that public goods can be more efficiently provided in the public sector, even if there is a prima facie case for at least considering the use of public sector provision or finance or for making payment for them compulsory.[32] As long as the constituency that benefits from a public good can be identified (for example, if it resides in a particular geographical area) public goods can be provided through subscription mechanisms, clubs and neighbourhood groups: this would, of course, accord with the principle of subsidiarity. Nevertheless, there is a case for *considering* some form of intervention to promote the provision of public goods, though taxation through *central* government would be a last resort, from

---

31 The classic example is street lighting – if one person in a neighbourhood puts up a street light, it will provide light for others in the neighbourhood.

32 Coase (1974), for example, showed how lighthouses, another classic public good, were much more effectively provided in the UK guided by private initiative than they were provided by the state in other countries.

the point of view both of economic efficiency and of Catholic Social Teaching.

Taxation can also improve economic efficiency where it is used to 'correct' for 'externalities'. For example, if certain economic activities (such as driving a car) impose costs on others, car use will exceed the efficient level because the car user does not bear all the costs. Certain activities may provide external benefits – it is sometimes suggested, for example, that primary education confers wider benefits on society. If this is the case, subsidising such activities, where the subsidy is financed through taxation, may lead to a more efficient use of economic resources.

Every economic activity confers some external benefits and costs and it is impossible for these to be calculated and for appropriate taxes and subsidies to be imposed to correct for externalities. Public choice economics (see below) also helps us to understand the limitations of the state both in providing public goods and in using taxes and subsidies to 'correct' externalities. A reasonable and pragmatic approach, compatible with the principle of subsidiarity and economic theory, would suggest that, where possible, markets or sophisticated social orders should be allowed to evolve to deal with problems created by externalities. Voluntary action should then be free to address problems where market solutions do not evolve.[33] If both these solutions are inadequate, taxes levied to deal with externalities should be explicit and used only where the externality is considerable. In some cases, such taxes can be regarded as a price for the use of shared resources and can be levied as charges rather than taxes.[34] Taxation or charges levied for these purposes, as a

---

33 The provision of Church schools, with subsidised places for the poor, is an obvious example in the case of primary education.

34 The best example here would be road pricing. A car user imposes congestion costs on other road users. It is the absence of a market in road space which creates the underpricing of road use. If possible, markets in road space should be facilitated. If not, a statutory authority (which should be the lowest level of statutory authority that will be effective for this function) should levy a charge for road use. Technically, this is not a tax but a 'charge'. Nevertheless, the revenue can be used to reduce other taxes, which impair efficiency. See Glaister and Graham (2004) for a thorough analysis of the application of road pricing to the UK.

'price for the consumption of shared resources', are effectively used to adjust the costs of private activity for the social costs associated with the activity. As such they are not necessarily a violation of property rights, nor do they necessarily impair economic efficiency.

Informing Catholic Social Teaching with economic theory: public choice economics

Public choice economics developed in a formal sense from the early 1960s. It is a discipline that should be at the forefront of the thinking of those seeking to develop Catholic Social Teaching for the simple reason that it examines the results of applying the assumption of the imperfectibility of man in political life: this manifests itself in the absence of perfect knowledge or the absence of omniscience and in the assumption of the pursuit of self-interest among political actors.[35]

The most important premise of public choice economics is straightforward. It is that we should not assume that people will behave in one way in the political arena and behave in a different way in the economic arena. In the economic arena we generally recognise that agents act in their own self-interest and that they have imperfect knowledge, thus leading to certain problems that governments may try to address. In the political sphere, however, agents will have these characteristics too: they will have a tendency to act in their own best interests and they will act with imperfect knowledge. That is not to say that all agents in the political sphere will behave only in their own best interests: altruism is possible in both the political and economic arenas. Nevertheless, it is prudent to adopt a working assumption of the pursuit of self-interest in both the economic and political spheres.

There are a number of implications from combining the adoption of the assumption of the self-interested participant in the political process with our understanding of various administrative aspects of the

---

35   It should not be thought that self-interest is the same as selfishness or a disregard of the needs of others (see Chapter 1).

political process.[36] The most important of these for our purposes are as follows:

- Electors have little interest in being perfectly informed about political issues because the probability of an individual's vote impacting on the result of an election is close to zero.
- Where the benefits of government regulation or subsidy are concentrated among particular voter groups, such voter groups have an incentive to lobby for regulation and subsidy – particularly if the cost is widely dispersed.
- Politicians will, other things being equal, respond to the preferences of the 'median voter'.
- Politicians may act in their own best interests when designing and supervising regulatory agencies.
- Bureaucrats cannot 'correct' the failure of markets to find efficient outcomes or socially desirable outcomes, even if they wished to do so, because they lack the information to know what the outcome of the market process would have been, had the 'failure' not existed.
- Bureaucrats will act in their own best interests, taking courses of action that will lead to promotion and advancement, including increasing the size and power of their regulatory bureau.
- Because of this, there are information asymmetries between regulatory bureaus and those to whom they are ultimately accountable (electors) – thus electors are at a relative disadvantage when assessing the merits of proposed regulations and other political decisions.

In many areas of political life it is possible to see how these problems manifest themselves. The EU Common Agricultural Policy is an example of a policy that confers concentrated benefits on farmers and dispersed costs on people throughout the world. Local Education Authorities and

---

36   See Tullock et al. (2000), reprinted, with revisions, in the USA as Tullock et al. (2002), for a clear and full discussion of these issues.

central government bureaucracy, which account for about one third of all UK education spending, seem to many to be risk-averse organisations that not only frequently do not act in the best interest of parents, but which cannot know the diverse objectives and aspirations of parents and thus cannot, even if they should have the desire to do so, act in the best interests of parents.

Public choice economics does not lead to specific and strong conclusions. Rather, it leads in the direction of some important cautions about the role of government, as well as towards the view that some forms of institutions are likely to give rise to better results than others. The main caution can be outlined as follows:

> One [area of policy into which public choice economics has been integrated] is simply a lack of enthusiasm for government as a solution to problems. The view that government is the automatic perfect solution to innumerable problems no longer exists. Not very long ago, the simple proof that the economy did not function perfectly was regarded as an adequate reason for governmental action. Today, we start from the knowledge that the government also does not function perfectly and then make a selection between two imperfect devices ... (Tullock et al., 2002: 11–12)

It seems that this fits in very well with the general thrust of Catholic Social Teaching on the role of government and, more specifically, with the principle of subsidiarity. As has been discussed above, there is a general scepticism in Catholic Social Teaching about the ability of a 'big state' to resolve economic and social problems. Public choice economics provides us with a rigorous framework that should strengthen such scepticism. The framework is based on assumptions that accord with a Christian view of human nature. In Catholic Social Teaching, there is a general presumption in favour of private property, the market economy and individual and family autonomy. There is also, however, an obligation to pay special attention to the plight of the poor. Public choice economics suggests that, even where the market produces an outcome that may seem unsatisfactory for the poor, intervention, including intervention using taxation and redistribution, may not produce a better outcome, as a political and bureaucratic process being used to allocate resources may favour the poor even less than the use of the market.[37]

There is an important moral lesson from public choice economics too. Frequently, as has been noted above, taxation and government spending are regarded as a seamless extension of charitable activity. Community and society are treated as synonymous with the state and the government. Public choice economics shows how government action replaces resource allocation through individual economic decisions by resource allocation through majority political decisions.[38] Both the market and the political process will be affected by self-interest. There is no reason to suppose that self-interest will be pre-eminent in the economic sphere but not in the political sphere. The majority will, or the will of the political or bureaucratic bodies that take and implement government resource allocation decisions, is not, of course, destined to fulfil God's will. Indeed, it may behave in a way that is fundamentally opposed to God's will.[39] When government initiative

---

37   Education and health are perhaps good examples of this. Health outcomes and services are known to be better in the UK in richer areas. With regard to education, also allocated through the political system in the UK, better-off parents can improve their children's education through the purchase of private education, through moving house to the catchment area of a better school, or through lobbying either the school or the local political authority to improve the service: none of these options may be available to the poor, particularly if they are not self-confident and articulate. The absence of a market means that the right of exit and freedom of choice are also not available to poor parents to help them improve education services for their children. Whereas the poor buy similar-quality television sets to the rich, they have dramatically worse educational outcomes.

38   Via the political and bureaucratic structures set up for the purpose.

39   An obvious example would be the provision of abortion funded by government health services, but there are many other examples. I have not come across mainstream teaching on whether it is legitimate to withhold taxes used to finance ends that are objectively evil: given the extent of state spending and the nature of the services on which taxpayers' money is spent, this is an area that should be given urgent attention. There should be a distinction, of course, between ends that are not immoral in themselves (for example, the conduct of war) but of which individual Catholics may disapprove and ends that Catholics regard as always objectively evil – such as abortion.

supplants and displaces individual initiative, individuals have their realm of moral choices reduced and may be required to finance choices that are immoral.

Conclusions: taxation and the role of the state

Our understanding of economic theory confirms the central importance of the principle of subsidiarity and private property while not contradicting the legitimacy of some role for the state in the provision of public goods and in income redistribution. Government must ensure, however, that all have the right to economic initiative and that taxation to finance redistribution and the mechanisms of redistribution themselves do not undermine this right.

It is difficult to be specific about the proportion of GDP that involvement by government in legitimate areas might entail. Reducing the role of the state in the UK, to financier of last resort for welfare and education provision, however, combined with some income redistribution, would probably reduce spending to less than half of what is currently spent in the UK on such items (see Congdon in Booth (2006) for some estimates). As has been noted, when *Rerum novarum* was published, government spending was around one fifth of current levels as a proportion of a much smaller national income.

The current tax system in the UK is not compatible either with the provision of appropriate incentives or with the maintenance of family independence. It seems clear that Catholic Social Teaching supports giving the poor the means to purchase education and health provision, although this should not necessarily mean universal free access and certainly not state provision of these services.

A flat-rate tax with a relatively high allowance would enable the objectives of taxation to be met while not destroying the reward for economic initiative. The granting of additional tax allowances for children and transferable allowances for married couples and cases where families look after elderly relatives would allow the phasing out of many cash benefits and remove the discrimination in the tax and benefit system against families living under one roof.

Taxes might be appropriate on certain economic activities that cause harm to those not party to the activity. Such taxes, or charges, need not violate property rights or reduce economic efficiency. Public choice economics might suggest, however, that alternative ways of dealing with such problems should be found, if possible by trying to widen the scope and role of private ownership (perhaps in common – though not through the state) of shared resources: this is compatible with the principle of subsidiarity.

More generally, the Church is aware of the limitations of political structures, something that is studied in detail in public choice economics. Certainly, the idea that political structures, so long as they are democratically elected, should have no restraints on their power in the economic realm is explicitly rejected: 'Experience shows that the denial of subsidiarity, or its limitation in the name of an alleged democratization or equality of all members of society, limits and sometimes even destroys the spirit of freedom and initiative' (Pontifical Council for Justice and Peace, 2005: para. 187). Indeed, state action is regarded as the exception and not the norm and certainly not an ideal for which we should aim; 'state action in the economic sphere should also be withdrawn when the special circumstances that necessitate it end' (ibid.: para. 188). On the issues discussed in this chapter there is much scope for prudential judgement. Catholic Social Teaching, however, informed by economic theory, provides little succour for those who believe that taxes should be raised further from their current level of between 40 and 60 per cent of income in most of the EU.

References

Bartholomew J. (2004), *The Welfare State We're In*, London: Politico's.
Booth, P. M. (ed.) (2006), *Towards a Liberal Utopia*, London:
    Continuum in association with the Institute of Economic Affairs.

Catholic Church (1994), *Catechism of the Catholic Church*, London: Geoffrey Chapman.

Charles, R. (1998), *Christian Social Witness and Teaching: The Catholic Tradition from Genesis to Centesimus Annus*, Leominster: Gracewing.

Coase, R. H. (1974), 'The lighthouse in economics', *Journal of Law and Economics*, 17: 357–76.

Glaister, S. and D. J. Graham (2004), *Pricing our Roads: Vision and Reality*, Research Monograph 59, London: Institute of Economic Affairs.

Hayek, F. A. (1944), *The Road to Serfdom*, London: Routledge and Kegan Paul.

Heath, A. and D. B. Smith (2006), *At a Price! The True Cost of Public Spending*, London: Politeia.

Heitger, B. (2002), 'The impact of taxation on unemployment in OECD countries', *Cato Journal*, 22(22): 333–54.

Hinze, C. F. (2005), Commentary on *Quagragesimo anno (After Forty Years)* in K. R. Himes (ed.), *Modern Catholic Social Teaching: Commentaries and Interpretations*, Washington, DC: Georgetown University Press.

Leech, D. and E. Campos (2003), 'Is comprehensive education really free?: a case study of the effects of secondary school admissions policies on house prices in one local area', *Journal of the Royal Statistical Society*, Series A, 166(1): 135–54.

Miles, D. and A. Scott (2002), *Macroeconomics: Understanding the wealth of nations*, Chichester: Wiley.

Morgan, P. (2007), *The War Between the State and the Family: How Government Divides and Impoverishes*, Hobart Paper 157, London: Institute of Economic Affairs.

Pontifical Council for Justice and Peace (2005), *Compendium of the Social Doctrine of the Church*, London: Burns & Oates.

Rothbard, M. N. (1960), *Readings on Ethics and Capitalism*, Unpublished memo to the Volker Fund, USA.

Spieker, M. (2005), 'The universal destination of goods: the ethics of property in the theory of a Christian society', *Journal of Markets and Morality*, 8(2): 333–54.

Tullock, G., A. Seldon and G. L. Brady (2000), *Government: Whose Obedient Servant? A Primer in Public Choice*, IEA Readings 51, London: Institute of Economic Affairs.

Tullock, G., A. Seldon and G. L. Brady (2002), *Government Failure: A primer in public choice*, Washington, DC: Cato Institute.

Woods, T. E., Jr (2005), *The Church and the Market: A Catholic Defense of the Free Economy*, Maryland: Lexington Books.

Part Two
BUSINESS, THE CONSUMER AND CULTURE IN CHRISTIAN LIFE

6   FREE MARKETS AND THE CULTURE OF CONSUMPTION

Andrew Yuengert

'In his riches man lacks wisdom; he is like the beasts that are destroyed'

PSALMS 49:13

Introduction

The Catholic tradition's warnings about wealth are based on two principles, each confirmed by millennia of sad experience. The first principle is that material goods do not guarantee happiness; they are not by nature bad, of course, but they do not give meaning to life, and great wealth often leads to great emptiness. The second principle is that wealthy people often forget the first principle. They firmly attach themselves to this world, and detach themselves from God and the treasures of heaven.

One of the distinctive features of modern times is the large number of people who are exposed to the spiritual dangers of material riches. The development and spread of free markets have generated tremendous increases in material prosperity, and wider access to that prosperity. Along with all this new wealth, we have seen the rise of consumerism – large numbers of people acting as if goods alone will make them happy, and organising their lives primarily around the pursuit of more and newer things. No one can begrudge the multitude (to which most of us belong, after all) their release from grinding material poverty, made possible by free markets. At the same time, it is disheartening to see people released from poverty by markets, only to embrace the consumerist lifestyle.

It should not be surprising to anyone in the Judaeo-Christian tradition that many squander the abundance of modern industrial society on an empty consumer lifestyle. The Jewish and Christian scriptures predict as much, and this chapter offers no new insight into human sinfulness and folly. Instead, I address a more modern concern: do free markets play a *direct* role in the rise of consumerism, apart from their indirect role in making widespread access to consumption possible? A closely related question is: what does consumerism imply for the regulation of free markets? This essay seeks answers to these questions in Catholic Social Teaching, particularly in the encyclicals of John Paul II.

Theories of consumerism and free markets fall along a continuum. At one end is the libertarian position (von Mises 1998; Rothbard 1971; Kirzner 2002). Libertarians, out of respect for individual liberty, privilege the desires and preferences on which consumers act in markets. Markets give people what they want; if they want material consumption, markets give it to them; if they want moderation, markets will also give that to them. From this perspective, any problems of consumerism are problems of culture, not of markets. Moreover, since markets are not the problem, restrictions on markets are not the solution.

The other extreme is illustrated by the attitudes of the anti-market left and conservatives in the Southern agrarian tradition (Schindler 2003; Berry 1990; O'Neill 1998). Both these groups are suspicious of markets: the spread of the market, with its arm's-length exchanges and rationalistic logic, erodes the fellow-feeling necessary for community and culture to flourish. In this account, markets directly cause consumerism, by undermining the conditions for true community. Any cultural initiative to address consumerism must therefore modify the market substantially, replacing its impersonal exchange with something more personal. The bonds of culture cannot withstand the solvent of the market.

Catholic Social Teaching adopts neither of the extremes outlined above. On the one hand, it recognises that markets effectively meet consumer preferences, which are backed by money, but it is not shy about criticising the content of those preferences, or about expressing reservations about the role of advertisers in distorting consumer preferences. On the other hand, the Catholic tradition recognises that there are important human goods which cannot be produced in markets, and which require protection from markets, but it stops short of drawing a necessary connection between markets and the decay of culture. John Paul II is especially confident in the ability of a renewed culture to resist any threat to its foundations from markets.

Catholic Social Teaching on consumerism and markets can be summarised in six points. The first three points address its nature; the second three address its causes and consequences. First, consumerism is the expression of a materialistic, secular world-view, part of a system of belief that exalts the things of this world without reference to eternal, spiritual realities. Second, although consumerism is new in the sense that it is the expression of a modern world-view, it is at the same time a chapter in an old drama – that of original sin. Concupiscence makes us vulnerable to consumerism and the world-view that supports it. Third, consumerism is a real problem, a real threat to happiness in developed economies. The critique of consumerism cannot be dismissed as a cranky, elite rejection of new things, based on a false nostalgia for simpler, more virtuous times.

The last three points address the consequences of consumerism for culture and markets. First, consumerism is primarily a problem of culture. The modern materialistic world-view can offer no source of meaning other than material consumption, and no other forum in which to pursue meaning other than markets. Second, although markets do not generate consumerism, there are important goods that can be produced only outside markets: any cultural renewal that makes consumerism less widespread will entail restrictions on the extent of markets. Finally, government restrictions on markets may play a role in addressing consumerism, but only in support of a renewed culture – not as a substitute for culture. Respect for the principle of subsidiarity (sorely lacking among most legislators and bureaucrats) reduces the sphere of government action on this issue.

Catholic Social Teaching is unwilling to entrust all of life to markets, but neither does it despair that a healthy culture might harness market exchange towards the promotion of happiness. Culture is primary in papal teachings on consumerism; John Paul II in particular places the hope for combating materialistic consumerism in the renewal of culture (*Sollicitudo rei socialis*, 36).

Papal encyclicals on consumerism

The first significant treatment of the dangers of consumerism is Paul VI's 1967 encyclical *Populorum progressio*. At that time there were a host of newly established countries, freshly freed from colonial rule. Although these countries were poor, some economists and others were optimistic that they would soon become prosperous through statist, protectionist economic policies. Although these policies have since been discredited, at the time many assumed that they would work, and Paul VI thought it necessary to put economic development into a moral context.

The encyclical reaffirms the age-old warning that material abundance can lead individuals to forget that goods are not the ultimate purpose of human existence. Wealth is only instrumentally good – good insofar as we use it to meet the most important human needs. This list of needs includes life, of course, but also the goods of society and culture: family and community, the pursuit of truth and beauty, the worship of God and love of neighbour. It is an unfortunate fact of human existence that, when life is easy and goods are abundant, men often lose sight of the full range of human goods as they unreflectively pursue more material goods.

Thus, material want is not the only evil to be avoided: one can have too many things as well as too few, if one forgets the purpose of things: 'Every kind of progress is a two-edged sword. It is necessary if man is to grow as a human being; yet it can also enslave him, if he comes to regard it as the supreme good and cannot look beyond it' (PP 19). It is a great tragedy when a society frees itself from a great material evil – subsistence poverty – only to embrace a moral evil – consumerism (PP 21). Paul VI encourages developing nations to strive to become, not just richer, but better places.

In the first encyclical of his pontificate, *Redemptor hominis*, John Paul II addresses the phenomenon of consumerism again, although he does not treat it in depth until later encyclicals. Technological progress and material prosperity have improved the material lot of many, but

> ... there is a real perceptible danger that, while man's dominion
> over the world of things is making enormous advances, he should
> lose the essential threads of his dominion and in various ways
> let his humanity be subjected to the world and become himself
> something subject to manipulation in many ways ... (RH 16)

A modern dynamic is at work here: the human person is somehow diminished by his own technical, economic progress (*Gaudium et spes*, 4). He becomes less an acting person, who reasons about his good and pursues it in the world, and more a person who is *acted upon*, ruled by passions, and subject to outside manipulation of his desires.

John Paul II describes a grim contrast, between the material evil of abject poverty in the developing world (poverty that is an affront to human dignity) and the surfeit of goods in the 'consumer civilisation' of the developed world (consumption that diminishes those who buy into its materialistic premises). According to John Paul II, the world situation is the parable of the rich man and Lazarus writ large (RH 16). Caught up in his feasting, the rich man of the scriptures does not see the important human good outside his door – a man in need of basic material goods.[1]

---

1   In *Redemptor hominis* John Paul II asserts in passing that terrible poverty is somehow a
     necessary condition of material abundance in the developed world, and not simply a con-
     dition that calls for renewed efforts by the First World to help the Third World develop
     (RH 16). This claim is based on the same economic theories of dependency and exploita-
     tion that gave rise to the failed development strategies of the sixties. As they have fallen
     out of favour in the theory of economic development, they have disappeared from papal
     encyclicals. In *Sollicitudo rei socialis* (published in 1987), in his discussion of consumer-
     ism, John Paul II makes the contrast without asserting a necessary connection, and in
     Centesimus annus in 1991 he does not make the contrast at all in his long treatment of con-
     sumerism. The obligation of the First World to help the Third, even at some significant
     material cost, is a grave one (as the parable of Lazarus attests); those who are rich in this
     world's goods bear a heavy responsibility towards those who have nothing. This moral
     responsibility need not be based on theories of neocolonial dependency and exploitation,

In *Sollicitudo rei socialis*, John Paul II both celebrated the twentieth anniversary of *Populorum progressio* and developed Paul VI's teaching on consumerism more fully. In the section entitled 'Authentic Human Development', he begins by noting that the 'naïve mechanistic optimism' that inspired the development schemes and political programmes of the 1960s had been replaced by 'a well-founded anxiety for the fate of humanity' (SRS 27). This anxiety has many causes, but chief among them is the discovery that economic growth does not necessarily lead to moral improvement:

> ... the 'economic' concept itself, linked to the word development, has entered into crisis. In fact there is a better understanding today that the mere accumulation of goods and services, even for the benefit of the majority, is not enough for the realization of human happiness. (SRS 28)

Although man has at his disposal more productive technology and economic systems capable of making full use of that technology, more than ever he needs 'a moral understanding and ... an orientation toward the true good of the human race' to put material abundance into moral perspective (SRS 28).

At this point John Paul II repeats the comparison of *Redemptor hominis*, between the 'miseries of underdevelopment, themselves unacceptable' and '*superdevelopment*, equally inadmissible' (SRS 28).

> This superdevelopment, which consists in an *excessive* availability of every kind of material goods for the benefit of certain social groups, easily makes people slaves of 'possession' and of immediate gratification, with no other horizon than the multiplication or continual replacement of the things already owned with others still better. This is the so-called civilization of 'consumption' or 'consumerism,' which involves so much 'throwing away' and 'waste.' (SRS 28)

---

however: that is, it should not be assumed that underdeveloped countries are poor because developed countries are rich.

In this passage, John Paul II makes three points. First, an abundance of goods makes people vulnerable to consumerism, or slavery to possessions. The seeming plenitude of choice in prosperous economies can mask restrictions on the person's inner freedom. Second, consumerism is essentially an inability to see beyond material goods: human beings have no broader 'horizon' against which to see material goods in perspective. Third, there is a restlessness in consumerism: it generates a constant search for new products, and an excessive 'throwing away'.[2]

Although consumerism generates in many a 'crass materialism', its most important effect is a 'radical dissatisfaction', according to the Pope. The dissatisfaction with material goods is radical because it has a perverse effect. Instead of moderating consumption when it fails to satisfy, the slave to consumption seeks out more goods, even as 'deeper aspirations remain unsatisfied and perhaps even stifled' (SRS 28).

Echoing Paul VI, John Paul II takes pains to note that material goods are not bad in themselves, and that the desire to have more is not in itself sinful: 'having' and 'being' are not mutually exclusive: 'The evil does not consist in "having" as such, but in possessing without regard for the *quality* and the *ordered hierarchy* of the goods one has' (SRS 28). The value of goods is measured against man's vocation. Human dignity and purpose are the appropriate 'horizon' against which to put goods in perspective.

It must be noted that John Paul II paints here an exalted vision of the potential of material goods to promote human happiness. The human need for basic food and shelter by no means exhausts the usefulness of material goods. Just as human beings are meant for more than subsistence, the goods of this world can contribute to man's good beyond keeping him alive. New products can open up 'new horizons' for man,

---

2   I must express some scepticism about the criticism that modern societies throw too many perfectly serviceable products away. When a person buys a new car, the old one is sold on a used car lot. The existence of yard sales and the spectacular success of eBay attest to the strong desire *not* to throw things away. Consumer societies may be too eager for 'the latest thing', but rarely do they throw the old things away while they are still useful to someone.

contribute to his full development (SRS 29). The true value of material goods, however, depends crucially on man's willingness to place those goods at the service of his true dignity. John Paul II characteristically locates this dignity in the creation of man, male and female, and in the dominion granted to them over the material world.

The dominion granted to Adam and Eve was not absolute, however. The original sin of Adam distorts the relationship between man and the material world (SRS 29). Consumerism is therefore another chapter in the ongoing drama of original sin and redemption:

> It is logical to conclude, at least on the part of those who believe
> in the word of God, that today's 'development' is to be seen as
> a moment in the story which began at creation, a story which is
> constantly endangered by reason of infidelity to the Creator's will,
> and especially by the temptation to idolatry. (SRS 30)

The person who piles up goods for their own sake, thinking they are the key to happiness, rejects God's dominion over his life, and denies his own nature as a human being called to communion with God. Human development consists in 'subordinating the possession, dominion and use to man's likeness and to his vocation to immortality' (SRS 29). It is one of the paradoxes of sin that, granted the immense bounty of the earth to develop through work and ingenuity, human beings make an idol of material goods, and reject the happiness intended for them by the One who grants the bounty.

In *Sollicitudo rei socialis*, John Paul II ends his meditation on the nature of consumerism, not with hand-wringing over its dangers, but with a call to substitute for it a truer vision of the nature of the human vocation, and the legitimate role of economic development in that vocation. The task of promoting true development is made arduous by original sin, but our duty to promote man's true happiness is not diminished by the difficulty of the task set before us (SRS 30).

The four years between the publication of *Sollicitudo rei socialis* in 1987 and *Centesimus annus* in 1991 saw the fall of communism and the discrediting of the totalitarian project in Europe. In *Centesimus annus* John Paul II took the opportunity to reflect on the errors of socialism and on the requirements of true freedom in democratic, market-oriented societies. It is here that he discusses most fully the problem of consumerism and the role of the market.

The error of socialism, and the source of its downfall in Europe, was not in its failure to 'deliver the goods':

> ... the fundamental error of socialism was anthropological in nature. Socialism considers the individual person simply as an element, a molecule within the social organism, so that the good of the individual is completely subordinated to the functioning of the socioeconomic mechanism. Socialism likewise maintains that the good of the individual can be realized without reference to his free choice. (CA 13)

It was not the lack of goods which doomed communism: the low productivity of communist economies was a symptom of the real problem – the lack of true human freedom in the political and economic spheres. To blame the fall of communism on a lack of goods is to make the same mistake as the communists – to assume that human well-being depends on material consumption alone (CA 19). One of the goals of *Centesimus annus* is to combat this materialistic error – to encourage Christians to foster in free societies social institutions that will orient those societies towards true human development.

Centesimus annus begins its treatment of consumerism in the same way *Sollicitudo rei socialis* does, by contrasting poor subsistence societies with more prosperous ones. In a subsistence economy there is a limited range of options for production – a minimum of food and shelter are all the economy produces (CA 36). In developed economies, consumers choose from a much wider range of goods. How this choice is made reveals a society's values: 'A given culture reveals its overall understanding of life through the choices it makes in production and consumption' (CA 36).

What 'understanding of life' do Western cultures reveal through the choices they make? According to the Pope, the production and consumption patterns of modern culture reveal rampant materialistic consumerism:

> It is not wrong to want to live better; what is wrong is a style of life which is assumed to be better when it is directed toward 'having' rather than 'being,' and which wants to have more, not in order to be more but in order to spend life in enjoyment as an end in itself. (CA 36)

The Pope offers three pieces of dramatic evidence of the underlying consumerism in modern culture. The first piece of evidence is the prevalence of drug use and pornography in modern societies, which reveals a radically distorted view of happiness:

> Widespread drug use is a sign of a serious malfunction in the social system; it also implies a materialistic and, in a certain sense, destructive 'reading' of human needs. In this way the innovative capacity of a free economy is brought to a one-sided and inadequate conclusion. Drugs, as well as pornography and other forms of consumerism which exploit the frailty of the weak, tend to fill the resulting spiritual void. (CA 36)

The twin vices of pornography and drug abuse (one might include a third today, that of 'gaming') are extreme expressions of consumerism. Where the modern world glorifies expanded freedom of choice for consumers, John Paul II sees a lack of freedom; drug and pornography addicts are frail and 'exploited', both by producers and by their own disordered orientation towards goods.

A second phenomenon that reveals an underlying consumerism in society is the abuse of nature. In the same way that material goods are only good for man when they are put into proper perspective, the use of the natural environment to produce those goods must also be appraised in light of man's divine vocation:

> Man thinks that he can make arbitrary use of the earth, subjecting

it without restraint to his will, as though the earth did not have its own prerequisites and a prior God-given purpose, which indeed man can develop but must not betray. (CA 37)

One need not be a tree hugger, or embrace the Kyoto protocols, to see the sense in this. To misuse the gifts of nature, to use them as if man may do whatever he wishes with creatures and matter, is to thwart the benevolent purpose of the gift and, ultimately, to betray the Giver.[3]

The third piece of evidence that modern culture is in thrall to a materialistic mindset is the most telling. Central to the Pope's treatment of 'human ecology' is a discussion of the ills of the family. The decline of stable marriage, and a materialistic attitude towards the decision to have children, is the clearest evidence that people are putting material goods ahead of their most important purposes as human beings.

But it often happens that people are discouraged from creating the proper conditions for human reproduction and are led to consider themselves and their lives as a series of sensations to be experienced rather than as a work to be accomplished. The result is a lack of freedom, which causes a person to reject a commitment to enter into a stable relationship with another person and to bring children into the world, or which leads people to consider children as one of the many 'things' which an individual can have or not have, according to taste, and which compete with other possibilities. (CA 39)

Although the Pope goes on to condemn systematic anti-childbearing policies, here he notes that there appears to be an anti-childbearing mindset even in the free nations. Note that he characterises the decision not to marry and not to have children as a 'lack of freedom': many in the grip of consumerism are *not free* to marry, *not free* to embrace the married state. Both individuals and societies suffer as a result.

Whatever the arguments about the causes of consumerism or the

---

3   It must be noted that markets play an important role in the solution to environmental problems. The establishment of clearly defined property rights often forces individuals to take into account the environmental effects of their actions.

solutions for it, Catholic Social Teaching clearly teaches that it is a gravely disordered lifestyle, and a severe problem in modern society. People who give overriding prominence to material possessions are often so attached to material consumption that they neglect commitments to God, family and community that are critical to their own happiness and the health of society. Anyone who takes Catholic Social Teaching seriously cannot dismiss concerns about consumerism as mere differences in taste. The critique of consumerism is more than a fastidious, ascetic distaste for sports utility vehicles, fast food and cheap gadgets.

Consumerism and public policy

In light of the gravity of the problem, what solutions does Catholic Social Teaching suggest? To understand the solution, we must first locate the source of the problem. As noted in the introduction, two accounts bracket the possibilities. The first is that a materialistic, individualistic culture is the source of consumerism, and that markets merely reveal the problems of culture. The second is that market exchange, by its nature individualistic and anonymous, destroys culture, leaving individuals vulnerable to consumerism.

A close reading of the encyclical tradition favours the first account. Although the Popes do not deny that economic change can radically alter the cultural landscape – think of the Industrial Revolution – one does not find in their writings any conviction that the logic of market exchange is necessarily corrosive of culture. There are simply too many plausible alternative explanations: there is ample evidence for sources of cultural decay in the decline of religion and the philosophical dead-end of materialistic relativism, and the widespread material abundance made possible by free markets puts more people at risk of consumerism than ever before.

John Paul II is particularly adamant that the source of consumerism is the culture itself. Two excerpts from *Centesimus annus* confirm this point:

> A given culture reveals its overall understanding of life through the choices it makes in production and consumption. It is here that *the phenomenon of consumerism* arises ... (CA 36)

> These criticisms are directed not so much against an economic system as against an ethical and cultural system. The economy in fact is only one aspect and one dimension of the whole of human activity. If economic life is absolutised, if the production and consumption of goods becomes the centre of social life and society's only value, not subject to any other value, the reason is to be found not so much in the economic system itself as in the fact that the entire socio-cultural system, by ignoring the ethical and religious dimension, has been weakened, and ends by limiting itself to the production of goods and services alone. (CA 39)

In the first quotation, John Paul II asserts that the culture *chooses* consumerism – it 'reveals its overall understanding of life' through production and consumption. In the second quotation, he asserts that it is the logic of secular culture, not the logic of markets, which drives consumerism. A world-view that cannot see beyond this world – beyond man's animal nature to his spiritual and transcendent nature – will be unable to find meaning in anything other than material consumption. In such a world-view, the market becomes by reluctant default 'the centre of social life and society's only value'.

It is tempting at this point in the analysis to draw a libertarian conclusion; Christians have a responsibility to try to put the culture right, and leave market institutions alone: put consumer preferences right, and producers will then meet the new, improved, consumer desires. This reading of the Catholic social tradition is premature, though, for two reasons. First, John Paul II's set of market institutions does not include marketing or advertising: in the Pope's scheme these are instruments of culture, of mass communication and media, and they are an important proximate cause of consumerism. This means that both consumers and producers bear a responsibility for consumer culture. Second, a reformed culture will not place the market at 'the centre of social life', but will embed and circumscribe markets, putting them at the service of true human flourishing.

The Catholic tradition does not buy into an extreme account of consumer sovereignty in markets; nor does it treat advertising and marketing as mere exercises in discovering what consumers want. It certainly respects the ability of markets to respond to human needs, insofar as they are backed by purchasing power, as shown in the following passage:

> Certainly the mechanisms of the market offer secure advantages
> … above all they give central place to the person's desires and
> preferences, which, in a contract, meet the desires and preferences
> of another person. (CA 40)[4]

As effective as markets are in responding to human desires, marketers and advertisers, when they appeal to immediate sense experience and instinct, can distort the desires of consumers. John Paul II hints at the problem in *Sollicitudo rei socialis*, where he attributes consumerism to 'the flood of publicity and the ceaseless and tempting offers of products' (SRS 28). In John Paul II's analysis, marketers and advertisers are part of the cultural sphere, and they can affect consumer preferences for better or for worse:

> If … a direct appeal is made to human instincts – while ignoring
> in various ways the reality of the person as intelligent and free
> – then consumer attitudes and lifestyles can be created which are
> objectively improper and often damaging to the person's physical
> and spiritual health. (CA 36)

Because the problem of consumerism is not simply a problem of consumers wanting the wrong things or too many things, independent of producers, both producers and consumers must be part of the cultural response to consumerism:

---

4   See also CA 34.

Thus a great deal of educational and cultural work is urgently
needed, including the education of consumers in the responsible
use of their power of choice, the formation of a strong sense of
responsibility among producers and among people in the mass
media in particular, as well as the necessary intervention by public
authorities. (CA 36)

Of course, consumers must learn to put their purchasing and savings
choices at the service of their true vocation as children of God. Nevertheless, producers and others in the 'mass media' have a responsibility to
develop and sell products that are good for people. Advertising and sales
are not neutral activities; they help to build (or destroy) culture.

In the above quotation, a third party is in need of 'educational and
cultural work': the 'public authorities'. This brings us to the question of
the role of state regulation in correcting the tendencies towards consumerism in modern cultures. Although the culture is the primary source
of consumerism, and must therefore be the source of alternative world-
views, the state has some role to play in safeguarding the community
from consumerism and its effects.

Centesimus annus outlines the role of the state at length; in this
chapter we are concerned only with its role in promoting a non-consum-
erist culture. Central to the government's role in this area is the fact
that certain human goods cannot be produced in markets, although
feeble imitations of these goods are for sale. To understand the role for
the state outlined here, we must return to John Paul II's discussion of
modern culture's failure to resist consumerism.

A healthy culture generates in the person a love for ultimate goods
– the virtues, truth, beauty, goodness. It is not founded on the person's
autonomous choice of these goods; it orients him towards them. To this
extent, culture is founded on those vital things that we do not choose.
We inherit these things from family, community and religion. Because
modern materialism offers no wellsprings of meaning – no ultimate
goods – it does not orient the individual towards any goods beyond
those chosen by the individual himself; therefore, it allows the market

to dominate cultural life. In the event that a more humanistic culture emerges from the current societal chaos, one of its effects will be to push the market out of some of the areas of social life it currently dominates, or at least to regulate its effects. It may also lead to reforms of advertising and marketing practices. The state has a role to play in supporting these cultural initiatives: 'It is the task of the State to provide for the defence and preservation of common goods such as the natural and human environments, which cannot be safeguarded simply by market forces' (CA 40). Healthy cultures will not rely on markets for all their needs; indeed, they cannot rely on them for every human need.

It is here that conservatives of every stripe get nervous. Is the admission that the state has a role to play a warrant for any arbitrary regulation of markets in the name of 'human ecology' and 'spiritual good'?

The current over-regulation of society by government should not force us to renounce a legitimate role for the state in helping a resurgent culture to keep market-generated prosperity in human perspective. For example, a society infused with a renewed spirit of religion may call for public expressions of that consensus, in Sabbath laws restricting business activity on Sundays and holidays. It may also insist on restrictions on the ways in which advertisers use sex to sell products.

What is most important in all this is that the state does not get ahead of the culture, or attempt to replace it. The most important check on government activity in this area is the Catholic principle of subsidiarity (see also the chapters by O'Brien and Gregg in Part Three):

> A community of a higher order should not interfere in the internal life of a community of a lower order, depriving the latter of its functions, but rather should support it in case of need and help to coordinate its activity with activities of the rest of society, always with a view to the common good. (CA 48)

The institutions of culture are the subsidiary communities of society: families, churches, businesses, non-profits and countless professional and community associations. A government which takes upon itself to create and safeguard the culture misunderstands the principle of subsidiarity and, consequently, the nature of culture. Culture is not the business of government; government is neither the arbiter nor the creator of culture.

Life is lived in the wide, rich social space between the individual and the government (CA 49). It is here that the hard work of cultural renewal must take place, and from which any initiatives for government action in support of cultural renewal must come. Modern governments are philosophically ill suited to this supporting role. Many government activists are suspicious of these subsidiary communities – family and church, in particular – because they are not as comprehensive as the state, or are obstacles to utopian, rationalist programmes of social improvement. This statist philosophy of government is a misreading of society, and disregards the potential of subsidiary communities to renew culture. Active resistance to the attempts of subsidiary communities to affect the culture, under the guise of separation of Church and state or hostility to the family's role in the raising of children, is a serious impediment to the renewal of culture.

The most fundamental community of society is the family, and any renewal of society must begin with a renewal of family life. The *Compendium of the Social Doctrine of the Church* makes this point forcefully: 'the family is presented, in the Creator's plan, as "the primary place of humanization for the person and society" and "the cradle of life and love"' (Pontifical Council for Justice and Peace, 2005: 209). Any resistance to consumerism must begin with the family, supported by church and community. The state must safeguard the natural family in concrete ways, and allow the subsidiary communities, including the churches, a role in public life. It cannot simultaneously renew culture and suppress the institutions of a healthy culture.

Conclusion

Catholic Social Teaching has always taken culture seriously. It rejects the Marxist critique that culture is simply an elaborate justification for economic power. Similarly, it refuses to make culture a creature of the state, dependent for its existence and vibrancy on state initiative. Culture is prior to both economics and politics. It provides the virtues necessary for market production and exchange, and the common goods that give purpose to politics emerge from culture. It is the culture, and not the forum or the marketplace, which ought to orient us towards those things that make life worth living. After all, the Church lives in the culture, even though it is not the only cultural institution.

Because culture is so primary in Catholic thought, it naturally looks to culture for the roots of consumerism. The ascendancy of a materialistic, secularist world-view leaves the culture unable to find meaning in the things of the spirit, and thus culture turns to markets and material goods for meaning. A materialistic culture, widespread access to consumption in free-market economies and fallen human nature combine to create ideal conditions for consumerism.

A weak culture assigns a greater role to material goods and to the markets in which they are exchanged. This is not the fault of markets, but a renewed culture may look at markets differently, because the goods of markets will be seen in perspective – not as sources of ultimate meaning, to which the goods of family and society are sacrificed, but as supplemental means by which to attain the greater goods of life. The work of cultural renewal will affect politics, through demands to protect, or at least to respect, the institutions that strengthen culture.

The Popes would have us get to work on culture – on our families, our churches, our communities. A healthy culture provides the energy by which we can order the tremendous material abundance of modern economies towards true human development. Without this order, we will continue to live diminished lives of the saddest sort – those of people who have every material blessing, but are still desperately unhappy. We risk more than unhappiness, according to the Scripture verse at the beginning of this essay; the more we become like beasts, driven by unreflective instinct to seek material comfort for its own sake, the more we risk being destroyed by those very instincts. Freedom undisciplined by wisdom leads to inner slavery, and can lead a society towards political tyranny.

References

Berry, W. (1990), *What Are People For?*, New York: Northpoint Press.

Kirzner, I. (2002), 'Advertising', in E. Heath (ed.), *Morality and the Market: Ethics and Virtue in the Conduct of Business*, Boston, MA: McGraw-Hill.

O'Neill, J. (1998), *The Market: Ethics, Knowledge, and Politics*, New York: Routledge.

Pontifical Council for Justice and Peace (2005), *Compendium of the Social Doctrine of the Church*, London: Burns & Oates.

Rothbard, M. (1971), *Power and Market*, Menlo Park: Institute for Humane Studies.

Schindler, D. L. (2003), '"Homelessness" and market liberalism: toward an economic culture of gift and gratitude', in D. Bandow and D. L. Schindler (eds), *Wealth, Poverty, and Human Destiny*, Wilmington, DE: ISI Books.

Von Mises, L. (1998), *Human Action: A Treatise on Economics*, New York: Ludwig von Mises Institute.

7 BUSINESS AND THE COMMON GOOD
Robert G. Kennedy

Introduction

The social doctrine of the Catholic Church is not new. It is as old as the Church Herself and flows directly from the conviction that human persons, as images of the Trinity, are social creatures, impelled by their nature to live and flourish only in communities. As a branch of moral theology, the social doctrine has developed over a period of nearly two thousand years in response to a deepening understanding of the practical implications of the Gospel as well as to a variety of changes in the cultural, political and economic dimensions of social life.[1]

Until the modern era, reflections on the economic dimension of the social question were relatively primitive. The Church's main preoccupation was with a spectrum of political issues: the proper relationship of Church and state, the nature and limits of authority to govern, religious freedom, and so on. It was not until the sixteenth century, with the explosion in trade and wealth brought about by the European voyages of discovery, that theologians turned their attention to an analysis of the dramatic changes in the economic arena. Still later, near the end of the nineteenth century, the challenge of socialism provoked Pope Leo XIII

---

1   See Pontifical Council of Justice and Peace (2005: 72–4). The *Compendium* is the first authoritative and comprehensive exposition of the social doctrine of the Catholic Church. Where almost all official documents dealing with social questions in the past have been occasional, i.e. provoked by a specific problem or set of questions, the *Compendium* sets out to summarise the tradition as a whole. A number of private summaries have been prepared over the years, some of them quite well done, but the *Compendium* has an authoritative character that other treatments cannot claim.

to address contemporary economic issues in an encyclical letter.[2] Some of his successors, notably Pius XI, John XXIII and John Paul II, similarly wrote about economic questions in prominent encyclical letters of their own.

The thrust of the encyclicals, however, tended to be a defence of some elements of the moral tradition of the Church (e.g. the right to private property, the right to just wages, the integrity of the family) against socialism and other forms of statism, coupled with urgent expressions of concern about social justice. In their turn, the encyclicals inspired generations of theologians, religious and lay persons to become engaged in efforts to implement some of the principles they articulated. Still, it is probably fair to say that, while the social encyclicals were especially concerned with the dangers of socialism, advocates of social justice came to be more concerned in practice with critiques of free-market econo-mies.

In either case, what has been missing is a sustained and comprehen-sive consideration of the role of private enterprise in a modern society.[3] At best, some of the encyclicals have given attention to certain aspects of business and acknowledged in general that it has an important role to

---

2   This encyclical, *Rerum novarum* (1891), has real historical significance in that its publica-tion marked the first time that a Pope addressed contemporary economic issues in such an authoritative document. Many people mistakenly regard the letter as the starting point for the Catholic social tradition, at least in its modern form. Leo himself, however, had already written no fewer than six encyclicals on issues in the arena of politics and governance before the appearance of *Rerum novarum*, including one on the problems of socialism. Furthermore, to exaggerate the distinctiveness of the encyclical is also to over-look the pains that Leo took to emphasise that his teaching was a continuation of, not a departure from, the Catholic tradition of moral theology.

3   In the ancient world, indeed in Western civilisation up to the nineteenth century, com-merce and trade were often regarded with suspicion and disdain by the nobility and the Church. Respectable wealth came from the land and entailed a variety of customary re-sponsibilities. The new wealth that came from commerce and trade was thought often to be the result of deception and dishonesty. This attitude of suspicion has diminished a bit over the past two centuries as business activities have become such a large part of modern economies, but it has not entirely been dispelled. One important area for development for the Catholic social tradition, therefore, has to do with the marketplace.

play in the community.[4] At worst, many advocates of social justice have regarded business with suspicion in principle and ironically turned to socialist analysis in an effort to craft a better society.[5] There has been, however, no systematic theory of business to rival the theory of law and governance that the Catholic social tradition has elsewhere developed. The elements of such a theory are present in the tradition but they have not been effectively drawn together. The purpose of this chapter is to address one part of this larger project, namely to explore the relationship of business to the common good of civil society in light of the principles of the Catholic social tradition.

Catholic social thought and the good society

Businesses of every sort exist only in the context of a larger social body, a civil society. At the same time, every business, even a publicly owned corporation, is composed of individual persons who conceive of the organisation, assemble the resources to make it possible, make decisions about strategy and operations, and execute those decisions. The organisation does not interact with an impersonal environment; persons representing the business interact with other persons external to the organisation. As a consequence, the nature of a business becomes clear only when it is examined in the context of the persons who bring it to life and in the context of the society in which it lives that life.

---

4 Prominent in this regard are Pius XI, *Quadragesimo anno* (1931), and John Paul II, *Centesimus annus* (1991). Though much less well known, the occasional speeches and radio messages of Pius XII and John Paul II often gave attention to specific questions concerning business.

5 Note that while the social doctrine of the Church is a product, strictly speaking, of the Magisterium (i.e. the Pope and the bishops in union with him), there are countless additional witnesses to the Church's concern with social questions. These witnesses include individual bishops, clerics, theologians and faithful laity, many of whom have made it part of their life's work to translate the principles of the social doctrine into practice. Not every witness, however, is an authoritative representative of Catholic thought. In particular, the bias against business and the marketplace that has become a common feature of advocates for social justice should not be regarded as a formal element of Catholic doctrine.

What, then, makes a society good? The Catholic social tradition conceives of the ideal human society as an integrated whole, a network of relationships between individuals, their families and a wide variety of other associations (Pontifical Council for Justice and Peace, 2005: 185). Society arises as a natural result of the individual's pursuit of personal fulfilment and its function, its only reason for being, is to facilitate that fulfilment. Good societies can take many shapes since there are a great many avenues for human fulfilment but all good societies have some common traits.[6] Bad societies – the tradition has no doubt that there are indeed bad societies – all fail in critical ways to support authentic human development.

One of the marks of a good society is respect for the primacy of the person. Catholic doctrine insists that human persons each have a transcendent destiny, which is to share in God's life for time without end.[7] No society is an end in itself; each is instrumental and exists to serve the ultimate end of the persons who are its constituent members (ibid.: 132). Societies and social structures betray this principle when they frustrate the destiny of some of their members for the sake of the perceived well-being of others. Prominent examples of such flawed societies are the communist and fascist governments of the twentieth century, in which the state claimed primacy and acted to subordinate the most critical human rights of its citizens (to life and liberty, to property, to freedom of religion, and so on).

---

6   In the Catholic view, no society short of the Kingdom of Heaven can be a *perfect* society. This conviction, which is not unique to Catholicism, has sometimes served as an excuse to avoid giving attention to the genuine ills and injustices of a particular community and to focus energy instead on private piety. While acknowledging that all human lives, and therefore all human communities, are blemished by sin, the Church nevertheless insists that an essential part of its mission is to work for the reform of society. Even something that cannot be made perfect can still be made better. By the same token, the fact that every society is flawed does not support the conclusion that no societies are better than others or that none is more readily improved than others. In the end, Christians have a clear duty to work constantly for the reform of the societies in which they live. See Pontifical Council for Justice and Peace, 2005: 52–66.

7   This conviction is captured by the Second Vatican Council, which said that 'man is the only creature on earth that God has wanted for its own sake'. See *Gaudium et spes*, 24. See also Pontifical Council for Justice and Peace, 2005: 47.

Another mark of a good society is variety and plurality in relationships and associations among its members. While human beings have an ultimate end in common – God – there is a broad spectrum of genuine human needs that can be addressed in a virtually infinite number of ways.[8] For example, people have a range of material needs related to life and health. We have to eat and drink, find shelter and clothing, receive medical care, and so forth. We also have needs for knowledge, beauty, play and friendship, to name a few. A good society offers possibilities for satisfying a very wide range of authentic human needs and it typically does this by encouraging and supporting families as well as a great many clubs, businesses, charities and specialised associations of all sorts. Some of these organisations may be very small and local, while others may be quite large and national or international in their scope. Each of the organisations is in some way a manifestation of the energy and creativity of individuals and a means for their self-expression.

According to the Catholic tradition, the family is the fundamental and irreplaceable association at the core of a good society. Its stability and flourishing must be encouraged as an essential foundation for the health of the community. In addition, the good society must have formal government but also a number of non-governmental associations that pursue aspects of human welfare, such as church-related and other charitable organisations, universities and cultural associations, and so forth. It must also have a variety of associations engaged in market activities, for example businesses that aim at producing a profit and creating wealth by addressing human needs. Thus the good society will include the family and the state as well as intermediate bodies engaged in both market and non-market activities. Seriously defective societies seek to

---

8   We have a 'need' for any good thing that genuinely contributes to our development and
     well-being as persons. Needs are not merely those things without which we die. Needs
     may be very general (we all need to eat but we can satisfy this need in a great many ways)
     or very specific (we need a particular medication here and now). Frequently needs must
     be distinguished from wants. Sometimes we really need less of something than we want.
     Sometimes we want something that actually adds nothing to our development or well-
     being.

suppress one or another of these categories of associations, usually the intermediate bodies.

The myriad associations that flourish in a good society inevitably give it a hierarchical character. The idea of hierarchy is in disfavour today but that is because it is usually taken to refer to a situation in which an authoritarian figure (or group) dominates the rest of society, suppressing legitimate liberties and self-expression. This is an unfortunate caricature of hierarchy and quite different from that which the tradition recognises. In the tradition, every ordered society – and no good society can be disordered – is hierarchical, and appropriately so. On the one hand, order requires coordination, which in turn demands some principle of authority for resolving disagreements. A well-ordered society in this respect will have levels of authority, increasingly broad in application, that exist to resolve these disagreements when compromise and concession fail. On the other hand, a society with a great many associations, some local and highly focused in their activities, others regional or national and comprehensive in their interests, naturally manifests a different sort of hierarchy. Here, for example, a local golfing club might reasonably defer to a regional or national association in regard to the rules of the game in order to preserve a uniformity that serves everyone well.

It is certainly the case that persons in positions of broader application and greater power can and do abuse their authority. The Catholic tradition is well aware of this and so insists that the bedrock principle guiding the exercise of authority in any community or society is subsidiarity (ibid.: 185–8). Underlying this principle is the conviction that a good society demands the flourishing of this wide variety of associations. As a consequence, every superior authority has a twofold duty. First, it must provide assistance as needed to subordinate associations to enable them to perform their functions as effectively as possible. Second, it must always exercise restraint in its use of power so that the legitimate activities of these subordinate associations are never destroyed or absorbed. If the principle of subsidiarity is properly observed, the good society will be an organic whole in which small associations multiply and flourish, quite distinct from a centralised organisation in which subordinate units are merely extensions of the dominant power.

The person and the common good

The nature of the contribution that a good business makes to society depends upon what the human person is understood to be. Given the primacy of the person in the Catholic social tradition, it is necessary to be clear about what the tradition teaches on this question.

At the very foundation of Catholic doctrine on the person is the conviction that each and every person is an image of God, created for his own sake and therefore possessed of a value (dignity) as an end in itself. While persons, or their activities, may also function as instruments for the achievement of other goals, they are never merely instruments. Instruments always have contingent value. They are valued for their capacity to achieve goals and may be discarded once they lose this capacity. Even though persons may sometimes be useless as instruments, they nevertheless always have value as reflections of the divine.

As mentioned above, human persons also have a destiny that transcends material creation and physical life. This destiny contributes to the intrinsic value of each person but also implies that persons are never completely fulfilled by created goods or even by other creatures. While created goods are necessary to sustain physical life and contribute in important ways to human happiness (we are *embodied* spirits, after all), they are not enough. The deepest human desires and fulfilments transcend the material world and, by implication, no one should concentrate so strongly on obtaining created goods so as to close off the possibility of obtaining the transcendent good.

All creation is a reflection of the Creator but human persons are unique images because they possess intellect and will, their two most Godlike characteristics. As a consequence, an essential part of human well-being consists in knowing the truth and choosing well. This is really the foundation for the principle of subsidiarity, for a superior authority frustrates human flourishing if it suppresses freedom of action in individuals. By the same token, such an authority does violence to individuals, in a way, if it deceives them or distorts and conceals the truth they ought to know.

Because they can know the truth and choose freely, human persons can be independent actors and are fulfilled in part by the productive activities in which they engage. The Catholic tradition insists that each person is called by God to work, to be a collaborator in the unfolding of creation. This fact of vocation has implications for both businesses and the state, for each has a responsibility, at minimum, not to interfere unreasonably in the efforts of individuals to obtain good work and to respond to their vocations.

Furthermore, properly human work and indeed the whole effort of an individual in pursuit of fulfilment are understood to be collaborative because human persons are social by nature. In this they are once again reflections of God since the Trinity is a community itself. The conviction that human persons are social and not atomistic individuals brings the Catholic tradition into sharp contrast with some modern political and economic theories. At the same time, the conviction that individuals matter enormously and that the function of the state is to facilitate the flourishing of these individuals brings the tradition into conflict with another set of political and economic theories. The result is a body of doctrine that, on the one hand, defends the primacy of the person and the right to private property and, on the other hand, emphasises the importance of the common good and solidarity.

Finally, the larger Catholic tradition acknowledges that the human being is a fallen creature, a creature whose natural capacities have been maimed by his sinfulness, a creature in need of salvation, and in the end a creature who has been saved by God made man. This reality accounts for the unavoidable defects in human societies, human associations and social systems, but it also provides another reason for respecting the dignity of individuals, who were each worthy of God's saving acts.

Based on this understanding of the human person, the Catholic social tradition has something to say about the world of creation. In the first place, the material world is the proper sphere of human operation and human dominion. The world, in all its complexity and richness, is the object of human work and creativity. Its resources, living and non-living, are to be cultivated for the sake of general human well-being, and never to be put to wasteful uses. Moreover, the Christian God is a God of abundance, not a God of scarcity. The material resources of the created world are more than sufficient to meet the needs of the human population, though it may well require ingenuity, work, restraint and solidarity actually to provide the necessary resources to each person.[9]

Common goods and the common good

The nature of the human person as a social being who must seek his fulfilment in community with others places a set of demands on society (ibid.: 164–5). As a consequence of what people are, every civil community must have certain characteristics if it is to serve effectively as a context in which individuals can develop and flourish. While it is not primarily in the larger civil arena that individuals pursue their proper ends – families and the various intermediate bodies are more likely to be

---

9   While this may seem at first to conflict with a fundamental principle of economics – which assumes scarcity rather than abundance – the apparent conflict is not difficult to resolve. In the first place, economics concerns itself with the allocation and distribution of things that are scarce in particular instances, and more or less ignores things that are abundant. Scarcity and abundance are relative terms, comparing the available quantity of a thing with the amount desired. When more is desired than is available, the thing is scarce; when more is available than is desired, the thing is abundant. Economics has little or nothing to tell us about the absolute quantity available of any resource or about whether that quantity will in the future be sufficient or insufficient to meet human needs. While acknowledging that physical resources are finite in some way, Catholics nevertheless believe that, in an absolute sense, creation is not deficient nor is the Creator miserly. The earth provides enough for every human person to have a reasonable share. In a fallen world, however, scarcity of one sort or another is the common experience at the practical level. It is here that economics can suitably inform theology. See Pontifical Council for Justice and Peace, 2005: 323–9.

the actual communities in which people flourish – it is still true that this arena provides the foundation on which all other communities depend. The name we give to this set of characteristics is the 'common good', but in truth this is only one common good among many.

A common good by definition is one that is, or may be, shared (owned, used, enjoyed or pursued) by a number of people (we might say that a private good, by contrast, is one that is not or cannot be shared with other members of a group). Since human persons are naturally social beings, and their genuine fulfilment inevitably involves a community of some sort, common goods are always important.

Goods, or a good, may be described in a number of ways.[10] Both private goods and common goods, for example, may be *actual* or *potential*. Actual goods are those that, at a given point in time, really are owned, used or enjoyed. Potential goods are those that, while not presently owned, used or enjoyed, are seen as real possibilities: they are goals. Potential goods serve to motivate goal-directed action, and potential common goods motivate collaborative action. Indeed, underlying any genuinely collaborative action (as opposed to an aggregate of individual actions aimed at the same goal such as a gold rush) there must be at least one potential common good.

Common goods may also be *instrumental* or *final*. An instrumental good is one that is valued for its capacity to help us obtain something else that we want, while a final good is the ultimate object of our actions.[11] Potential common goods (i.e. goals) are valued by the individuals who pursue them in collaboration with others because they are always understood to promote private goods. Players work together in a team because each wants to be part of a winning effort or at least each wants to share

---

10   It can be a mistake to speak of *the* common good, as if there were one good (or collection of goods) that composed the common good. The Catholic social tradition does speak of *the* Common Good as a sort of shorthand for the common good of a civil community. This is a legitimate usage but it should not obscure for us the fact that there are many other important common goods.

11   Money is the model of an instrumental good. We value it only because it can be exchanged for other things we want.

in the camaraderie of the group. Employees work towards the success of a business for similar reasons but also so that they can participate in the financial rewards.

On a larger scale, peace, order and justice in a society are valued because they promote individual flourishing, not because they have an intrinsic value apart from their utility in supporting human well-being. Individuals may make extraordinary sacrifices to bring such common goods into being and to protect them, but it is because they understand and rightly value the private goods that follow.[12]

The common good of a society has a distinctive character. Since societies are intended to endure over time and through a succession of generations, their characteristic common good does not consist in a goal to be achieved once and for all. While there may be something potential about this common good, it is not a goal that, were it to be achieved, would mean the end of the society. Moreover, as the function of the society is to support the flourishing and fulfilment of its members, its common good is instrumental. That is to say, it is not a final good valued in and for itself (as basic goods are, for example), but it is something valued, supported and protected by the members of the society for what it permits them to do and to be.

More precisely, the common good of a society is *constructive*, which means that it is a set of conditions that makes possible the individual flourishing of each and every member of the community.[13] To the extent

---

12 Totalitarian states make the serious mistake of regarding such common goods as absolutely final, and so in the end become willing to sacrifice all manner of private goods for their sake. Even in wiser societies, caution must always be exercised in crafting and applying positive laws so that the conditions that must exist in a society to promote the flourishing of its members are adequately protected while at the same time private goods are not threatened. To be sure, in any society, some private goods are incompatible with sustaining these public conditions and so may be legitimately curtailed – but a prudent balance must nevertheless be maintained.

13 See Pope John XXIII, *Mater et magistra*, 65, for a classic definition of the common good of political communities: '[The common good] embraces the sum total of those conditions of social living whereby men are enabled more fully and more readily to achieve their own perfection.' As a practical matter, this set of goods includes such elements as peace, justice, universal education, participation in culture and public life, and so on.

that some necessary conditions are not present in a society, or that the well-being of some members is not addressed, the common good has not been achieved. We recognise as a practical matter that in a fallen world the set of goods and conditions that constitutes this common good is never fully achieved and so remains a goal for the members of the community. Even if it were to be achieved, the continued maintenance and support that it would require would still make it a goal of ongoing collaboration.

Potential common goods not only shape the collaboration of members of an organisation, they also define organisations and communities. In particular, the potential common goods that define business organisations make them quite different from other kinds of communities.

A specialised association, as the name implies, is ordered not to the integral fulfilment of its members, but rather towards attaining some human good or limited set of goods.[14] A business organisation is a specialised association, but so is an army, an orchestra, a charitable organisation, a bowling club, a university, a criminal syndicate, and virtually an indefinite number and variety of human organisations.

Our understanding of the relationship between a specialised community and a political community needs further refinement. Until relatively recently (perhaps in some places as late as the nineteenth century) specialised associations played only a small role in human life.[15]

---

14 The *Compendium* and some elements of the Catholic social tradition seem to prefer the term 'intermediate' to refer to 'associations', 'bodies', 'entities' or 'groups' that exist and function between the family and the state. This term of art suggests, in English at least, an organisation that acts as an intermediary between the domestic society and the civil society. Some intermediate groups do function in that way but the majority simply focus on, or one might say 'specialise in', a specific set of human goods. Furthermore, the tradition has tended not to give much attention to businesses as intermediate groups though they certainly belong in this category. As a result, the term 'specialised associations' seems to me to be more inclusive and so a better one.

15 The triumph of the nation-state in Europe after the seventeenth century diminished the role of what had been a rich web of specialised associations (villages, churches, guilds, and so on). In this earlier period, people tended to shape their personal identities from their membership in these associations and therefore saw themselves as integral and

In the twentieth century, however, that role has expanded greatly, in terms both of the size of specialised associations and of their numbers. In developed societies today, virtually everyone is dependent upon specialised associations, directly or indirectly.[16]

Specialised associations differ from political communities and families in several important respects. First of all, there is the difference in purpose. A specialised association is always organised in order to pursue some particular good or set of goods, at least for those who collaborate in the association and often for others as well. Where the society or family functions to sustain a set of conditions within which persons may mature and seek their own fulfilment, a specialised association is directed to the creation of actual goods that its members can possess or enjoy.

Second, the nature of specialised associations makes their potential common goods (i.e. the goals of the organisation) more important for their day-to-day functioning than would be the case in other communities. In business, for example, specific kinds of collaboration are required because of the organisation's goals. In order to elicit this collaboration, the goals must be clearly understood and they must be compelling. The success of the organisation will require a certain kind of active contribution from each member, where the common good of a society can often be supported by the choices of citizens *not* to engage in behaviours that undermine this common good.

Third, specialised associations have a clear relationship to the societies in which they exist and function. It is sometimes assumed that, to

---

important parts of small wholes. After the seventeenth century, many people tended to see themselves as small parts of large wholes (which were the nations). It is easy to exaggerate the significance of this change, however, since it is also the case that these earlier specialised associations never achieved the size and extent of so many contemporary organisations.

16 Which is not, however, to say that we lead lives that are socially richer. In many cases, while we may do what we do in the context of an organisation of some sort, we do these things not as members of a true human community but as strangers in a crowd. Robert D. Putnam (2000) has described the curious decline of community at a time of the increased importance of organisations.

be legitimate, specialised associations must serve the common good of the society in all that they do. This, however, is a misunderstanding.

The common good of a society is oriented to the flourishing of all its members. This flourishing, however, entails the flourishing of the organisations and associations formed by members of the society to seek and obtain private goods (ibid.: 168). These associations derive their legitimacy from the authentic human goods they seek, not from their contribution to the general common good. Indeed, the general common good must create the circumstances in which these organisations can function.

As a result, in a good society, these organisations should have considerable freedom in identifying and pursuing goods, which, to the extent that they serve to focus and motivate collaboration, will genuinely be common goods for that organisation. To be morally legitimate these common goods must be true human goods (and not merely apparent goods, such as revenge or pornography) and they must be pursued by morally sound means (so a criminal organisation might pursue real goods but do so by immoral means). Of course, the pursuit of these goods cannot undermine the constructive common good of the larger human community. Insofar as the goods pursued really are human goods, however, it is not necessary that the goods of a specialised association intentionally and directly support the common good of the larger community. They may quite legitimately do nothing more than facilitate the attainment of private goods by those associated with the organisation.[17]

---

17   That is, while the common goods of smaller communities must ordinarily be subordinated to the common good of the larger community within which they exist, it is not the case that the common goods of smaller communities must always be directed to serve the common good of the larger community. To put it another way, the actions of smaller communities or associations must not be such as to undermine the common good of the larger communities of which they are a part, although their actions need not always aim deliberately to enhance that common good in particular ways in order to be morally sound. Business organisations, therefore, need not use their resources to address social problems in order to be morally worthy associations. They are morally worthy if they pursue authentic goods in ways that properly respect other private goods and the common good of the larger community.

These private goods may include the direct satisfaction of a variety of human needs, as well as opportunities for good work. Also included, and not least in importance, is the creation of wealth.

The contribution of business to the common good

Something new has emerged in the modern world: a sophisticated commercial system that makes possible the creation and distribution of products and services on an unprecedented scale. The significance of this development, and the possibilities inherent in it both for promoting and for undermining human well-being, have not been correctly or sufficiently recognised within the Catholic social tradition. While some official statements, notably the 1991 encyclical by Pope John Paul II, *Centesimus annus*, acknowledge in broad strokes the potential of the new system, most discussions, whether official or unofficial, represent a primitive view of modern economic realities. This is one area in which the tradition urgently needs updating.

Even though a business need not make a direct contribution to the common good of the civic community in order to be good and legitimate, business as a system in fact does make such contributions. The system organises and integrates a number of separate elements for the sake of the common good. These elements include:

- a business culture in which individual businesses, from small to large, create an environment in which certain procedures and values are shared for the sake of more effective collaboration and even competition;[18]

---

18   Despite some dramatic exceptions, contemporary business relationships and operations are facilitated by a culture in which certain attitudes and practices are taken for granted. These include respect for market mechanisms, an attitude of service, and commitments in practice to transparency and good record keeping, honouring promises, and so on. By way of illustration, as formerly communist countries worked to re-enter a global market-place in the 1990s, one of the things businesspeople were particularly keen to learn from the West was the set of habits required to compete and be taken seriously.

- a stable financial infrastructure, which depends upon sound fiscal and monetary policies and international cooperation;
- a system of laws and regulations concerning business operations that are stable, economically sound and ordered to the common good;
- the effective application of technology, especially in the areas of communication and transportation, that serves to facilitate business operations.

The history of the development of modern business need not concern us here. It is sufficient to say that the invention and spread of the limited liability corporation made possible the creation of the large organisations required for the production of many modern products and services.[19] These organisations could survive their founders and the principle of limited liability encouraged investors to take risks. The early successes of these organisations gave some indication of the possibilities (and the perils) that lay ahead. Over time we came to realise that exploiting the potential of this new way of doing business would also require the cooperation of government in setting in place sound financial policies as well as sensible laws and regulations. It was also important, in some areas, for government to take a hand in shaping the institutional framework, and sometimes facilitating the provision of infrastructure, in which new technologies would facilitate business operations. The appropriate role of government here is arguable but it can include facilitating the development of railway networks, roads and motorways, and air travel, as well as aspects of the Internet and modern telecommunications.

Much of the government interest in the development of the modern business system was motivated, or at least justified in public discussion,

---

19 Many of the foundations of modern life would be impossible without large business organisations. From railways, automobiles and aircraft to telecommunications, computers and modern medicine, much of what we take for granted cannot be produced entirely by small companies. The limited liability corporation made practical the assembly of financial resources required by these large businesses.

by a concern for the common good of the community. Like any powerful tool, this system can be abused and turned against the common good. This fact should not be ignored but neither should we make business the natural enemy of society and overlook the real good it is capable of doing. When it functions well, the modern system of business contributes to that common good in two principal ways.

First, the system of business greatly augments the wealth-producing capacity of the community. In the Christian tradition, wealth is not understood simply as money but rather as an abundance of the material goods required for a good human life (see Kennedy, 2006). To create wealth is to apply human labour and ingenuity to the resources of creation in order to produce the goods that satisfy human needs. To have an abundance of these goods is to be prosperous and in the most important sense prosperity is a sought-after condition of communities and societies, not merely of individuals (Pontifical Council for Justice and Peace, 2005: 323–9). The wealth-producing capacity of a society, therefore, is its ability to bring into being the abundance or prosperity necessary to sustain the good life for each of its members.[20]

Business may do this in two ways. First, it often seeks ways to organise human work more effectively, which at its best makes work more productive without necessarily demanding more time and energy from the worker.[21] Second, business in many societies has the task of

20   One might argue that this abundance of goods is impossible to achieve because human wants are unlimited; as soon as one desire is satisfied another one can arise. A truly good life for an individual, however, is not the satisfaction of every desire but rather the reasonable satisfaction of the desires of a virtuous person. Since the deepest human desires, the ones that are properly unlimited, are spiritual and intellectual, not material, it remains possible in principle to generate an abundance of goods. That even 'wealthy' societies fail to do this may say more about the reasonableness of their desires than about the capacity of the society to create prosperity. Furthermore, as a practical matter unlimited goods would require unlimited productive labour. While a good life requires some good work, it also requires leisure properly understood. Therefore, in a prosperous society material goods are available in abundance, making a good life possible, but desires are moderated by virtue as well, making unlimited goods unnecessary.

21   Needless to say, businesses are not immune to the disorganisation and inefficiency that are found in other sectors. Incentives to deal with these problems are, however, more

converting common resources (whether natural like oil or virtual like bandwidth) into useful products and services.[22] Developed economies generally recognise that business manages this conversion better than the public sector and therefore contributes more to the common good by doing so. Thus in more highly developed economies a great many activities are privatised that once were conducted by a branch of government.

Business does not have a monopoly, so to speak, on productive human labour. Wealth can be created by any segment of society but business by its nature focuses on wealth-creating activities. While well-managed businesses aim at particular goods for their members and customers, they also augment the capacity of a society to create general prosperity, which is indeed an element of the common good.

The second broad contribution that the system of business makes is related to the first. Business organises work and resources to generate not only *more* products and services to address the material needs of members of the community but also better and more sophisticated ones.[23] This is exemplified by the healthcare industry in which so much progress has been made over the last few generations. From extraordinary new technologies to creative surgical techniques to breakthrough medications, the industry has made routine what was once thought impossible. Similar things have happened in communications, transportation and information management. Though some are commissioned by the public sector, most of these innovations are actually produced by private business, which also does a great deal of fundamental research.

All this is a significant contribution to the general common good, but from the perspective of the Catholic social tradition it does carry with it a

strongly present in business settings than in most non-profit or government organisations. Very few people, if any, recommend that businesses study government agencies or university faculties to find models of efficiency and effectiveness.

22 That is, societies convey to businesses in some fashion the right to extract or exploit a resource owned by the community. In doing so, the society may benefit from a fee paid to acquire the rights as well as from the relatively efficient conversion of the resource into something that serves human welfare.

23 On the desirability of this, see *Centesimus annus*, 36.

certain risk. This is the danger of losing sight of what genuinely contributes to human well-being and instead employing our enhanced technological capacities merely to respond to wants. Medical technology, for example, can be turned to frivolous cosmetic surgery or communications technology can produce and distribute ever-increasing amounts of pornography. Neither business nor engineering has internal compasses that can direct practice unerringly to good ends (ibid.: 360, 376). Instead, they both depend upon external ethical guidance, which can be supplied by the social tradition, among other sources.

By the same token, the Catholic social tradition is at risk of becoming impractical and esoteric unless it is informed by practical disciplines such as business, economics, engineering and politics. The tradition does indeed have something to teach these disciplines but it also has some important lessons to learn. We turn to that now.

What the Catholic social tradition has to learn from business and economics

The ultimate measure of the success of a business is neither its margin of profit nor the market price of its shares. Its true success lies in the human needs that its activities satisfy, including the needs of workers, customers, investors and others. This is a moral criterion but then business, and the economic arena in general, is not simply a technical exercise; it should also be truly moral. The Catholic social tradition reminds us of this (ibid.: 338–40). The tradition and its advocates, however, are often less mindful that there are crucially important lessons to be learned from the social sciences and the professions, such as management (ibid.: 378).[24]

---

24   It should be noted that while, at some level, the Church acknowledges the need to learn from the social sciences and other disciplines, this has often not translated into a real appropriation of what these disciplines have to teach. Too frequently a passion on the part of advocates for better economic outcomes has resulted in commitments to policies that are unwise, even if well intentioned. The problem is compounded when such a policy preference is later understood to be a necessary entailment of the Church's social teaching.

Indeed, to be morally good in the fullest sense an activity or a practice must not only be oriented to genuine goods, it must also employ morally sound means to achieve these goods. And a morally sound means must be both effective and efficient.[25]

Consider, for example, the doctrine of the just wage (ibid.: 302). The idea that a worker ought to be paid fairly for his work is at least biblical in origin.[26] During much of the Middle Ages wages for labourers were established not so much by agreement between employer and employee as by law or custom. Until the modern era prices were comparatively stable and labourers rarely suffered from inflation. In the modern era, however, as fairly rapid inflation became a fact of life and as developed countries moved away from customary forms of labour to industrial employment, the question of just wages became more acute. It was no longer quite enough to encourage employers to pay a just wage when such a wage was being set by a market of sorts.[27] The doctrine of the Church evolved somewhat to demand that the wages paid to a full-time worker be sufficient to permit that worker, and his family, to live a minimally decent life, taking into account the time and place. Simply relying on the market was not enough since a market mechanism alone could result in wages below a subsistence level.

One response to this problem which was championed by many advo-

---

25 Cardinal Ratzinger (now Pope Benedict XVI) made a similar observation many years ago: 'A morality that believes itself able to dispense with the technical knowledge of economic laws is not morality but moralism. As such it is the antithesis of morality. A scientific approach that believes itself capable of managing without an ethos misunderstands the reality of man. Therefore it is not scientific. Today we need a maximum of specialised economic understanding but also a maximum of ethos so that specialised economic understanding may enter the service of the right goals.' See Ratzinger (1986).

26 See Leviticus 19:3, Deuteronomy 24:14–15, Judges 5:4.

27 While acknowledging the legitimate freedom of persons to negotiate the terms of contracts, there was some initial suspicion among Catholic thinkers of negotiated wages and wage contracts. Some theologians argued that wage contracts were immoral, but this view was definitively rejected by Pius XI in his encyclical *Quadragesimo anno*, 64. Nevertheless, the Church has always insisted that negotiation by itself does not make a wage just and that other, non-negotiable, factors must be considered: see Calvez and Perrin (1961: 282–5).

cates of the social tradition early in the twentieth century was a legislated minimum wage. This policy recalled the medieval practice of legally determined wages and in principle offered some protection to workers who were vulnerable in the absence of unions. Nevertheless, despite the fact that minimum wage legislation had (and has) the energetic support of a number of priests and bishops, it remains merely one policy option that follows from the general principle that workers ought to be paid fairly. As a policy option, not a moral principle, it ought to be examined for its effectiveness and its consequences in the times and places in which it might be imposed (see Chapter 4). There is considerable evidence to suggest that minimum wage legislation increases unemployment while not accomplishing as much as it was once thought to do to ensure that workers are paid enough. If that is the case then perhaps alternative policies ought to be considered. At the very least, we should keep in mind that the social tradition is ordinarily not committed to policies and practices at this level. Advocates should be prepared to revise their preferences in the light of sound economic evaluation while at the same time remaining firmly committed to the relevant moral principles.

Numerous other examples could be cited concerning such topics as corporate taxation, executive compensation, marketing and accounting practices, and so on. There are three important broad areas concerning business and the common good, however, in which we might say that economics and business practice can inform the social tradition.

The first of these has to do with the importance of wealth creation in a society (ibid.: 332, 334). The tradition acknowledges that wealth may be created, not merely distributed, and recognises that the true and ultimate source of wealth is human ingenuity and the capacity for work (see CA 32). Still, the tradition has not fully appropriated the significance of this idea. It remains more concerned with the distribution of wealth and income than with its creation. It is similarly concerned with the danger posed by a materialism that springs from prosperity. One answer to both concerns (which are indeed real enough) is to urge people in developed countries, by law or by persuasion, to adopt simpler lives and to share more of what they have. Both may have some benefits (especially if not coerced) but policies that expand the sum of wealth to be shared may be wiser and more effective. This could be especially true if coupled with cultural models, perhaps inspired by Christian teaching and preaching, that discourage excessive consumption through personal moral restraint and encourage people to bend their energies to obtain genuine human goods rather than empty consumption.

The second area is related to this. No one disputes that there are indeed problems of poverty and deprivation that urgently need attention. In parts of the world there are people who need help – food, shelter, healthcare – immediately. There is no time to wait for the development of these countries, as there is an urgent need for relief: material resources for their relief must be brought to bear, transferred, without delay (see the chapter on foreign aid by Booth for a discussion of development aid, which is different in character from this form of relief). Not every situation, however, is so urgent. In many cases the resolution of immediate problems needs to be accompanied by an appreciation of the importance of economic initiative and responsibility.

Once again, the tradition recognises this but does not always explore the full implications (ibid.: 187). Human persons, as images of God, are endowed with intelligence and freedom. An important element of their flourishing as persons is the exercise of these capacities, including their exercise in the economic arena. This means that people have a need to solve problems, to make choices, to be creative, and to express themselves, especially through their work. An implication of this on one level is that the full dignity of the person is not respected when welfare replaces work (assuming an individual is able to work). Far better for the person that he or she exercise all the capacities that are the gift of God rather than be a passive recipient of what others share.

This has implications, too, for policies quite removed from concerns about poverty. There is considerable evidence from business practice, for example, that procedures are more effective and more efficient when the creativity of employees is released and when they have a significant degree of freedom in which to do their work. Government policies that unnecessarily constrain business practices or that stifle creativity, to say nothing of management practices that do the same, are wasteful, or worse. They smother the human spirit and ignore the fact that the economic segment of life produces more than merely material goods: it also shapes the soul of participants. The Church understands this, again at some level, but a tight focus on distribution of resources in practice tends to obscure some of the deeper and more human goods meant to be served by an economy or a business (ibid.: 189–91).

One last consequence of the creativity and freedom of individuals, one that modern economics has come to appreciate far more strongly than the social tradition, is change in technology, in work and in economic relationships. A society in which creativity and freedom are suppressed, whether by design or by circumstance, is also a society in which much is stable. This is probably a convertible proposition: a stable society is one in which creativity and freedom are not adequately enjoyed by the population (and in which the common good is defective to that extent). A healthy society is dynamic and characterised by Schumpeter's 'creative destruction'. This does not mean that the economy in such a society needs to be brutal but perhaps that what is to be preferred is a sort of dynamic equilibrium rather than economic stasis. In contrast, some elements of the social tradition of the Church have had a wistful longing for economic relationships that belong to an earlier era and which would not be possible today without sacrificing some of the benefits of modern civilisation.[28]

A third area in which the Church could learn from economics, and perhaps the most direct area, has to do with what we might call the economic realities of a fallen world. The world in which we live is not the Kingdom of Heaven: it is populated by men and women who are not only sinners but whose perceptions and inclinations are damaged by original sin. Economic relationships and behaviours are shaped by this reality.

---

28 One thinks in this regard of the economic nostalgia of Chesterton and Belloc, or of the romantic attachment that the Church often has to agriculture as a way of life.

While it is certainly true that the economy must, in the end, be at the service of man, it also functions the way it does because of who man is.

From Kant we have inherited the idea that genuinely moral actions cannot at the same time be self-serving. In other words, the moral act cannot and should not benefit the person acting. On this analysis, most business activities are non-moral at best and immoral at worst since they aim at obtaining benefits for employees and shareholders through service to customers and communities. Catholic moral theology, however, has never adopted this view. It does not see a conflict, in principle, between moral behaviour and self-interested behaviour (though such a conflict can certainly exist in particular cases). On the other hand, neither does it fully subscribe to Adam Smith's notion of a tradesman indifferent to the welfare of his customers. Moral business people, in the Catholic view, attend to the well-being of their customers and understand that their own well-being, both spiritual and material, is intimately connected with the excellence of their work.

Economics, for the most part, would not dispute this analysis but it has a greater appreciation of the degree to which even good people fall short of seeing and pursuing the good in every case. This leads to an appreciation of the importance of incentives.

In a world populated by saints, people would make economic choices that reflected a sound understanding of and a deep commitment to what is truly good, for themselves and for everyone affected by their actions. In the world in which we really live, we often make choices that are not so much self-interested as selfish. We prefer the good for ourselves even when our actions deny the good to others, and we often prefer our private goods to the common good.

As a practical matter, then, leaders in an organisation or a community must provide some additional motivating factors to assist people to work for the good of others and for the common good. This entails providing incentives that channel behaviour in more appropriate directions. One difficulty with the practical side of the social tradition is that it too often relies on persons to act with the most saintly motives and too often is frustrated when they fail to do so. Sometimes this frustration results in a desire to provide legislated incentives of a different sort.

It would be far better for advocates of the tradition to understand more deeply the ways in which people, in the aggregate, respond to economic pressures and opportunities in order to craft more effective and respectful incentives.

Finally, the social tradition needs to overcome its apprehensions and hesitations about markets. Again, at an abstract level, the tradition recognises that markets play an important role in society (ibid.: 347–50; see also CA 42). There remains in practice, however, a very considerable conviction that markets are inevitably abusive and that freedom in the marketplace is to be avoided, that profitability is morally suspect, and so on.[29] In fact, as we can learn from economics, it is not so much free markets which are abusive as defective markets, such as those in which monopolies persist or competitors are prohibited from entering or where information is deficient.[30] Nevertheless, markets do respect human dignity and do reward human creativity, initiative and virtue (e.g. fairness, industry, self-discipline, and so on) while at the same time efficiently providing for human needs. The social tradition needs to acquire an appreciation of the value of markets and wean itself from its long infatuation with planned economies.

---

29 See Ratzinger (1986: 201–2). Consider, too, the criticisms commonly levelled against companies in the energy or pharmaceutical industries when they profit from high prices in their markets.

30 To be sure, even free markets, properly understood, can result in harms to participants when unscrupulous people cheat. Their cheating is not really a failure of the market and over time market mechanisms will introduce corrections. On the whole the market will function but in specific cases individuals may be harmed in the meantime. One can support free markets and at the same time acknowledge the necessity of external authorities to impose rules for the common good and correct for bad behaviour. But bad behaviour also occurs in regulatory authorities, of course, sometimes without self-correcting incentives. We therefore have to choose between different imperfect mechanisms. Who regulates the regulator? (see Chapter 10).

Conclusion

The Catholic social tradition is an integral element of the Church's teaching on moral matters. Its concern with the societies in which people live and work and pursue holiness is a legitimate part of its mission to continue the work of Christ. One major thrust of this tradition is a project to describe the nature of a good society and help people in particular places and particular times to bring that good society into being. Within this tradition the practice of business has a place. Good businesses address genuine human needs directly and form communities of work in which investors and employees can use their resources, their talents and their energies to support human well-being. Good businesses also make vital contributions to the common good of the societies in which they operate by creating wealth, by providing opportunities for good work and by making efficient use of the resources of the community.

The Church can play an important role in carrying forward its own mission and in making societies better by helping people to understand how business contributes to individual well-being and to the common good. To do this more effectively in practice, the Church needs to learn from disciplines like economics about the obstacles to and the practical means for supporting healthy businesses.

References

Calvez, J.-Y. and J. Perrin (1961), *The Church and Social Justice*, Chicago, IL: Regnery.

Kennedy, R. G. (2006), 'Wealth creation within the Catholic social tradition', in H. Alford et al. (eds), *Rediscovering Abundance*, Notre Dame, IN: University of Notre Dame Press, pp. 57–86.

Pontifical Council for Justice and Peace (2005), *Compendium of the Social Doctrine of the Church*, London: Burns & Oates.

Putnam, R. D. (2000), *Bowling Alone: The Collapse and Revival of American Community*, New York: Simon & Schuster.

Ratzinger, J. (1986), 'Church and economy: responsibility for the future of the world economy', *Communio*, 13: 199–204.

8 THE ENTREPRENEUR IN THE LIFE OF THE CHURCH AND SOCIETY

Anthony Percy

Introduction

There can be no doubt that the Church definitely has a bias against consumerism. In his encyclical letter on the Fatherhood of God – *Dives in misericordia* ('Rich in mercy') – the late Pope John Paul II noted that 'side by side with wealthy and surfeited people and societies, living in plenty and ruled by consumerism and pleasure, the same human family contains individuals and groups *that are suffering from hunger*' (DM 11).[1]

The Catholic Church has long had a deep concern for the poor. In fact, as Rodney Stark has discovered, one of the reasons why the Catholic Church had great success in evangelising the world in the first few centuries of its existence was its love and care for the poor. Survival rates among Catholics, for instance, after famines and plagues in the ancient world, were higher than among other groups in society. Catholics put into practice the *Mandatum novum*. They loved one another, cared for one another and thus had greater survival rates (see Stark, 1997: 74–5). Loving one another had practical consequences.

But it doesn't quite follow that railing against consumerism and having a preferential option for the poor means that you are against business, businessmen, entrepreneurs or money. After all, it is wealth which alleviates poverty. And poverty is what we want to remove. Wealth creation, therefore, should be promoted as a significant contrib-

---

1   All citations of the encyclicals of Pope John Paul II are from Miller (2001).

utor to the good of the human person and the common good. Wealth is a *means* to an end.

Besides, and perhaps surprisingly so, the Word of God is quite clear about this. Consumerism is not fuelled by money itself. Rather, it is the *love* of money which causes the problem. According to St Paul's first letter to Timothy, 'the *love of money* is the root of all evils' (1 Timothy 6:10). It is a warning whether you happen to be an entrepreneur or not.

The entrepreneur

Needless to say, having an interest in money (a commercial focus) and in making money is an important ingredient in what makes an entrepreneur tick. Along with this interest, an entrepreneur is extremely creative, and alert to information and new possibilities in the marketplace. He or she will be good at bringing both people and the factors of production together for a project, and will not be overawed by the risk – usually large – of undertaking such a project. Finally, and importantly, the Christian entrepreneur should carry out his work conscious of the common good.

The entrepreneur and the Word of God

The Word of God deals with God's saving action among us and it has a preoccupation, as regards social justice issues, with caring for widows and orphans. One would not expect, therefore, to find the latest investment or share advice in the sacred text. Still, all is not darkness with respect to the entrepreneur. We do find, particularly in the Wisdom literature, small rays of light with respect to his activity: 'These are the things you should not be ashamed of ... of making small and larger profits, or gaining from commercial transactions' (Sirach 42:1, 5).

Besides affirming commercial exchange and the profits that flow from it, this pithy text alerts us to the fact that each generation of businessmen and businesswomen does face a particular challenge: people are generally suspicious of anyone who makes money from commerce.

Why else would the biblical author counsel the reader to avoid feelings of shame?

The New Testament, too, alludes to the value of the entrepreneur. The parable of the talents (see Matthew 25:14–30) encourages diligence in the use of our God-given gifts. We are to avoid all forms of fear so that we are fruitful. To be sure, the parable has an eschatological flavour about it. But this should not stop us from recognising that the Lord, in telling the parable, made use of a measure of wealth – a talent. Other parables include two that run side by side in the Gospels:

> The kingdom of heaven is like treasure hidden in a field, which a man found and covered up; then in his joy he goes and sells all that he has and buys that field.
>
> Again, the kingdom of heaven is like a merchant in search of fine pearls, who, on finding one pearl of great value, went and sold all that he had and bought it. (Matthew 13:44–6)

These parables are evidently about the offer of eternal life – it is worth doing everything to gain it. But, as Bernard Lonergan has pointed out, they utilise the *principle of sublation* (Lonergan, 1972: 241). That is, the parable does indeed introduce something new and distinct (i.e. eternal life), but it does not interfere with or destroy the work of the businessman and merchant. On the contrary, the parable needs and preserves their work and activity and brings them to a fuller realisation. Thus there is an *implicit* approval of entrepreneurial activity in the scriptures.

The entrepreneur in the Fathers of the Church

Much the same can be said of the writings of the Church Fathers. On many occasions they approve of entrepreneurial work – implicitly. For instance, Basil the Great (329–79) approves of the work of merchants within the paradigm of the Creator's garden:

[T]he sea is good in the eyes of God ... because it brings together
the most distant parts of the earth, and facilitates the inter-
communication of mariners. By this means it gives us the boon
of general information, supplies the *merchant with his wealth*, and
easily provides for the necessities of life, allowing the rich to export
their superfluities, and blessing the poor with the supply of what
they lack.[2]

The merchant, his work and his wealth are praised within a general
theology of the creation. At the same time the poor benefit from such
activity. The work of the merchant is thus of great service to humanity
– particularly in its alleviation of poverty.

John Cassian (360–435) describes – quite remarkably – some 'infant'
Christians who were searching for perfection and found it among a
group of Christians whose only activity, it appears, was business. They
were businessmen by weight of necessity and used their intelligence for
survival. In some way, they must be considered the forerunners of the
Dutch:

And so we came by a very lengthy voyage to a town of Egypt named
Thennesus, whose inhabitants are so surrounded either by the
sea or by salt lakes that they *devote themselves to business alone* and
get their wealth and substance by *naval commerce* as the land fails
them, so that indeed when they want to build houses, there is no
soil sufficient for this, unless it is brought by boat from a distance.[3]

The entrepreneur and the virtue of magnificence

From a preliminary perusal of the tradition, then, it would appear that
those involved in business were not regarded as ogres. Rather, there seems
to be a healthy appreciation – albeit an implicit one – of their activity.

2   St Basil the Great, 'Nine homilies on the Hexaemeron', Homily IV (Upon the gathering
    together of the waters), in Schaff and Wace (1999: 75) (one finds similar thoughts in the
    writings of Chrysostom and Jerome).
3   John Cassian, 'Description of the town of Thennesus', in ibid.: 415.

St Thomas Aquinas (1225–74) adds weight to this claim in his treatment of the virtue of magnificence.[4] He lived at a time when a market economy was beginning to emerge (Charles, 1998: 197f). His analysis – remarkably – anticipates modern corporate finance theory with its emphasis on the relationship between risk and return, which was developed some seven centuries later.

According to Thomas, to carry out a 'magnificent work' requires both form and matter: largesse of soul (form) and largesse of outlay (matter). Thomas says, rather strikingly and incisively, that people would never carry out such works if they had not first *moderated their love for money*. If they truly loved money, then, according to St Thomas, they would never assume such a grand undertaking with its consequent risks. They would, presumably, be content to protect their sum by banking the money and obtaining the interest. It is precisely the ability to moderate one's love for money which leads an entrepreneur to engage in large and risky projects. Clearly, St Thomas thought there was virtue in the type of work and activity that we call 'entrepreneurial'.

Social doctrine and the entrepreneur

If circumstances and changes within society led St Thomas to consider more thoughtfully the importance of works of magnificence in the field of business and economics, then the Industrial Revolution in the eighteenth and nineteenth centuries definitely forced the Catholic Church, as well as many other institutions, to rethink – seriously – relationships in the social order. This was particularly true of the relationship between capital and labour. Pope Leo XIII was to focus his thoughts on this precise relationship in what became the Catholic Church's first and most famous social encyclical. It was called *Rerum novarum* and means 'Of new things'.

Society had been predominantly agrarian up until the eighteenth century, but changes late in that century meant that it was shifting

---

4   See *Summa Theologica*, 2, 2, Q. 134 (especially Article 3).

towards being an industrial society. Men no longer worked from home; technology and inventions contributed to vast changes in the quality and quantity of production; the means of production settled in the hands of a few; capital, not labour, was being considered as the main resource; wealth was increasingly focused in the hands of those in control of capital; inevitably tension developed between the new class of industrialists and a new – poorer – class of workers.

In 1891 Leo, with the encouragement of many of the world's bishops, was to respond to this massive shift in society with his famous and groundbreaking encyclical. It was some time in coming, but according to the late Pope John Paul II has provided the Church with a lasting paradigm for Catholic social thought (*Centesimus annus*, 5).

Two issues preoccupied Leo's thoughts. First, he defended the rights of workers to a just and fair wage. Second, he provided compelling arguments against socialism. The socialists reacted to the Industrial Revolution by promoting the socialisation of the means of production. They thought this was the best chance they had of fighting the inequalities between the emerging working class and the new class of wealthy industrialists.

The issue of socialisation is of interest to entrepreneurs, since Pope Leo defended vigorously the right to private property. He saw this right as flowing from human nature itself and wisely judged that if this right were taken away, human beings would lose all interest in their welfare. They could no longer call anything their own. His reasoning, to this day, is compelling.

Forty years later, Pope Pius XI wrote another social encyclical to coincide with the anniversary of *Rerum novarum*. It was called *Quadragesimo anno* and means 'Forty years' (or strictly speaking, 'In the fortieth year'). The year was 1931 and the world was in a mess.

> In 1931 Pius faced a very different situation. World War I had shattered liberal confidence. Parliamentary democracy seemed almost helpless in the face of the mass movements of fascism and communism. And the economy of the Western world lay in the ruins of a worldwide depression. (O'Brien and Shannon, 2000: 40)

Addressing the problems, Pius's encyclical was on the restructuring of the social order. While Leo had developed marvellously the right to *private property* in the social order, Pius moved to a defence of *private action* in the social order. This itself was a clear development in Catholic social thought, occasioned by culture and political factors.

The right to private action and initiative was threatened in a world filled with Nazi predators and communistic wolves. Moreover, the depression and its resultant despair opened the door to a particular political temptation: that of abolishing private initiative and the replacing of it with the installation of the welfare state.

Pius resisted the temptation forcefully. He reaffirmed, and developed for generations yet to come, the *principle of subsidiarity*. Subsidiarity derives its meaning from the Latin word *subsidium*. It means 'to help'. Thus the state is there to help and *not replace* the role and work of private citizens. The state is there to provide the *conditions* under which private enterprise can flourish. In this way the state serves and does not suffocate both private initiative and the common good.

And so, within 40 years two critical developments took place in the social teaching of the Church with respect to the entrepreneur and his work. First, the right to private property and private action was vigorously defended and affirmed. In the face of a rapidly changing world, and in response to the challenge of socialism and other 'isms', the Church taught clearly that no one should have their right to private property denied. Likewise, their right to private initiative must be considered sacrosanct. The good of the person and society depended on this being the case. Second, the Church clearly articulated what we now call the 'two arms' or 'two wings' of her social teaching – the *principle of solidarity* and the *principle of subsidiarity*. The Church could not stand idle at a time when the rights and dignity of workers were threatened. She defended the right to a just wage[5] and the right to private property

---

5   Whether a just wage should be one decided by agreement, with the state removing impediments to free negotiation, or have other characteristics too has been debated through the ages: see Chapter 4.

to ensure the material well-being of humanity, and these were the bases of the principle of solidarity. John Paul II would deepen the Church's understanding of solidarity in his three social encyclicals.[6]

Equally important was the principle of subsidiarity. How could poverty be eliminated if there was not freedom of action in the social and economic sphere? Who would create wealth? The enunciation of this principle proved to be more than prophetic with the collapse of the Berlin Wall in 1989. That wall was a symbol of stupidity, closed-mindedness, state enslavement and suffocation. It led to mass poverty. It took years of immense suffering in communistic societies for people to realise the truth of Pius's words in 1931.

The wisdom of Pope Pius XII

Between the years 1950 and 1956 Pope Pius XII made a significant contribution to the development of Catholic social doctrine with respect to business, banking and the entrepreneur.[7] His teachings on these matters come to us not in encyclical form, but rather in the form of radio addresses and talks to specialised groups of people.

What distinguishes Pius's addresses from the writings of both Popes Leo XIII and Pius XI is their *concreteness*.[8] He moves beyond principles and speaks very specifically about particular types of business and entrepreneurial activity. To my knowledge, he is the first Roman pontiff to use the word 'entrepreneur'. This is important since many commentators have suggested that it was Pope John Paul II in his encyclical letter *Centesimus annus* (1991) who shifted the Church's thinking to a

---

6   *Laborem exercens, Sollicitudo rei socialis* and *Centesimus annus*.

7   For a full treatment of Pius's teaching and the relevant references, see Percy (2004).

8   Like his predecessors – Leo XIII and Pius XI – Pius forcefully articulates the principles of private property and private initiative. He also introduces the principle of the *universal destination of material goods*. The material riches of the world are an endowment made by the Creator to every human being – and not just those who happen to lay their hands on them first. Nevertheless the principle of private property is not in conflict with that of the universal destination of goods: the latter principle does not mean that all people have a right to all goods.

more favourable assessment of the workings of business and the market economy. Some even see it as a radical shift in papal social thought.

In the brief material that I present below, and indeed from what I have said about the encyclical letters *Rerum novarum* and *Quadragesimo anno*, one can see that this latter claim is a touch wide of the mark. It is true that an encyclical letter carries more weight than a papal audience or papal address. For that reason, people tend to take more notice of an encyclical. Still, both an encyclical letter and a papal address form part of the ordinary teaching Magisterium of the Popes and of the Church and because of this both should be duly acknowledged. As we shall see, Pope John Paul II did indeed affirm a society of *free work, enterprise and participation* in his encyclical letter of 1991. Entrepreneurs and those working for free societies must have jumped for joy on reading the Pope's thoughts.

But we should not overlook the wisdom of Pius XII some 40 years prior. His addresses on the dignity of business and entrepreneurial activity are like the treasure hidden in the field that Jesus spoke about in chapter fourteen of Matthew's gospel. Upon reading these addresses, no budding entrepreneur would want to do anything other than sell what he had and enter the world of money and thus serve the needs of others.

Let me cite two of Pius's addresses.[9] A section of his address to an International Congress on Credit Questions on 24 October 1951 is worth quoting at length. His address has a similar flavour to that of St Thomas Aquinas in his treatment of the virtue of magnificence. The message is forceful: money should not be hoarded but is there to be used for the greater good of society; risks should be taken, fear set aside. I have highlighted some key points in italics:

> How much capital is lost through waste and luxury, through selfish and dull enjoyment, or *accumulates and lies dormant without being turned to profit*! There will always be egoists and self-seekers; there will always be misers and those who are *short-sightedly timid*. Their number could be considerably reduced if one could interest those

---

9   See note 6 above for a fuller treatment of Pius's teaching and the references it contains.

who have money in *using their funds wisely and profitably, be they great or small*. It is largely due to this *lack of interest that money lies dormant*. You can remedy this to a great extent by making ordinary depositors collaborators, either as bond or share-holders, *in undertakings whose launching and thriving would be of great benefit to the community*, such as industrial activities, agricultural production, public works, or the construction of houses for workers, educational or cultural institutions, welfare or social service. (Pius XII, 1951: 121)

And then, in what must surely be regarded as an extraordinary address with respect to its affirmation of the entrepreneur, Pius XII in his address of 20 January 1956 to the First National Congress of Small Industry had these things to say. Again, emphasis added is mine:

Among the motives that justified the holding of your convention, you have given the first place to '*a vindication of the indispensable functions of the private entrepreneur*.' The latter exhibits in an eminent degree the *spirit of free enterprise* to which we owe the *remarkable progress* that has been made especially during the past fifty years, and notably in the *field of industry*. (Pius XII, 1956: 50)

The Church is a 'joy and hope'

Pius XII died in 1958 and was replaced by Pope John XXIII. Between the years 1962 and 1965 the Second Vatican Council took place in Rome. It was a Church council with many of the world's bishops in attendance. Unlike previous Church councils, however, the Second Vatican Council faced no specific doctrinal or disciplinary issues. Rather, John XXIII called the Council to deepen the Church's understanding of Herself and of Her age-old truths. He was concerned that the 'treasure' or deposit of faith was not reaching the hearts of Her people. In a rapidly changing world, moreover, he was deeply concerned as to how the Church could best communicate these truths and so reach the 'inner sanctum' of the faithful.

In this sense it is probably more accurate to say that the Council was a 'spiritual' rather than a 'pastoral' council. It issued sixteen documents on various ecclesial matters. Two documents took centre stage. One of the them was entitled *Lumen gentium* – the Church is a 'light to the nations'. The other received the Latin title *Gaudium et spes* – the Church is a 'joy and hope to the world'.

While *Lumen gentium* dealt with the very nature of the Church Herself, *Gaudium et spes* directed its attention to the relationship between the Church and the modern world. A small section in this document discusses the entrepreneur and his activity. Again, it is an affirmation of private initiative, although the term now employed for this is *spirit of enterprise*. The Council taught:

> [T]herefore we must encourage technical progress and the *spirit of enterprise*, we must foster the eagerness for creativity and improvement, and we must promote adaptation of production methods and all serious efforts of people engaged in production – in other words of all elements which contribute to economic progress. The ultimate and basic purpose of economic production does not consist merely in the increase of goods produced, nor in profit nor prestige; it is directed to the *service of man*, of man, that is, in his totality taking account of his material needs and the requirements of his intellectual, moral, spiritual, and religious life. (GS 64)[10]

This passage is interesting, not only for its employment of the term *spirit of enterprise* but also for its rejection of what I would call 'economism'. Economism is the ideology of making economics or money the standard around which we judge all reality. Having an interest in money is important. So is the study of economic theory. It is important to put fear aside, so that a spirit of enterprise embeds itself deeply in a society and its culture. Also, the rejection of goods and profit as the 'ultimate and basic purpose' of enterprise is not to say that the price

---

10   Citations of Vatican II documents are from Flannery (1992).

mechanism and the profit signal are not fundamental in directing enterprise towards promoting the common good. The authors of the Vatican II documents would not regard it as their role to make a definitive judgement on this. The extent to which the price mechanism and the profit signal are best fitted to direct enterprise in the service of man is a matter for economists and political economists to debate.

But all this should be subordinate to the *service of man*. And man, as the Church likes to remind us, is not just a 'consumer'. Man is also a 'creator' – of sorts. That is, he has a profound spiritual centre. He is gifted with a powerful intellect and the ability to reason things through. He can remember things and so foster the virtue of hope. His spiritual centre – according to the Word of God – is his heart, and so he has an immense capacity to love and forgive. Putting these marvellous attributes together, we come to the conclusion that, like no other creature on earth, man can transcend material things. In fact, he can transcend himself and thus reach out to touch the divine.

Man, then, cannot be analysed solely from an economic perspective, important as that may be. The laws of demand and supply are important. So, too, is the relationship between risk and return. But these realities do not capture the total reality of what it is to be human. Man is part of the material world and subject to laws of the human sciences, but not a slave to them. He in fact transcends them because he is made in the image and likeness of God and called to a destiny beyond this earthly life. The divine law imparts its authority, too. This is what the Church means by putting technological, productive, economic and financial advances at the service of man.

The Pope from Galilee – John Paul II

In the year 1978 the Catholic Church experienced the end of the pontificate of Pope Paul VI, the rise and fall of the pontificate of Pope John Paul I (he lasted just thirty-three days) and the election of the first non-Italian Pope for over four hundred years. The new Pope was the first

Polish Pope elected in the history of the Church and he would reign on the throne of Peter for almost twenty-seven years. The sorrow of losing Paul VI and John Paul I gave way to the joy of expectation. The new Pope was just 58 years of age. He was vigorous and healthy in appearance and exuded the confidence of a rock star. His charisma was simply extraordinary. Through his pastoral visits and writings he reminded the Church and the world that the Magisterium of the Church is not primarily juridical, but *prophetic*. This is particularly true of his social teaching and with regard to the entrepreneur.

He issued three social encyclicals. This brings to eight the number of social encyclicals since 1891. The first of John Paul's social encyclicals was issued in 1981 and was called *Laborem exercens* – 'On human labour'. It was the first encyclical devoted exclusively to the nature and meaning of *human work*. The second social encyclical was published in 1987 and was called *Sollicitudo rei socialis* – 'On social concerns'. The third of the Pope's social encyclicals is *Centesimus annus*, meaning 'The hundredth year'. This encyclical letter, published in 1991, was timed for the 100th anniversary of *Rerum novarum*.

Laborem exercens is significant for three things. First, the Pope establishes that work has an objective character. He means by this two things. On the one hand, in our work we take something, act upon it and produce something new or significantly altered from its original state. We are responsible for the new 'status' or 'nature' of the transformed matter. This is important for us as human beings. We naturally like to make a difference and you cannot do so if you do not work. Hence unemployment is not only a scourge for its obvious material deprivation, but also for the loss of dignity that people feel when their natural gifts are not put to good use.

Work has another objective meaning flowing from the biblical text. In the Book of Genesis, Adam is commanded to work. John Paul II sees human work as a 'mirror' of God's work. When human beings work they are reminding others of God's creating work. In a frenetic society, this second aspect of objective work is well worth reflecting upon. God wants to speak to us as we work and particularly as we observe others work. Work is not just an objective transformation of things, but it is an action that is in accord with God's creative action. For this reason, work is like a sacrament. People should be led to God when they see and experience others working. We don't often think like this, but John Paul II encourages us to do so.

Next, John Paul II articulated in *Laborem exercens* the subjective meaning of work. That is, when we work we are not just transforming matter, but we are – most importantly – transforming ourselves. We are called to perfection – to bring our humanity to its fulfilment – and work plays a large role in achieving this.

Man has to subdue the earth and dominate it, because as the 'image of God' he is a person, that is to say a subjective being capable of acting in a planned and rational way, capable of deciding about himself, and with a tendency to self-realisation. As a person, man is therefore the subject of work. As a person he works. He performs various actions belonging to the work process. Independently of their objective content, these actions must all serve to realise his humanity, to fulfil the calling to be a person that is his by reason of his very humanity (LE 6).

It is this subjective meaning of work which allows John Paul to develop what he calls the *personalist argument*. It argues for the priority of labour over capital. *Capita* originally referred to the heads of cattle, but had come to mean the natural resources of the earth and the means of production that would transform them. This argument was, we recall, part of the battle that Leo XIII had entered into some 80 years before. John Paul II puts a name to this deeply rooted gospel principle. Human beings – whether they be managers or workers (to use traditional terms that are not entirely necessary these days) – are far more important than capital.

This subjective meaning of work is, of course, intimately related to the objective meaning of work. All work begins in the human person, proceeds to transform matter in one form or another, and then produces a finished product or service with a view to aiding human persons.

So work *begins* with us and it is *for* us. In addition, the *way* we do our work will influence whether we do really perfect ourselves – whether we honour the subjective meaning of work. Put bluntly, sloppy, slapdash work won't perfect us and neither will it get the job done! We will fail in our divine calling to perfect ourselves and we will fail in producing something for the good of humanity. The objective and subjective meanings of work, therefore, are intimately tied to each other.

The third significant contribution of the encyclical lies in the fact that it tries to articulate a spirituality of work. The Benedictines had done so years before – emphasising work, worship and reading as part of one's daily routine. So, too, had the founder of Opus Dei in the twentieth century. St Josemaria Escriva, a Spanish priest, taught that work has a triple dimension: we are called to sanctify our work, sanctify ourselves and thereby sanctify others in and through our work.

It was not uncommon, therefore, for various groups and persons in the life and history of the Church to attempt to develop a spirituality of work and thus highlight its meaning. But the waters were uncharted for Popes. John Paul II, in *Laborem exercens*, decided to broach the topic and in doing so elevated the lay vocation. Vatican II had taught that all the baptised are called to be saints, and John Paul II was suggesting that work forms an intricate part of the call to sanctity.

Unfortunately, however, much of what he had to say about a spirituality of work was lost in the English translation of the official Latin text. For in the Latin text the Pope contrasted work as *opus* with work as *labour*. As human beings we experience work as something necessary and fatiguing. God's work, however, is neither necessary nor tiring. Rather, his work is an *opus* – it is free, without any form of compulsion or exhaustion. It is a consequence of his inner life with the Son and the Spirit and it is a result of his love for humanity.

Human beings are called not only to offer their necessary and exhausting tasks to the Creator and Father of all. In this they can imitate Christ's work of redemption on the cross. Work has a redemptive meaning and Christians are called to discover it and teach it. But also, with the aid of divine grace, they are called to acknowledge and experience their work as an *opus*. We are called to see our work as a participation in God's totally free and gratuitous love. In this we imitate our God and so make him present throughout the world. We participate in God's creative work and thus begin to understand that work is and can be an expression of love.

Centesimus annus was the third of John Paul's social encyclicals. It contains six chapters. The first recalls Leo's famous encyclical. The second and third deal with the current changes in society, especially the collapse of communism in 1989, while chapter four revisits the Church's position on private property and material goods. It is this chapter which raises the profile of entrepreneurial work. Chapter five presents an excellent summary of the relationship between the state and the Church and chapter six returns to a favourite theme of the pontificate and is headed 'Man is the Way of the Church'.

Besides chapter four, the following passage from chapter two, entitled 'Toward the "new things" of today', is of the utmost importance. It is critical, not just for a correct understanding of why the Church sees merit in entrepreneurial work, but also for insight into how Pope John Paul II has deepened the Church's social doctrine. From the passage it becomes clear why socialism must be rejected. Not only does it devalue the principle of private property, but it also denies the freedom of the human person. That is, the reason socialists scorn private property is because of their inadequate and reductionist understanding of the human person. Upon reading this most enlightening papal text, we recognise the Pope's own personalist philosophy; his experience of living under a socialistic and atheistic regime; and the wisdom of 100 years of Catholic Social Teaching.

> [T]he fundamental error of socialism is *anthropological in nature.*
> Socialism considers the individual person simply as an element,
> a molecule within the *social organism*, so that the good of the
> individual is completely subordinated to the functioning of the
> socio-economic mechanism. Socialism likewise maintains that the

good of the individual can be realized without reference to his *free choice*, to the unique and exclusive responsibility which he exercises in the face of good or evil. *Man is thus reduced* to a series of social relationships, and the concept of the person as the *autonomous subject of moral decision disappears*, the very subject whose decisions build the social order. From this *mistaken conception of the person* there arise both a distortion of law, which defines the sphere of the exercise of freedom, and an opposition to private property. A person who is deprived of something he can call 'his own,' and of the possibility of earning a living through his own initiative, comes to depend on the social machine and on those who control it. This makes it much *more difficult for him to recognize his dignity as a person*, and hinders progress towards the building up of an authentic human community. (CA 13)

Importantly, and this cannot be overstated, the essential error of socialism is a *defective* and *deceptive anthropology*. The error of socialism lies not only in its *overplay* of the state, but also in its *underplay* of the human person. This insight we owe to John Paul II and it is well worth treasuring and remembering as we begin the 21st century.

With this passage in mind, it becomes clear that John Paul II will affirm the entrepreneur and – to some degree – free markets and free societies, not just because they produce more wealth and thus alleviate material poverty. Rather, he affirms them because they come closer to recognising the profound truth of the human person made in the image and likeness of God. In this sense, it becomes clear to any serious student of the Pope's writings that John Paul is entirely consistent in his thought and philosophy. For, more than any other Pope in history, he wants to recognise, proclaim and defend the dignity of the human person made in the image and likeness of God. This he has done in each of his fourteen encyclicals, but it is especially true in *Redemptor hominis*, *Veritatis splendor* and *Evangelium vitae*. He has done this also in *Centesimus annus*, as the above citation demonstrates admirably.

Let us now move to the fourth chapter of the encyclical and in doing so complete our argument. Unfortunately, many of the papal insights into the relationship between the factors of production cannot be commented upon here. We restrict ourselves to the following passage. Entrepreneurs will not be left in two minds. The Church deeply appreciates their work and efforts.

> A person who *produces something* other than for his own use generally does so in order that others may use it after they have paid a just price, mutually agreed upon through free bargaining. It is precisely the *ability to foresee* both the needs of others and the *combinations of productive factors* most adapted to satisfying those needs that constitutes another important *source of wealth* in modern society. Besides, many goods cannot be adequately produced through the work of an isolated individual; they require the cooperation of many people in working towards a common goal. *Organizing* such a productive effort, *planning* its duration in time, making sure that it corresponds in a positive way to the demands which it must satisfy, and taking the necessary *risks* – all this too is a source of wealth in today's society. In this way, the role of disciplined and *creative human work* and, as an essential part of that work, initiative and *entrepreneurial* ability becomes increasingly evident and decisive. (CA 32)

Conclusion

Catholic social thought has been in existence since the time of Christ. Indeed, since revelation began. But it is in the last 100 years or so, beginning with Pope Leo XIII, that the Church's social teaching has undergone a marvellous and breathtaking development. Both changes in society and insights from the Popes have occasioned this development.

Wisdom would dictate that we be somewhat cautious in making an assessment of these recent developments. Thomas Stransky, in his preface to Pierre Blet's revealing work on Pius XII, cites Walter Raleigh and then Chou En-lai:

> Any writer of modern history who treads too closely on the heels of

events may get his or her teeth knocked out. And one ponders the calm reply of Chou En-lai when a European intellectual had asked the premier of China what he thought of the eighteenth-century French Revolution: 'It's too early to tell.' (Blet, 1999: xi)

We do not want to be hasty. None of us likes getting our teeth kicked out. But the weight of evidence in the last 100 years of Catholic social thought strongly suggests that entrepreneurs can take their place in the life of Church and of society without any fear whatsoever. Their task is a noble one – building their own humanity and constructing the common good.

The path travelled in these last few years of the Church's history is, to say the least, impressive. It begins with a robust defence of *private property* and a devastating critique of socialism by Leo XIII. Then Pius XI moves to defend and highlight the importance of *private action* in the social sphere. Pius XII, that much maligned Pope, steps into the social ring as a heavyweight and has no qualms in naming the entrepreneur as crucial to social advancement. Vatican II praises the *spirit of enterprise*, while Pope John Paul II proves the true prophet by alerting us to the spiritual meaning and significance of work in general and entrepreneurial work in particular. We are well placed as we begin this new century.

References

Blet, P. (1999), *Pius XII and the Second World War: According to the Archives of the Vatican*, trans. Lawrence J. Johnson, New York: Paulist Press.

Charles, R. (1998), *Christian Social Witness and Teaching: The Catholic Tradition from Genesis to Centesimus Annus*, Leominster: Gracewing.

Flannery, A., OP (ed.) (1992), *Vatican Council II: The Conciliar and Post Conciliar Documents*, new revised (study) edn, New York: Costello Publishing Company.

Lonergan, B. (1972), *Method in Theology*, New York: Herder and Herder.

Miller, M. J. (ed.) (2001), *The Encyclicals of John Paul II*, Huntington: Our Sunday Visitor Publishing Division.

O'Brien, D. and T. Shannon (eds) (2000), *Catholic Social Thought: The Documentary Heritage*, Maryknoll, NY: Orbis Books.

Percy, A. (2004), 'Private initiative, entrepreneurship, and business in the teaching of Pius XII', *Journal of Markets and Morality*, 7(1): 7–25.

Pius XII (1951), 'Function of bankers', *Catholic Mind*, LII(1094): 121–2.

Pius XII (1956), 'The small business manager', *The Pope Speaks*, 3(1): 49–52.

Schaff, P. and H. Wace (eds) (1999), *Sulpitius Severus, Vincent of Lerins, John Cassian*, 14 vols, vol. 11: *Nicene and Post-Nicene Fathers*, second series, Peabody: Hendrickson Publishers.

Schaff, P. and H. Wace (eds) (1999), *Basil: Letters and Select Works*, 14 vols, vol. 8: *Nicene and Post-Nicene Fathers*, second series, Peabody: Hendrickson Publishers.

Stark, R. (1997), *The Rise of Christianity: How the Obscure, Marginal Jesus Movement Became the Dominant Religious Force in the Western World in a Few Centuries*, San Francisco, CA: HarperCollins.

9 EDUCATION AND THE CATHOLIC CHURCH IN ENGLAND AND WALES

Dennis O'Keeffe

Introduction

The Catholic Church's great intellectual gift to mankind has been the individualism implicit in the doctrine of the unique, immortal soul of each person.

Of all history's institutions the Catholic Church embodies the greatest intellectual and cultural achievement. The Church has been itself a vastly accomplished teaching agency, as befits a body in receipt of Christ's instruction that Catholics should teach all nations. One essential strand in this pedagogic success has been the Catholic tradition of the individual soul. Xavier Martin has argued that traditional Catholic approaches to education are far more individualist than the philosophy of the French Enlightenment, which in the main espoused a view of man as manipulable.[1] He quotes Jacques Maritain on the Thomist educational doctrine that 'in any discipline and in any form of teaching the master merely offers external assistance to the principle of immanent activity which is present in the pupil' (quoted in ibid.: 78). Such 'external assistance' will include a knowledge of subject matter and of the rules and conventions of scholarship superior to those possessed by the pupil. It is this knowledge which creates the teacher's authority. The pupil is the active focus, however, in whom crucial powers of learning and human creativity are located.

Even sceptics have often agreed subsequently that the unique indi-

---

1   Martin surveys all the main voices of the French Enlightenment and finds in them an anthropology according to which the human animal needs direction by experts, employing a programme external to the person being taught. See Martin (2001).

vidualism of the West, without which the Renaissance, the Enlightenment and the extraordinary economic development of recent centuries
would all have been impossible, is a bequest to the world of the Christian
doctrine of the individual human soul (Minogue, 2003).

Presenting Catholic influence on civilisation in this way is in marked
contrast to the better-known modern tendency to dichotomise Catholic
experience, between pre-Vatican II and post-Vatican II notions. The
traditionalists claim that modern Catholic education is an empty set,
leaving the Catholic population disastrously ignorant of their religion.
The modernists claim that traditional Catholic schooling involved little
more than unenlightened rote learning and stifling bigotry. The traditional versus modernist claims are well presented in Gerald Grace's
book on modern Catholic education (Grace, 2005: chs 2, 3). Professor
Grace does not, however, deal with the incomparably more important
question of the role of Catholicism in the protection of civilisation. This
chapter examines the most crucial features of present Catholic teaching
on education alongside the practice of teaching in Catholic schools. How
well do Catholic educational attitudes and practice secure our vital civilisation and heritage?

We cannot pursue at length the question of how far there is a global
Catholic view of education or how far Catholic educational practice
differs between countries. There is no comprehensively binding educational consensus among Catholics in individual countries, let alone
worldwide agreement. The only manageable focus of this essay is
Catholic education in its British context, though it must necessarily pay
some attention to opinions from Rome and elsewhere. It seems entirely
proper to look at the variations in British Catholic opinion on education. We need also to examine how well our Catholic schools in general
seem to transmit the Catholic faith. In practice, education in England
and Wales must serve as an approximate guide for a general British
account. As we shall see, England and Wales have learned useful lessons
from Scottish experience. While the ideal would be to examine Catholic
education at all levels, I will speak mostly about the bedrock primary

and secondary levels. The Catholic Church in this country does not have a very large presence at the tertiary level.

The practical situation in England and Wales appears generally a good one. There is now a very strong and successful Catholic middle class in this country. Many well-known figures are Catholics, and the ancient prejudices seem mostly buried. Catholic schools have enjoyed a large growth in numbers (Burn, 2001: 37). Moreover, from north of the border we have the admirable example set by the late Cardinal Winning, ensuring that the shortcomings of Catholic teaching in Scotland were brought to public attention, and reform set in motion for his Glasgow diocese.

Winning spoke of 'post-conciliar confusion' and pointed to the virtual collapse of doctrinal transmission in the schools in the 1970s – 'a catechetical desert' in the Cardinal's words – making it impossible for many parents to participate subsequently in the Catholic education of their children.[2] This observation – of unplanned incompetence – should be flanked by another one, made to me in May 2006 by the headmaster of a Catholic independent school in southern England, to the effect that many parents, including nominally Catholic ones, are interested only in the *secular* education Catholic schools provide. There have long been non-Catholic pupils at Catholic schools, including maintained ones. It was also clear in the past that many nominally Catholic children did not go to church, yet clearly their parents wanted them at a Catholic school. Today, however, the numbers of non-Catholics and even non-Christians at Catholic schools are higher than ever. As to tokenism by Catholics, how could we ever really know its magnitude? In any event, it seems that it is often the *trace elements* of Catholic education, the famous discipline, intellectual rigour and community ethos, which appeal to Catholic and non-Catholic parents alike. How far the system and its attraction to parents is driven by Catholic spirituality is debatable.

---

2   Eric Hester, 'Religious education in crisis', *Catholic Times*, October 2004.

In the popular view this connects with the stronger moral ethos in the voluntary aided sector. This perception has served to increase the popularity of Catholic schools and to swell the numbers of non-Catholics who attend them. The Holy See has, moreover, long looked with favour on applications of the voluntary principle. The non-private Catholic schools are clear exemplars of mutual compromise and understanding between the Roman Church and the British state.

This secular superiority of Catholic schools does not mean, however, that they are good at teaching the Catholic faith

Their secular superiority does not, however, make Catholic schools effective in religious education. Mr Ken Connelly, formerly Head of English at St Benedict's, Ealing, later Deputy Head at the Oratory School and subsequently employed as a civil servant specialising in the drafting of government bills,[6] has been active on the Education Committee of the Catholic Union. He has a distinctly low opinion both of the general secular legislative apparatus that affects *all* schools and of the religious teachings in the ascendant in Catholic ones. He thinks most educational legislation is at best useless and at worst highly destructive.[7] Given the officially available evidence on the millions who have emerged both illiterate and innumerate from the system (Bartholomew, 2004), we are surely entitled to wonder just how all this legislation can be represented as aiding the learning activities of our schools.

It is the weakness and distortion of *Catholic* teaching which most worry Connelly, however. This is seen, for example, in many of the English and Welsh Bishops' public statements, which seem to interpret the promotion of the 'common good' in socialist terms, despite papal teaching that emphasises the importance of achieving the common good through institutions such as the market economy, voluntary exchange and the family (see Chapter 10). Indeed, the emphasis on the family is

6   For the Department of the Environment.
7   In a private interview with the author, 14 May 2006.

supremely important. It is the family, not the state, which the Church
sees as the prime agency for promoting basic morality. In his attempt
over many years of retirement to promote a traditional teaching of
Catholic morality and values, in particular with regard to the role of
the sacraments and grace, Connelly's criticisms of current teaching and
its emphasis on secular themes were generally met with great hostility.
It is ironic and regrettable that those who are often described by their
opponents as 'liberals' seem to be most defensive and dogmatic in
maintaining the status quo that has now been established if it comes
under attack. The first Catholic priority is the redemption of the individual soul. Each individual salvation is unique. It is the facilitation of
individual salvation *collectively* which constitutes the common good. It
is this perspective which must underlie the Catholic view of curriculum
and pedagogy. It is far from clear that all or even most Catholic school
practice reflects these perspectives. Hence the anxiety felt by Professor
Grace and Mr Connelly.

The *Compendium of the Catechism of the Catholic Church* published by the Catholic Truth Society

It has been precisely deficiencies and strange priorities reflecting an
overemphasis on secular themes which alarm some Catholics. Despite
these shortcomings, good Catholic teaching material has recently
become available. On the question of good texts for teaching, things are
distinctly looking up. We now have at our disposal *The Compendium of
the Catechism of the Catholic Church* (Catholic Truth Society, 2006). Eric
Hester, a very experienced former headmaster of Catholic high schools,
has described the reissue of this book as 'a gift from God, a treasure, a
precious jewel'.[8] Like the familiar catechism of generations ago, the
Compendium is a model of clarity and simplicity, set out in straightforward question-and-answer form. The book contains the profession of

8   Eric Hester, 'Compendium of the Catechism of the Catholic Church', *Catholic Times*, 23
     April 2006.

faith, with all the main prayers, the celebration of the sacraments, life in Christ, with the elucidation of the Ten Commandments, and Christian prayer. The main prayers are in English and Latin. Then there are the Formulas of Catholic doctrine: the Eight Beatitudes; the Gifts of the Holy Spirit; the Fruits of the Holy Spirit; The Four Last Things; The Corporal and Spiritual Works of Mercy.

Hester insists that the *Compendium* should be used in *all primary and secondary classes* (my italics) in our Catholic schools. This would much relieve those of us who worry about the teaching of the faith. After all, there could scarcely be a clearer exposition of the Church's teaching. We need more traditional Catholic teaching on faith and morals and less by way of self-indulgent posturing. It is perfectly proper for children to understand the evils of prejudice between races and sexes. It is also imperative, however, that pupils should learn that opposition to such evils is fundamentally subsumed in the Ten Commandments.

Moreover, the wider community of scholars and administrators has recently severely reined in the former enthusiasm for 'multiculturalism', viewing some of its variants as threatening national solidarity and good community relations. We have to note that the support for multiculturalism was recently very strong in some Catholic circles. The Catholic Bishops of England and Wales once argued that 'All Catholic schools, regardless of their location, will need to give full attention to matters concerning multiculturalism and racism' (Catholic Bishops' Conference of England and Wales, 1997).

It looks as if history will pronounce multiculturalism a dangerous fashion. Is it improper to suggest that Catholic bishops should exercise a little more caution in the face of easy enthusiasms? In matters of secular education the turnaround of the present Labour government is astounding, given that the education system is Labour's central constituency. Streaming, whole-class teaching, single-sex education, rote learning, grammar, tables: all the practices in varying degree scorned for four decades are now resurfacing. Might not the preoccupation with racism follow multiculturalism into the latter's threatened oblivion?

Does racism need any further indictment than that implied by all humanity being made in God's image? Should not sexual prejudice fall at the first Christian fence too? We also need some hard-headed thinking on the political economy of education, a point to be driven home later.

Difficulties: Catholic, educational, sociological and economic

Our markers for discussion are thus the contrasting facts of the publication of the Compendium and the running down of our spiritual resources

The central need is a resumption of catechesis. The *Compendium* is available and the spiritual resources are depleted. These opposite facts are our initial markers. How well do our primary and secondary schools explain, justify and propagate the Catholic religion? I note with regret that I have not come across any specifically Catholic modern teachings such as might, if they were followed, play some part in attending to the notorious deficits in modern educational practices, those affecting all the advanced Western societies, these having long had predominantly market economies, combined oddly and *discontinuously* with mainly state-financed school systems. The level of illiteracy and innumeracy in the British case as elsewhere is of alarming proportions. Conservative scholars have long complained about this. These days it is the everyday stuff of official pronouncements. Two-thirds of the children taking public examinations in England and Wales in the General Certificate of Secondary Education (GCSE) do not pass in English or mathematics.[9]

Other deficits include lack of historical knowledge and widespread moral and intellectual relativism. These also connect with the bad behaviour now so widespread. Moreover, there is a neglected economic aspect to the problem. These deficits are indices of economic inefficiency. They suggest that resources involved in educational and intellectual transmission are seriously misused (O'Keeffe, 1999). Indeed almost no one would

9   'GCSE tables expose the truth about maths and English', *Daily Telegraph*, 11 January 2007, p. 1. Most of the candidates are sixteen years old.

presume to argue that school standards have risen over the last half-century. The one undenied truth is the vast increase in resource input. The implication is a drastically falling trend in productivity (see O'Keeffe and Marsland, 2003: 1–28; O'Keeffe, 1999). The question is not whether but *why* these things are so. I have located no Catholic opinion on this vital issue.

Some Catholic educationists want a socialist education system rather than a socialist society proper

Activists in Catholic education tend to fall into the same division between conservative and socialist which occurs in other fields of concern. The reflex conservatism I remember from childhood reflected the Church's very active, indeed *unbending*, hostility to Marxism and communism, a hostility long since abandoned by many Catholics. Thus the error obtains of treating the Marxist challenge as possessing intellectual authority. Indubitably learned writings make references to Marx (Harvey et al., 2005: 28) and Hobsbawm (ibid.: 47). The Catholic writings on education I have been reading mostly fall in with the correct general Western academic convention that Nazism and fascism are beyond the intellectual pale, such that pronouncements by their ideologues are simply absent from discourse, though James Hanvey's fine book does mention Martin Heidegger (ibid.: 88). There is *perhaps* a case for allowing any Catholic writer to refer to *any scholar of any persuasion*, provided the intention is to strengthen the Catholic viewpoint.

If we conclude, however, that the anathema on writers of Nazi persuasion is too strong to overturn, then at least we could extend the same treatment to Marxism and communism. In terms of the almost countless millions slaughtered by communism and its rabid hostility to our Christian faith, the argument here seems unanswerable. My case would be helped along if one could find among Catholic radicals any recognition of the common anti-totalitarian view that Nazism and its half-brother fascism are fundamentally *Marxist heresies* (Pipes, 1994:

ch. 5). Pipes is not a Catholic, though he is Polish by birth. In Catholic Poland the identification to which he inclines is widely made. If we were intellectually consistent we would maintain a general rule that no writer having totalitarian persuasions should feature in the literature of Catholicism, except by way of hostile analysis. In fact, however, much of the non-totalitarian radicalism one encounters in that literature is deeply suspect too.

The rejection of Marxism should follow from the empirical facts of communist experience, but even more crucially from the ferocious intolerance of the theory itself (see Kolakowski, 1988). This stance is precisely what many Catholic activists have *not* adopted. Since the 1960s such activists have not been outright communists: anti-anti-communist would be a better label. Indeed, the overall Catholic voice on politics is not even socialist in any society-wide sense. What many Catholic intellectuals want is *a socialist education system*. They want public finance and egalitarian ideology, the socialisation of mind as a surrogate for socialised property. This is not Marxist politics any more; rather it is a residual version, what the French call *Marxisant* politics.

The atmosphere of discussion among progressive Catholics is familiar: it is simply secular radicalism

The atmosphere of discussion in most Catholic educational circles is immediately recognisable to me, however, no matter how we label the ideology. There is much talk of 'gender'. Whatever arguments were employed when this term was plucked from its grammatical context, it is now merely an unjustified replacement for 'sex'. Grace does not use it extensively in his much-regarded text, though it appears in a subhead as an unproblematic category in bold type, Gender, Leadership and Catholicism (Grace, 2005: 229). Of the extensive use of the term in radical Marxist feminism as far back as the 1970s, and its hold today on virtually all feminist literature, however, there is no doubt. The modern use of the term perhaps comes from the seminal essay by Gayle Ruben,

'The traffic in women: notes on the political economy of sex', in which she coins the phrase 'sex/gender system' (Ruben, 1975). The use of the word 'gender' rather than 'sex' was strongly criticised by Cardinal Ratzinger in his booklet, because it attempted to diminish the importance of the created differences between the sexes (see Ratzinger, 2004).

The corrupting influence of 'rightsology' is widely apparent

The penetration of Church thinking on education by secular themes of a soft radical kind now reaches back nearly half a century. Thus the *Declaration on Christian Education* (*Gravissimum educationis*) proclaimed by Pope Paul VI on 28 October 1965 bears witness to the influence of secular speculation on human rights, a speculation since grown to gigantic proportions, harking back to the adoption by the General Assembly of the United Nations, on 10 December 1948, of the *Declaration of the Rights of Man*. Pope Paul VI noted in *Gravissimum educationis* that the rights of men to an education, particularly the primary rights of children and parents, are being proclaimed and recognised in public documents. On page two we learn that 'men of every race, condition and age ... have an inalienable right to an education'.

This proposition is grossly false. Perhaps MacIntyre's view that 'rights' are one with unicorns and fairies is too severe (MacIntyre, 1999). Perhaps our being human does entail limited rights. More important are the *duties* laid upon us by the Catholic faith as commands, vis-à-vis our treatment of others. We have inalienable duties as to other people. Inalienable rights are merely the shadows of these. So-called rights to education are non-existent. They presuppose individuals whose duties include the requirement that they educate others. This can be true only of parents. It cannot be true for others except by way of contract. So-called rights are mostly contractual and conventional, not inalienable.

Gravissimum educationis compounds this problem by saying that Catholics have an inalienable right to a Catholic education. Again this is only true in the sense that Catholic parents have a duty to educate their

Our depleted spiritual resources

Gerald Grace believes that the spiritual resources of the Catholic Church in this country have been greatly depleted.[3] I would agree with his analysis. The implication would seem to be that the spirituality of our Catholic schools has at the very least been attenuated. Grace has very usefully assembled much invaluable factual and analytical material on modern British Catholic education. What he calls depletion I would call 'decline'. There are still, nevertheless, powerful reserves available. The printed and intellectual materials we need for successful Catholic aspirations are not lacking. Unfortunately, we have often used inadequate material, such as *Weaving the Web*.[4] Nor does the primary text *Here I Am* inspire much enthusiasm. Few traditional Catholics speak highly of that other Catholic text, *Icons*, whose use spans primary and secondary schools. Book 1 defines twelve Hindu terms for the edification of young children. Book 3, which is the approved text for pupils aged eleven to fourteen, gives a careful explanation of the five pillars of Islam. It is hard to see much justification for this in *basic* Catholic texts, given the obvious time constraints and ongoing anxiety about how much our children know of their own faith. Such excursions may be well intended, but seem likely to cause further depletion.

Yet in secular terms praise of the Catholic schools is still due. Research findings supplied by official reporting reinforce the popular view. Catholic schools, like other Voluntary Aided Schools, are superior in academic terms to the Non-denominational Maintained Schools on the secular front; Catholic schools maintain a varying but distinct margin of advantage. Morris puts it thus: 'The superiority of Catholic schools, in respect of measures adopted by OFSTED [Office for Standards in Education] is very noticeable.'[5]

---

3   Grace (2005). Professor Grace's concerns are articulated through the notion of 'spiritual capital', a borrowing from the 'cultural capital' of Pierre Bourdieu, of which more later.

4   Ibid. One Catholic head I spoke to, however, claimed that *Weaving the Web*, while a limited resource, is satisfactory if it is backed up by more profound and central notions.

5   A. B. Morris, 'Catholic and other secondary schools: an analysis of OFSTED inspection reports, 1993–1995', *Educational Research*, 40(2): 181–90; quoted in Grace (2005: 106).

children in the Catholic faith where they can. Where parents are unable to educate their own children, it is difficult to see upon whom such a duty can fall. Certainly it is not clear that it should fall on the taxpayer. The truth is that people have a duty to permit religious freedoms to others, save where these others restrict the freedoms of other persons to perform their duties. We can pursue the goal of Catholic education for our children only because of our mutual reciprocal duties with regard to people of other persuasions. Thus parents do have a right to be allowed to educate their children in the faith. This is different from a right to children to a Catholic education. More generally, these aspects of the Vatican II Decree on Education are not very tightly argued, betraying a capitulation to lay fancies.[10]

What the Church does not talk about: Catholicism and tough social science

If Rome has positions on compulsory attendance, standards, private or state finance, vouchers, intellectual competition between students and between institutions, none seems to be on the agenda here at diocesan level. We know that Vatican statements on education have specifically stated that parents who use private education should get the same support from the state as those parents who use state schools – indeed, this is stated in the recent *Compendium on the Social Doctrine of the Church* (see also Chapter 5). This might, for example, imply a voucher system of support for education but it does not seem to figure in our diocesan debates. Indeed, there is in Catholic quarters a general failure to address crucial questions of economic and intellectual efficiency.

It is also the case, however, that Catholic writings on education do

---

10   The development of teaching on rights was most explicitly articulated in *Pacem in terris* (John Paul XXIII, 1963). There is room for debate about the merit of specific rights articulated in that document but, whilst it is clear that Catholic parents have a duty to provide Catholic education for their children, how can children have a right to a Catholic education financed and provided by the generality of the population that is not Catholic?

not seem to put any emphasis on a clear-sighted *economic* analysis of education more generally. The central structure of Grace's book is borne by his interviews with 60 teachers across three English archdioceses. On Grace's own admission, most of the heads of schools interrogated about the importance or otherwise to them of market-style competition denied any trust in such competition, though one bold spirit went so far as to say that the hierarchy was hypocritical in its opposition to severe competition and attempts to maintain superiority by certain schools by way of competitive ethos. He also said outright that it is the children who benefit most from competition and that schools 'do not look after each other', that is do not maintain mutual solidarity, proclamations to the contrary constituting a sham (Grace, 2005: 191).

If education is often malfunctional – doing proper things inade-quately – or even dysfunctional – doing improper things – the economic context is important. Failure to teach reading exemplifies the malfunc-tional, while worrying children about what race or which sex they belong to exemplifies dysfunctionality. We have been trying to manage educa-tion without property rights. In the absence of mechanisms of complaint, exit and correction, these faults are precisely the outcomes we encounter, often for decades on end, once the elite abandon competition. Education systems manifestly function less efficiently than they would if property rights did indeed obtain in schools and colleges and if competition existed within the system (O'Keeffe, 2003). Some Catholics, however, seem to have the problem precisely the wrong way round.

Markets versus centralised state control of resources

Where education is involved, some Catholic authors say there is a tension between the efficient operations facilitated in theory by market transactions – and most economists worldwide would now say in reality – and the 'common good'. This latter concept is much in favour with the Catholic Bishops' Conference of England and Wales. Indeed, they have produced a critique of 'market education' called *The Common Good in Education* (Catholic Education Service, 1997). There is nothing amiss with a belief in and promotion of the concept of the common good, of course. What is wrong, however, is to deny that the common good can be achieved through the mechanisms and institutions of competition and the marketplace – in education as elsewhere. The common good and family autonomy, leading to choice in education, should be in harmony, not in conflict. Grace too speaks of an 'attempted colonisation' of education by market ideologies in the 1980s and 1990s (Grace, 2005: 180). Those many writers hostile to market forces in education are, however, vulnerable on many counts. We now know beyond doubt that central power is a wholly inefficient means of organising scarce resources, above all because there is no way of knowing what the public wants. As Hayek has shown, no one knows, nor could know, this information (Hayek, 1948). Discussion of this problem is simply missing in this Catholic literature.

Why, we may ask, should education be held to escape the proven results, some might call them 'iron laws', of socialism? Private enterprise works far better than the socialist planning of communism. Why should not free enterprise work better in education for the same reason than do our socialist arrangements? The centralisation of power, the abolition of markets, the absence of property rights, the reduction of money exchanges and varying degrees of suppression of the division of labour did not lead to human emancipation but to murder and wickedness and vast waste. If these are the results of society-wide socialism, on what grounds is socialism to be applauded and furthered in relation to the transmission of knowledge and culture in free societies? If socialism must be pursued in education, why not also in the wider society? If not in the wider society, why should it be pursued in education?

The mantra runs that something about education necessitates public finance. But what? It cannot be the necessity of education, since economic science knows no distinction between necessary and luxury goods. Anything said about education as a special case can equally be said about food or holidays. Some argue that education is a public good, and therefore subject to externalities that require public finance. I cannot retain for myself all the benefits of being educated, therefore the state must pay some contribution to the cost of my children's education.

In fact education is a thoroughly private good. It is not even certain that the overall outcomes of mass-financed education are not dysfunctional. Such eminent scholars as Milton Friedman and E. G. West thought so and provided a substantial body of historical evidence and economic analysis to back up their case. It may be the case that zero action by the state, with neither public funding for education nor compulsory attendance for children, would secure better outcomes.[11]

There is another, in some ways even more important, mistake made by progressive educationists. They seem to assume that socialised education must be hostile to competition. This is not so. Indeed, the key difference between free enterprise and socialism is that the former is always competitive, while the latter is so only under special circumstances.

There was little talk of markets in the 1940s and 1950s when I received respectively my elementary and secondary-school education. In my elementary school, by the age of eleven every child could read. That is rather rare in primary schools today in my very extensive experience.[12] The fierce and non-stop competition, backed up by ferocious discipline on the part of the nuns who dominated the school, forced standards upwards. At my private Catholic secondary school, competition was equally fierce, though the discipline was much milder. Perhaps there are comprehensives today which match its standards, but these are few and far between, and rare in London.[13]

It is also a commonplace that competition in education was far fiercer under the communist regimes than it is in the education systems of most

---

11   Much of this can be found at the website of the E. G. West centre: www.ncl.ac.uk/egwest/.

12   See the evidence of children unable to pass the basic English examination for sixteen-year-olds, in note 10 above. This presupposes low English standards in primary schools.

13   I had 27 years' experience as a teacher of education in London.

market economies. The reasons need not concern us. While it is hard to imagine any kind of private production which is not competitive, in the case of publicly financed education the intentions of the elite are all-important. Competition, often savage competition, is not inconsistent with socialised schooling, whether we mean by this publicly funded compulsory education in predominantly market economies, or straight-forwardly socialist education as in generally socialist societies. The elites decide. It is not that communist education systems were not corrupt. But the freewheeling pseudo-bourgeoisie of state schooling in the free societies, who experiment using *other people's money* and are never or rarely held to account for their offences (O'Keeffe, 1990), were absent in communist societies proper. The communist elite simply forbade such freewheeling. Under the *patina* of Marxism on the communist curriculum there was an old-fashioned set of European ideas. Add this reality to a continued reliance on didactic teaching and the secret of communist education stands revealed. It is not that communist education systems were good overall. But for a complex set of reasons they functioned better than our kind of socialist educational arrangements do.

Gerald Grace believes that the spiritual resources of the Catholic Church in this country have been greatly depleted. I have agreed completely. Grace speaks of a declining 'spiritual capital' on the lines of Bourdieu's famous 'cultural capital' (Grace, 2005: 65). Here we part company somewhat theoretically. The original explicit suggestion from Bourdieu was that the 'cultural capital' of those who possess it works alongside 'economic capital', in the differential social positioning of the population. I object not to the proposition that culture or spirituality can be capitalised, but to the category error in Bourdieu's contrast.

Category errors, wrong theorising and the loss of the sacramental

The trope itself in cultural or spiritual 'capital' is in error. All capital is economic by definition, in the sense of deliberated and costly decisions having been made in pursuit of economic advantage. Bourdieu and

Grace may be referring to uncalculated stocks, formed spontaneously in the ordinary lives of children in educated families, conferring undoubted economic advantage, but involving no capital calculus. Alternatively, they may be referring to pondered capital formations, with regard to education. The very use of the word 'capital' presupposes this latter case. Thus 'cultural' and 'spiritual' capital are *sub-categories* of the general category 'capital'. In the functional (*sic*) sense this matters not a jot, of course, and Grace is quite correct that the Church has run down its intellectual and spiritual reserves. Nevertheless, it is worth pointing out the mistaken terms in which some functionally correct arguments are sometimes put.

Such category errors seem trivial when we compare them with the dysfunctional fare of contemporary sociology, and even this latter fault fades into insignificance alongside my central anxiety, namely that Catholic education has today lost most of its sacramental character and that those who should support its reassertion prefer a soft radical alternative secular agenda. In my view, these disasters cannot be corrected within the present structure. Let us conclude with a brief examination of why this is so.

The socio-economy of public finance

Since the time of Schumpeter few economists have dabbled much in the borderlands of economics and sociology. This absence has largely vitiated the contemporary sociology of knowledge, especially the Marxian version till recently so common in the study of education (O'Keeffe, 1999; O'Keeffe and Marsland, 2003). The key variable requiring investigation is public finance. In a free society the public finance of the transmission of knowledge and culture has a number of most undesirable results, once public and elite opinion become separated, as in this country happened in the 1960s.

First, public finance affects educational decision-making. It hugely enhances the power of the educational elite, especially in a free society with a tradition of reverence for experts. Using resources that are not its own, this elite becomes a kind of irresponsible pseudo-bourgeoisie, which privatises education decisions according to its own priorities and predilections, socialising the costs when policies fail. The rise of soft social science at all educational levels is a function of the activities of this elite, as is the disastrous 'progressive' education and a teaching of mathematics as woeful as the way we have been teaching reading.

On the crucial demand side consumption motives are magnified at the expense of investment. This is exemplified in the choice of soft rather than hard subject matter, with students choosing sociology rather than physics or modern languages. From the supply side inferior teaching and curriculum cause waste, often by under-equipping the children or by baffling parents and children alike, by rendering the activities of the classroom opaque to non-initiates of the progressive scene, a point Bernstein noticed 30 years ago, though he did not object to the mystification (Bernstein, 1975). It is hard to see how the system can be rectified without an infusion of property rights, unless the elite are converted wholesale.

In all these cases the absence of property rights and of the institution of bankruptcy effectively prevent exit. These defects are, like the other shortcomings of our educational arrangements, largely a result of the operations of public finance. No policy that does not include a very substantial element of privatisation has any hope at all of improving things. Markets can breed improprieties. These are dwarfed by those of socialism. Nor should we forget that an aim of many forms of socialism has been the eradication of all kinds of religion, perhaps especially in the case of the Church of Rome. This is becoming increasingly clear as the political and educational establishments become more radically secular in the UK.

There is an attenuation of Catholic tradition in Catholic schools, illustrated at its most frightening by the absurd claim that Catholic schools are themselves somehow the new Church (quoted in Grace, 2005). This contention is utterly heretical. The schools are the instrument of the Church. Not least an issue is that people are forced to go to schools but they are not forced to go to church. Having an institution that people are forced to attend as the main focus for worship and witness is completely contrary to free will.

Markets, Catholicism and mercy

Most important of all though is the perverse misunderstanding of markets on the part of Catholics and in particular their failure to grasp that economic efficiency is imperative to those who view the predicament of their fellow human beings in a spirit of mercy. There is above all a grave loss of spontaneity in socialised education. As Bastiat puts it: 'Let men work, trade, learn, form partnerships, act and react upon one another, since according to the decrees of Providence, naught save order, harmony, and progress can spring from their intelligent spontaneity.'[14]

What Christian charity is there in rejecting so notable a gift of Divine Providence as the spontaneously operating market economy, the only system known to history which can replace poor societies with rich ones?

References

Bartholomew, J. (2004), *Getting out of the Welfare State We're In*, London: Politico's.

Bernstein, B. (1975), 'Class and pedagogies: visible and invisible', *Class, Codes and Control*, vol. II, part II, ch. 6, pp. 116–56.

Burn, J. (2001), 'Church schools: a critique of much current practice', in J. Burn, J. Marks, P. Pilkington and P. Thompson, *Faith in Education*, Civitas, p. 37.

Catholic Bishops' Conference of England and Wales (1997), *Catholic Schools and Other Faiths*.

Catholic Education Service (1997), *The Common Good in Education*.

14   Frédéric Bastiat, *Harmonies*, trans. W. Hayden Boyers, ed. George B. du Huszar, Princeton, NJ, 1964, p. 12.

Catholic Truth Society (2006), *The Compendium of the Catechism of the Catholic Church*.

Grace, G. (2005), *Catholic Schools: Mission, Markets and Morality*, London: Routledge and Falmer.

Harvey, J. et al. (2005), *On the Way to Life: Promoting and Supporting Catholic Education in England and Wales*, Catholic Education Service.

Hayek, F. A. (1948), 'Economics and knowledge', in *Individualism and Economic Order*, London: Routledge.

Kolakowski, L. (1988), *Main Currents of Marxism*, Oxford: Clarendon.

MacIntyre, A. (1999), *After Virtue*, Chicago, IL: Open Court Press.

Martin, X. (2001), *Human Nature and the French Revolution*, trans. P. Corcoran, London: Bergbahn Press.

Minogue, K. (2003), 'Christophobia in the West', *New Criterion*, 21(10).

O'Keeffe, D. (1990), *The Wayward Elite*, Adam Smith Institute.

O'Keeffe, D. (1999), *Political Correctness and Public Finance*, Studies in Education no. 9, London: Institute of Economic Affairs.

O'Keeffe, D. (2003), 'Education and modernity', *Economic Affairs*, 23(2), June 2003, pp. 34–9.

O'Keeffe, D. and D. Marsland (2003), *Independence or Stagnation: The Imperatives of University Reform in the United Kingdom*, London: Civitas.

Pipes, R. (1994), *Russia under the Bolshevik Regime: 1919–1924*, London: Harvill.

Ratzinger, J. (2004), *On the Collaboration of Men and Women in the Church and in the World*, Congregation for the Doctrine of the Faith, London: Catholic Truth Society.

Ruben, G. (1975), 'Notes on the political economy of sex', in R. Reiter (ed.), *Towards an Anthropology of Women*, New York: Monthly Review Press.

Part Three
**SUBSIDIARITY AND SOLIDARITY – THE ROLE
OF THE INDIVIDUAL, THE COMMUNITY AND
THE STATE**

10 SUBSIDIARITY AND SOLIDARITY
Denis O'Brien

Introduction

The concepts of subsidiarity and solidarity arose in the context of concern about the distributive implications, and the working conditions, in nineteenth-century economies, especially in northern Europe. While the full implications will be clear only from a detailed discussion, it will perhaps be helpful to indicate briefly what these terms mean.

By *subsidiarity* is meant the principle that responsibilities should be devolved to the lowest viable level – the individual if possible. This stems directly from the Christian concept that the individual is of over-riding importance because the individual is unique, born with free will, and is of infinite value to God. The principle of subsidiarity is therefore rooted in a Christian understanding of the nature of the human person made in the image of God. By *solidarity* is meant the idea that no man is an island, and that mankind has the need and duty to bind together in common action to achieve aims that cannot be achieved by single individuals. Subsidiarity then requires that the smallest possible level of communality necessary to achieve a particular end should be employed. Action at state level is essentially a last resort. This is essentially because the Church has always favoured voluntary association, springing from individual decisions to act in conjunction with others. Action by the state carries with it a number of dangers, notably that the inescapably coercive character necessarily overrides individual decision-taking – and thus individual moral autonomy.

Leo XIII and Pius XI

Leo XIII was alarmed by nineteenth-century economic developments, with the appearance of a huge urban proletariat, and a small wealthy class (*Rerum novarum*, 2). Unconsciously echoing J. S. Mill, he stressed that it was the poor that needed protection in the dangerous situation which had come about (RN 32). The rich were well able to protect themselves. He sought to work out remedies for these developments, in the context of Catholic teaching, in his great encyclical *Rerum novarum* of 1891; and he was followed 40 years later by Pius XI, who in his *Quadragesimo anno* of 1931 also sought remedies for the inequality he observed in industrial society (QA 25, 63).

Both Popes were not merely clear but strongly emphatic that socialism provided no answer to the problems that had emerged. It was truly dangerous and based upon false premises (RN 3–12, 15). Socialism involved 'a remedy far worse than the evil itself, [which] would have plunged human society into great dangers' (QA 10). Capital and labour worked together and labour had no right to be the sole claimant on income (QA 53). Class conflict should be avoided, not fostered; at the same time, employees should be treated as equals by those who hired them (RN 16). Indeed, though a competitive labour market was legitimate, it was desirable to work towards a system of profit sharing and partnership (QA 64–5) (another unconscious echo of J. S. Mill – Mill, 1923 [1848]: 764–94).

Socialism was even worse than the evil that it purported to remedy; and at a time when members of the influential British left, notably George Bernard Shaw, were in denial over this, Pius XI referred trenchantly to the horrors of communist regimes. Where socialism had led to communism, the results had been terrible:

> Communism teaches and seeks two objectives: Unrelenting class warfare and absolute extermination of private ownership. Not secretly or by hidden means does it do this, but publicly, openly, and by employing every and all means, even the most violent. To achieve these objectives there is nothing which it does not dare,

nothing for which it has respect or reverence; and when it has come to power, it is incredible and portent like in its cruelty and inhumanity. The horrible slaughter and destruction through which it has laid waste vast regions of eastern Europe and Asia are the evidence; how much an enemy and how openly hostile to Holy Church and to God Himself is, alas, too well proved by facts and fully known to all. (QA 112)

Pius insisted that fundamentally socialism, even in its toned-down form, was irreconcilable with the teachings of the Catholic Church. 'Whether considered as a doctrine, or an historical fact, or a movement, Socialism, if it remains truly Socialism ... cannot be reconciled with the teachings of the Catholic Church because its concept of society itself is utterly foreign to Christian truth' (QA 117).

The fundamental reason for this, which is indeed the key to the whole intellectual apparatus constructed by the Popes, is that it is the individual who should be at the centre of consideration, and whose salvation provided the ultimate moral standard. The ultimate aim was the salvation of individual souls: 'Socialism, on the other hand, wholly ignoring and indifferent to this sublime end of both man and society, affirms that human association has been instituted for the sake of material advantage alone' (QA 118). The individual must never be regarded as a cog in a machine, with the guiding standard being instead some kind of measure of state achievement.

Leo began his encyclical with a forceful defence of private property as of central importance to the family, the family being the context of the individual (RN 5–7, 9–10, 35). In turn this was echoed by Pius XI (QA 44–5, 49). Recognition of the importance of private property in Catholic teaching goes back as far as Aquinas (RN 19), but it assumes much greater prominence in the two encyclicals. At the same time, possession of property, it was emphasised, was not an absolute right; its possession implied social obligations. But this did not justify collectivisation. The property right was fundamental (QA 46–7).

The state did have a role in providing good government based upon moderate taxes and protecting the stable ordering of economic life (RN 26–35). But it should not interfere with families, except to alleviate distress (RN 11). This was stressed very strongly by Leo. Subsidiarity – the primacy of the individual – must be overriding. It was entirely wrong to interfere with it. But the same principle applied at every level of organisation from the individual upwards. 'Just as it is gravely wrong to take from individuals what they can accomplish by their own initiative and industry and give it to the community, so also is it an injustice and at the same time a grave evil and disturbance of right order to assign to a greater and higher association what lesser and subordinate organisations can do' (QA 79).

Precisely because the state was incapable of regulating itself, it must be hesitant about interfering (QA 88). Moreover, it was not the only source of material welfare when assistance was required; the Church had an important role as well (RN 24). Leo stressed that state intervention should go no further than was required to equilibrate a disequilibrium situation. Private interests were paramount. In particular, the state had no authority to swallow up either the individual or the family (RN 28–9). It could certainly help them in a crisis; but there was also an important role for charity in addition to the state (QA 137).

Both encyclicals, however, encouraged not only the establishment of trade unions – an exercise in worker solidarity – but also the development of labour laws. Leo's encyclical undoubtedly led to the development of these, and this was approved in turn by Pius XI (RN 34; QA 28). There was a natural right of association with which the state should not interfere (RN 37). At the same time many trade unions were socialist in orientation, with an emphasis on class conflict; and the Popes looked to the development (which did follow) of Catholic trade unions (RN 38–44; QA 36).

Such an exercise in solidarity would in turn help to provide a level of wages which not only supported the family but (and this is of great importance in Leo's encyclical) provide also a sufficient margin for saving, leading to the accumulation of property by the wage earner (RN

35). Thus a more equal distribution of income would lead to a more equal distribution of property, something which both Popes considered to be vital (QA 61–3, 74). In addition, and both Popes stressed this as well, taxation should be at moderate levels in order to leave scope for saving and the acquisition of property (RN 35). This was designed to raise the welfare of the lower-income groups. According to Pius XI, 'it is grossly unjust for a State to exhaust private wealth through the weight of imposts and taxes' (QA 49).

The wage level had not only to be sufficient to leave a margin for thrift: it had also to be at a level to provide both for the employee *and his family*. (This comes out much more clearly in the encyclical by Pius XI; QA 71.) Women should not be forced to undertake paid work when they would prefer to nurture the all-important family.

The Popes thus looked to reform rather than to an overturning of property rights. There is a root-and-branch condemnation of socialism; but acceptance of the operation of a market economy is qualified. It was an absolutely fundamental requirement that the market should operate within a framework like that envisaged by the English classical economists, one of law, religion and custom, which limited the pursuit of self-interest through competition, in order to protect social interest (RN 26; QA 49, 88).Without this restraint, free competition was not acceptable. The market system was 'not of its own nature vicious'. But it was so if the owners of capital hired labour 'scorning the human dignity of the workers, the social character of economic activity and social justice itself, and the common good' (QA 101).

Nonetheless, *given* such a framework, there was no objection to increasing wealth in a just and lawful manner through the operation of the market system (QA 136).

John XXIII and John Paul II

The themes in the encyclicals of Leo XIII and Pius XI were further developed in four major encyclicals in the second half of the twentieth century: *Mater et magistra* (1961) from John XXIII , and *Laborem exercens* (1981), *Sollicitudo rei socialis* (1987) and *Centesimus annus* (1991) from John Paul II. Socialism was again explicitly rejected; it was the individual who was of prime concern, the focus of attention and not a mere cog in a machine (CA 13). The class struggle was contrasted with the achievement of genuine social justice, which must be the aim (CA 14).

Social justice involved recognition of human rights to take private initiative, to property and to freedom in economic life (MM 109; LE 52; SRS 86; CA 24, 30, 31, 43). It was again argued that workers should be given scope to save in order to become property owners, and indeed the state should encourage widespread property ownership (MM 109, 115). As in the earlier encyclicals, ownership of property is qualified by the social obligations that it imposes (MM 119–20; CA 6, 30); but the right to own property is an important part of the consolidation of the power and initiative of the individual vis-à-vis the state (MM 105–9).

Nonetheless, and despite the fact that inequality should be reduced as prosperity increased (MM 73), there was a continuing need for solidarity, and individuals should recognise the need to commit themselves to social as well as individual aims. Solidarity was based upon the need to recognise a common humanity. In particular, the poor needed protection, and solidarity should help to provide this (SRS 38–40, 74–80; CA 10). Catholic trade unions should deploy countervailing power in this cause, rather than seeking to pursue a class struggle (MM 100–101; LE 26–7; CA 7, 15, 24, 34).

But solidarity extended beyond trade union activity to social reforms. Such reforms were achieved through employing the agency of the state (MM 60–61; CA 16); but John Paul II, like Leo XIII and Pius XI, stressed the priority of the individual, of the family and of society over the state (CA 11). The state should provide a framework, including labour laws; and it should provide things like unemployment relief (MM 52, 54; CA 15). But it should not seek to control individuals. The family, as the nurturer of individuals, and as the primary level of solidarity, had a key role (CA 39). Like earlier Popes, John Paul II stressed that women should not be forced to enter the labour market and forsake their role as the centre of the family (SRS 69; CA 8, 34, 43).

All this, then, involves a forceful restatement of the principle of subsidiarity. This principle is contrasted with its diametrical opposite, totalitarianism, of which John Paul had first-hand experience, first as a subject of the Nazis, and then of the communists. Totalitarianism was identified as the antithesis of subsidiarity (CA 44–5).

John Paul went well beyond his predecessors in asserting the efficiency of the free market. Although 'there are many human needs which find no place in the market', nonetheless, 'It would appear that, on the level of individual nations and of international relations, the *free market* is the most efficient instrument for utilizing resources and effectively responding to needs' (CA 34; emphasis in original).

Indeed, he pointed to the damage done by the suppression of the pursuit of self-interest. 'In fact, where self-interest is violently suppressed, it is replaced by a burdensome system of bureaucratic control which dries up the wellsprings of initiative and creativity' (CA 25).

Moreover, he stressed the importance of entrepreneurial ability. '[T]he *role* of disciplined and creative *human work* and, as an essential part of that work, *initiative and entrepreneurial ability* becomes increasingly evident and decisive' (CA 32; emphasis in original).

He recognised a legitimate role for profit. 'When a firm makes a profit, this means that productive factors have been properly employed and corresponding human needs have been duly satisfied' (CA 35).[1]

If individual economic initiative were suppressed, this harmed the common good. The damage occurred through a process of 'levelling down', and through dependency creation (MM 55–7; CA 13).

> In the place of creative initiative there appears passivity,
> dependence and submission to the bureaucratic apparatus
> which, as the only 'ordering' and 'decision-making' body – if not
> also the 'owner' – of the entire totality of goods and the means
> of production, puts everyone in a position of almost absolute

---

1   The role of profit as a resource allocation signal seems to be recognised here.

dependence, which is similar to the traditional dependence of the worker-proletarian in capitalism. This provokes a sense of frustration or desperation and predisposes people to opt out of national life. (SRS 24)

Of course, it was necessary that the free market should operate within a framework of law, religion and custom, to distinguish it from raw capitalism. 'Economic activity, especially the activity of a market economy, cannot be conducted in an institutional, juridical or political vacuum' (CA 35, 48).

In the choice of appropriate economic system, the presence or otherwise of such a framework was decisive. In considering whether 'capitalism' should be the way forward, this was the key issue:

> If by 'capitalism' is meant an economic system which recognises the fundamental and positive role of business, the market, private property and the resulting responsibility for the means of production, as well as free human creativity in the economic sector, then the answer is certainly in the affirmative, even though it would perhaps be more appropriate to speak of a 'business economy', 'market economy' or simply 'free economy'. But if by 'capitalism' is meant a system in which freedom in the economic sector is not circumscribed within a strong juridical framework which places it at the service of human freedom in its totality, and which sees it as a particular aspect of that freedom, the core of which is ethical and religious, then the reply is certainly negative. (CA 42)

John Paul stressed that such limits could be at the level of subsidiarity through the exercise of consumer choice (CA 36). He explicitly mentioned drugs and pornography as things through which consumers, by not choosing them, could help to limit the operation of the market for the better. A sense of solidarity could also temper the profit motive (SRS 38). Insofar as the framework of economic activity involved legislation, it must involve sovereign law, which could not be subverted by the arbitrary will of individuals (CA 44). In this he was unconsciously echoing

Adam Smith (1979 [1776]: 825–6); but the lessons, no doubt learned in communist Poland, are of far wider application in an era when tax authorities seek to make retrospective changes to tax regimes.

The role of the state is thus carefully circumscribed. In particular both John XXIII and John Paul II warned against the excessive development of the welfare state. Such development offends against the principle of subsidiarity. Indeed, according to John Paul it posed the danger of the 'social assistance state'.

> In recent years the range of such [state] intervention has vastly expanded, to the point of creating a new type of State, the so-called 'Welfare State' ... However excesses and abuses, especially in recent years, have provoked very harsh criticisms of the Welfare State, dubbed the 'Social Assistance State'. This development is the result of an inadequate understanding of the tasks proper to the State. Here again the *principle of subsidiarity* must be respected: a community of higher order should not interfere in the internal life of a community of a lower order, depriving the latter of its functions. (CA 48; emphasis in original)

John XXIII warned too of the danger of creating dependency (MM 63–5). This was unacceptable, because it made the individual permanently subservient to the state and its decisions.

Thus we return to the idea that the state can assist, but must not take over, people's lives. It can support and coordinate, but it must not directly interfere (CA 48, 49).

It can legitimately provide public goods (CA 40). These include justice, and sound money, both of which are mentioned by several Popes. But the scope for public goods may be rather constrained by the discovery that the category itself is far more limited than had previously been thought – in particular there is the famous case of lighthouses, endlessly invoked by economists as a classic case of a public good that turns out to have been initially provided largely by private enterprise (Coase, 1974).

The economic model

The basic model which emerges from all this is remarkably similar in a number of aspects to that found in the writings of the British classical economists. This is a parallel which the Popes would not have recognised; it is evident that they believed northern Europe to be in the grip of an extreme form of laissez-faire. German economists, as devotees of what they regarded as a morally superior *Sozialpolitik*, caricatured English classical economics as advocating an extreme form of unregulated competition which they called 'Manchesterism' (Schumpeter, 1954: 765, 888); and this caricature seems to have been taken at face value south of the Alps.

Yet the basic model which emerges from the papal documents shares with the classical economists an emphasis upon security of property and decentralised decision-taking. In both cases the importance of individual initiative is stressed. The state should remedy defects in the competitive system as they emerge, but should not seek to take over the system. The labour market should respond to the preferences of individuals, not only in the provision of acceptable working conditions – stressed from Leo onwards – but also, and even more fundamentally, in not forcing women out of the home and into the labour market. Taxes should be at a moderate level (see also Chapter 5); this is consistent not only with the idea of encouraging individual initiative, but also reflects the concern to allow a margin for capital accumulation. The diffusion of property, which is a major concern of the encyclicals, is also one which accords with the outlook of the classical economists, who certainly did not see capital accumulation as the preserve of just a few individuals in society, and who witnessed the rise of many individuals from humble origins to commercial success.

At the same time, while stressing the importance of a legal and other frameworks for economic activity, the papal encyclicals are strong in their objections to state encroachment on individual activity, and emphasise that state assistance should be temporary and not become a permanent feature of economic activity. This has a parallel in the agonising of the classical economists over the Poor Law in England and Wales.

Again, while the classical economists fully recognised the need for a legislative framework for economic activity, they were very wary of direct state involvement outside limited areas, such as the provision of the currency. This accords with the outlook of the encyclicals. Indeed, Pius XI emphasised in 1931, decades before neoclassical economists had got away from the idea of the benevolent, omniscient state, that the state has one fundamental weakness above all in the economic sphere – it is incapable of regulating itself.

The emphasis by John Paul II on the supremacy of the rule of law, with its implication that economic activity must take place within a framework that is certain and not arbitrary (something which has come under threat in Britain in the last few years with the emergence of retrospective tax changes), is entirely in accord with Smith's view in the *Wealth of Nations*, one which was accepted by his successors. It is a corollary of the idea that security of property is vital, this in turn springing from the concept of the central role of the individual.

There are other aspects of the encyclicals which sit less easily with the liberal model. For instance, the social obligations of property ownership are mentioned from 1891 onwards, yet remain undefined and vague. The idea does, however, seem to reflect an aversion to the concept of the grim-faced entrepreneur, and a desire not only for harmonious relations in the workplace but also for profit-sharing and for cooperative enterprise. While this would have reflected the preferences of J. S. Mill, it cannot be said that Mill's views have enjoyed widespread support among economists or that cooperative enterprise has a particularly glorious history – or indeed that it necessarily provides better conditions for employees. Moreover, the emphasis on the encouragement of trade unions, entirely understandable as it was in 1891, and indeed in 1931, may seem a little strange to those who lived through the 1970s, particularly in Britain. But this may be something which can be interpreted in terms of the distinction in the encyclicals of Leo XIII and Pius XI between the activities of Catholic trade unions and those of socialist ones.

In addition, the British trade unions had remarkable legal privileges, and enjoyed, by virtue of these, powers of compulsion which effectively altered their character from that of voluntary associations to ones enjoying state sponsorship.

Lessons not learned – *Gaudium et spes*

Despite these problems, however, it is clear that the body of ideas worked out over a century provides an excellent guide to Catholic teaching on economic activity. It is then unfortunate that much of what was painstakingly built up seems to have dropped out of sight.

The starting point for this process would seem to be the document *Gaudium et spes* (1965), which was the product of the Second Vatican Council, and promulgated as *The Pastoral Constitution on the Church in the World of Today*. This document bears all the hallmarks of a committee document, and reflects very little of the carefully worked-out teaching previously discussed in this chapter. In particular it is imbued with 1960s corporatism, with an emphasis on state coordination, and with little emphasis indeed on the central concept of subsidiarity. It is clear that, where definitive statements are made on subjects such as economics and other social sciences, those making the statements have often gone outside their field of expertise and competence.

Though it defines the common good as individual fulfilment (GS 26), it does not relate this to concerns about the individual of the kind which informed the encyclicals of 1891 and 1931, and which were to be revived in the encyclicals of John Paul II. Sometimes the argument verges on the comic. At one point the reader is solemnly informed that 'Meanwhile every man goes on, obscurely recognising himself as an unanswered question' (GS 21).[2]

The document contains standard 1960s clichés about foreign aid (see also Chapter 3) and the arms race (GS 85–6). In connection with the

2   This is not written with regard to economic or social teaching but in the context of the difficulties that may face man in his life on earth. But it is an example of the kind of language in this document which is unintelligible and not typical of papal documents.

former it becomes apparent that there is serious ambiguity concerning the concept of solidarity, one which also surfaces at some points in the encyclicals of John XXIII and of John Paul II (MM 157; CA 22, 28, 51).[3] For both they and the authors of *Gaudium et spes* interpret solidarity as the protection of poor countries by richer countries (GS 87–8). Solidarity then becomes a top-down, government-driven, political exercise, a view which is consistent with the general 1960s corporatist outlook of the document (GS 65).[4] In the encyclicals of Leo XIII and Pius XI, however, and elsewhere in the encyclicals of John XXIII and John Paul II, solidarity is a bottom-up concept, originating in voluntary action, not state intervention. It is rooted in recognition of a common humanity, not in the political equivalent of *noblesse oblige*. The initial expression of solidarity is the family. Next there are associations for the promotion of particular objectives, and then the trade unions. Moreover, it is stated quite clearly that subsidiarity requires that, wherever possible, functions should be left with such low-level expressions of solidarity, and that the state should involve itself only where it is quite clear that these lower-level associations are not achieving desired aims.

In addition, *The Pastoral Constitution* appears willing to depart from papal teaching in the direction of what its authors believed to be new developments in social sciences. Thus the reader is assured that 'recent psychological studies explain human activity more deeply' (GS 54) and sociology is also recommended. Indeed, in view of what has recently been revealed about the role of psychology in bringing about the scandals that have afflicted the Church in the USA (Rose, 2002: 9, 31–40,

---

3 See also Paul VI, *Populorum progressio*, 43, 62–4.

4 This not unnaturally attracted some astringent criticism, notably from Peter Bauer (Charles, 1998, vol. 2: 455). Bauer concentrates his fire on Paul VI's *Populorum progressio* (1976) and on the Pontifical Letter *Octogesima adveniens* (1971). He notes in particular the reliance on 'top down solidarity', grounded in the naive belief (once held by economists) that governments always work for the best, the 1960s conventionalism resulting in recommendations that were neither distinctively Christian nor distinctively Catholic, and observes witheringly that 'Envy is traditionally one of the seven deadly sins. Vocal modern clerical opinion endows it with moral legitimacy and intellectual respectability' (Bauer, 1984: 73, 76, 78, 87).

129–44), it is deeply disturbing to find that the authors of *The Pastoral Constitution* suggested that those teaching theology in seminaries should 'cooperate intellectually and practically with experts' in psychology and related subjects (GS 62). At the very least, it is now clear that the naivety exhibited by those involved in drafting *The Pastoral Constitution* should be rapidly discarded and, just as Pope John Paul II looked again at the economic theory underlying pronouncements in *Gaudium et spes* in his encyclical *Centesimus annus*, the time has come to look critically at its pronouncement on other aspects of social sciences.

The hierarchy of England and Wales

Local Bishops' Conferences produce statements from time to time on matters that are related to economics and politics. These statements are intended to guide the lay faithful and politicians in their thinking by setting out the view of the hierarchy on particular matters. In this section some statements made by the England and Wales Conference are examined, and it is saddening to discover that an outlook of the kind to be found in *Gaudium et spes* seems to have exercised a greater influence on the local hierarchy than the papal encyclicals that both preceded it and followed it. For various pronouncements of the England and Wales hierarchy on the one hand pay no more than lip-service to the concept of subsidiarity while, on the other, endorsing a wide range of contemporary clichés.

This is all the more surprising because the 1994 *Catechism of the Catholic Church* followed correctly the lines of the encyclicals.[5] The *Catechism* rejects socialism, as did the encyclicals (para. 2425), emphasises subsidiarity (paras 1883–5, 2209, 2424, 2431), the family (paras

---

5   It is, however, rather interesting that neither *Rerum novarum* nor *Quadragesimo anno* is cited in the *Catechism*. This omission has only now been remedied with the publication by the Pontifical Council for Justice and Peace of the *Compendium of the Social Doctrine of the Church*. But full details of these and other encyclicals were available to the bishops in the magnificent study by Rodger Charles (Charles, 1998).

2209, 2434), the framework of market activity (paras 2425, 2431), and the legitimacy of a profit reward (para. 2432). In particular, it emphasises the importance of the individual, and the danger of excessive intervention by the state, and explains that the principle of subsidiarity is opposed to all forms of collectivism and sets limits to state intervention (paras 1883–5).

Yet, in the pronouncements of the bishops of England and Wales, there is a generalised distrust of the market economy and little scepticism about the level of taxation which, as a proportion of national income, is five times the level in the UK in 1891, when Pope Leo warned against excessive taxation sapping enterprise. This approach may well reflect, in part, pressure from the Catholic left in Britain,[6] which has been very prominent in British public and Catholic intellectual life. Subsidiarity is hardly mentioned. In this, the England and Wales hierarchy is faithfully reflecting the tone of *Gaudium et spes* (GS 75).

Indeed, the hierarchy, in contrast to mainstream Catholic teaching, seems to turn instinctively to paths involving taxation and the consequently inescapable state coercion. Documents produced by the hierarchy disregard voluntary association, despite the wealth of evidence concerning the good that this has done, especially in fields such as health and education. This is particularly marked in *Taxation for the Common Good*, which accepted without question the huge range of goods and services financed by taxation in the UK.

The bishops have also provided a ringing endorsement of EU

---

6   Thus, in response to the publication by the bishops of *Taxation for the Common Good*, a writer in the *Tablet* (as reported by the Catholic Communications Service, which, oddly, gives no precise source) claimed that 'Taxes pay for almost every amenity that makes life bearable in modern Britain', and concluded with a swipe at Mrs Thatcher. We should perhaps note, however, the irony of a body – the Church – supported by charitable donations, and thus exempt from tax on its income, being enthusiastic about tax. (It is interesting that the record of responses provided by the Catholic Communications Service included only favourable responses to the bishops' document.) Again, in *Vote for the Common Good* (Bishops' Conference, 2001: 5), we find the old canard about Britain having the highest prison population per head of population in Europe, whereas the relevant denominators are per criminal conviction, or per crime.

enlargement in a document that is, more generally, highly supportive of the EU as an institution (Bishops' Conference, 2004: para. 1), apparently unaware that both the Rome (Article 3) and Amsterdam (Protocol 7) treaties explicitly endorse subsidiarity but that in practice this is conspicuous by its absence from the operations of the EU.

The Bishops' Conference document *The European Common Good* (ibid.) mentions more than once the opportunity that enlargement will give rich nations to transfer resources to poorer nations. In doing so it cites the apparent success of this strategy in assisting the development of Ireland. Yet the main spur to the development of Ireland was significant reductions in tax rates: the rapid rate of growth began about 25 years after Ireland entered the EU. Regional policy of the sort recommended by the document has simply not succeeded. More crucially, nowhere in Church teaching is the application of the principle of 'solidarity' intended to imply that rich nations should assist slightly less rich nations through the transfer of money taken from families through taxation. Assisting the very poorest countries to develop is a continual theme of papal teaching, but such countries are not members of the EU. The bishops are so concerned with 'global poverty and deprivation' that they offer the view that considerations of this kind could affect whether a Catholic would vote for a pro-abortion candidate (Bishops' Conference, 2001: 3) – yet they fail to notice that the EU, through its trade restrictions and discrimination, is a major contributor to global poverty and deprivation (Bishops' Conference, 2003: para. 5), though there is a minor reference to the need for 'fairer trading conditions' in *The European Common Good*.

Not only is the EU credited with being a source of peace and prosperity (ibid.: para. 2) and EU travel held to have 'helped the UK immeasurably' (ibid.: para. 10) (hardly incontestable claims, and ones on which the bishops have no particular expertise), but the hierarchy goes so far as to hope that the proposed EU constitution would promote democracy (ibid.: para. 12). This aspiration is clearly at odds with the contents of the then-proposed constitution.

A possible, though contestable, case can be made that, for many countries in Europe, the EU and other European institutions have helped to preserve peace, democracy and justice. This, together with the importance of Europe's cultural and Christian heritage, has been a theme of both Pope Benedict and Pope John Paul II (see, for example, *Ecclesia in Europa*, 2003). The England and Wales Bishops' Conference statements may possibly be seen in that context. But there surely should be recognition that the political structures and economic policies of the EU are simply not conducive to implementing Catholic teaching on subsidiarity and solidarity. Furthermore, the England and Wales Bishops' Conference documents go much farther in praising the economic agenda of the EU than the related papal documents.

The bishops appear untroubled by the profoundly secularist agenda of the EU, culminating not only in the refusal to acknowledge Europe's Christian heritage in the constitution, but in the refusal to confirm a European Commissioner in office simply because he was a Catholic who had *private* beliefs that the EU establishment regarded as unacceptable. Such an action, taken on the basis of the private religious beliefs of an individual, would be serious enough; but, in addition, and in contravention of the principle of subsidiarity, the political structure of the EU enables its officials to impose this secularist agenda on citizens of member nations through regulation.

But the absence of any discernible influence of the encyclicals on the England and Wales hierarchy's pronouncements is nowhere more apparent than in its treatment of the family. The importance of the family is a major theme in encyclicals and in the developed position of the Catholic Church on social and economic issues. It is also an urgent policy issue in the UK. Yet the England and Wales hierarchy shows a solicitude for single mothers (Bishops' Conference, 2001: 3), and apparently sees no conflict between this solicitude and the need to strengthen family life.[7]

---

7   Such solicitude is all the more surprising in the present context, given the well-documented bias of the tax and benefit system against marriage. In fairness it should be added that in a later election document (Bishops' Conference, 2005) both the concern for single mothers

Again, there is little evidence in public statements that what many regard as the nationalisation of childhood taking place in Britain, a most flagrant violation of subsidiarity, concerns the hierarchy. Yet there is ever more detailed state control, in accordance with the criteria of the left-liberal agenda, of the upbringing of children in Britain. This is coupled with the relentless pressure on women coming both from regulation and from the tax and benefits system to hand over the care of their children to nurseries (themselves the subject of considerable state control, including Ofsted inspections, even when privately owned). Nor is there any apparent concern that the complex tax and benefits system created in recent years has produced the kind of welfare dependency against which both John XXIII and John Paul II emphatically warned.

A further document that shows vividly how the England and Wales hierarchy have trodden in areas where they have no special expertise, have not properly applied the concept of subsidiarity and have not taken on board developments in economics that are compatible with subsidiarity is the bishops' document on the environment (Bishops' Conference, 2002). We are told (Section II) that the environment is breaking down, cities are afflicted by smog, and so on. The section continues to deplore the apparent scarcity of natural resources that is 'threatening international stability' and expresses concerns about global warming threatening the planet. All the policy proposals in the document relate to government and international action through regulation. Kyoto is particularly recommended (Section V).

Pronouncements on this subject are justified by an appeal to solidarity; but a consideration of subsidiarity might have alerted the bishops to the potential loss of national income, were countries honestly to implement the Kyoto agreement, which is hardly a trivial consideration when balancing the costs and benefits of different courses of action, particu-

---

and the possibility of voting, with implied episcopal approval, for a pro-abortion candidate do not appear. There is, however, little that is explicitly Catholic about the document and, in particular, the support for marriage and the family is justified not on grounds relating to Catholic teaching but by sociological criteria.

larly for the 27 per cent of the world's population who do not have access to electricity. For such people the absence of energy supplies rather than global warming is the most urgent problem. Furthermore, most indicators of environmental quality have been improving dramatically in the last 40 years in developed countries that have systems of secure property rights and market economies. Market economies use resources more efficiently, including environmental resources. They are able to access cleaner technologies that can deal with environmental problems as they arise. The price mechanism promotes conservation and the development of alternatives to finite resources in the face of scarcity. Perhaps most importantly, environmental exploitation is generally a symptom of property rights not being properly defined or enforced – rainforests being an outstanding example of this. A true appeal to subsidiarity would have identified this problem. Instead, there is a single statement on property rights suggesting that *strict limits should be put upon private ownership*. Private ownership is vital for the safeguarding of the long-term sustainability of environmental resources. This can be seen from comparing the ability of privately owned land to produce crops year after year with the perilous state of fishing grounds, access to which is generally government controlled. The way in which the *absence* of property rights in many jurisdictions and over many environmental resources is leading to environmental degradation is not even considered in the document.

There is an urgent need for the England and Wales Bishops' Conference to think more carefully about these issues, taking on board both the principle of subsidiarity and an improved understanding of economics.

Conclusion

The concepts of subsidiarity and solidarity are absolutely central to Catholic Social (and indeed economic) Teaching. They provide powerful tools in dealing with a wide range of questions, and form the twin foundations of an impressive intellectual structure developed over a century in major encyclicals. It is abundantly clear that awareness of this structure, which is ably summarised in the *Catechism of the Catholic Church*, would be of considerable benefit to the hierarchy of England and Wales bishops, not only in dealing with social and economic questions, but indeed in indicating which areas fell within its competence. From such a start, other considerations might follow.

For example, the hierarchy might consider, when dealing with taxation, that the replacement of estate duty by legacy duty might well increase the dispersion of property ownership, as urged in the encyclicals. Again, the need for a certain and not arbitrary legal framework would not only call into question retrospective changes in tax regimes, but the whole operation of the secret family courts in which children can be removed from their families and put up for adoption. The general level of taxation, about which the hierarchy appears remarkably sanguine, and the provision of private (as distinct from public) goods by the state, notably in the fields of education and health, are areas where current policy would appear to conflict with the tenor of the encyclicals. Perhaps a start might be made by returning to the whole concept of subsidiarity. This should be embedded in the thinking behind all the hierarchy's documents and combined with an attempt to understand the compatibility of subsidiarity with different economic and political structures. From Catholic teaching it is also clear that subsidiarity should be balanced by solidarity but that solidarity progresses from the individual to the family through voluntary organisations. Only in the last resort should it be necessary to use the coercive forces of government to promote the common good. Furthermore higher levels of government should not act in areas that can be left to lower levels. This approach is compatible with the pursuit of the common good and with the Christian understanding of the human person who is, at once, unique and autonomous but also interdependent and part of a wider community.

References

Bauer, P. (1984), *Reality and Rhetoric; Studies in the Economics of Development*, London: Weidenfeld and Nicolson.

Bishops' Conference (2001), *Vote for the Common Good*, London: Catholic Bishops of England and Wales.

Bishops' Conference (2002), *The Call of Creation: God's Invitation and The Human Response. The Natural Environment and Catholic Social Teaching*, London: Catholic Bishops of England and Wales.

Bishops' Conference (2003), *Trade and Solidarity*, London: Catholic Bishops of England and Wales.

Bishops' Conference (2004a), *Responses to Taxation for the Common Good*, London: Catholic Bishops of England and Wales.

Bishops' Conference (2004b), *The European Common Good*, London: Catholic Bishops of England and Wales.

Bishops' Conference (2005), *The General Election. A Letter from the Bishops' Conference of England and Wales*, London: Catholic Bishops of England and Wales.

Catholic Church (1994), *Catechism of the Catholic Church*, London: Geoffrey Chapman.

Charles, R. (1998), *Christian Social Witness and Teaching: The Catholic Tradition from Genesis to Centesimus Annus*, Leominster: Gracewing.

Coase, R. H. (1974), 'The lighthouse in economics', *Journal of Law and Economics*, 17(2): 357–76.

Mill, J. S. (1923 [1848]), *Principles of Political Economy*, ed. W. J. Ashley, London: Longman.

Rose, Michael S. (2002), *Goodbye, Good Men. How Liberals Brought Corruption into the Catholic Church*, Washington, DC: Regnery.

Schumpeter, J. A. (1954), *History of Economic Analysis*, London: Allen and Unwin.

Smith, A. (1979 [1776]), *An Inquiry into the Nature and Causes of the Wealth of Nations*, ed. R. H. Campbell, A. S. Skinner and W. B. Todd, Oxford: Oxford University Press, 1979, reprinted Indianapolis, IN: Liberty Press, 1981.

11 CATHOLICISM AND THE CASE FOR LIMITED GOVERNMENT
Samuel Gregg

Introduction

Jesus Christ's famous words recorded in Luke's Gospel, 'render to Caesar what belongs to Caesar – and to God what belongs to God' (Luke 20:25), were literally revolutionary in their implications for how we understand the state. With good reason, Luke's Gospel records that Christ's 'answer took [his questioners] by surprise' (Luke 20:26). For, as observed by the nineteenth-century English Catholic historian Lord Acton, 'in religion, morality, and politics, there was only one legislator and one authority' in the pre-Christian ancient world: the polis and later the Roman state (Acton, 1948: 45). Separation of the temporal and spiritual was incomprehensible to pagan minds because categories such as 'temporal' and 'spiritual' did not exist in the pre-Christian world. As the twentieth century's leading historian of Catholic Social Teaching, Rodger Charles, SJ, notes:

> … in saying that God had to be given his due as well as Caesar, [Christ] asserted the independence of the spiritual authority from the political in all matters of the spirit, of faith, worship and morals. This was a new departure in the world's experience of religion. In the pagan world, the State had controlled religion in all its aspects. The kingdom of God that Christ had announced was spiritual, but it was to have independence as a social organization so that the things of God could be given at least equal seriousness to those of Caesar.… When events led to conflict with the State on this issue, and the Christians faced martyrdom, the political effects in theory and in practice did much to determine the shape of European political culture and through it that of the modern world. (Charles, 1998: 36)

Throughout the Graeco-Romano world, the widespread ascription of divine characteristics to the polis or the Roman state was often paid lip-service. The Roman authorities, recognising the strength of Jewish resentment concerning the token emperor-worship required of all the empire's subjects, exempted Jews from such acts. Yet there were times when the pagan synthesis of religion and state caused immense difficulty for people in the ancient world. People were not, for instance, able to appeal to a divine law that transcended the polis or the state.

By universalising the Jewish belief that those exercising legal authority were as subject to Yahweh's law as everyone else, Christianity achieved the hitherto unthinkable: the de-sacralisation of the polis and the Roman state. From Scripture, we know that early Christianity was respectful of the Roman state's authority. Both St Paul and St Peter underlined the divine origin of the state's legal authority (Romans 13:1–6; 1 Peter 2:13–17). Nevertheless, Christianity also quietly insisted that Caesar was not a god and might not behave as if he was God. Though Christians would pray for earthly rulers, it was anathema for Christians to pray to such rulers. While Christians regarded the state as the custodian of social order, they did not consider the state itself to be the source of truth and law (Ratzinger, 2006: 59). Thus, as the then Cardinal Joseph Ratzinger once observed, Jews and Christians viewed the state as an order that found its limits in a faith that worshipped, not the state, but a God who stood over the state and judged it (ibid.: 240). When Constantine gave religious liberty to the Church in his Edict of Milan (AD 313), he did not subject Christianity to himself. Instead Constantine effectively declared that Caesar was no longer God.

Throughout the centuries, there were instances when the Catholic Church associated itself with the exercise of temporal power to varying degrees. Charles notes that both the post-Constantinian Roman state and its successors used the Church's organisation and personnel to address many social and economic problems. Church courts, for example, were notoriously more efficient than the empire's civil courts, and noted for giving fairer judgments (Charles, 1998: 63). In the wake of the breakdown of political order after the Western Roman Empire's gradual disintegration following the waves of barbarian infiltrations and invasions that began in the late fourth century AD, the Church was perhaps the only institution capable of wielding significant moral and legal authority throughout much of western Europe during this period. Hence, it was not surprising that Catholic clergy such as St Ambrose of Milan and St Augustine of Hippo found themselves assuming social and political roles once reserved to Roman officials.

And yet despite this association the vital distinction between the claims of God and Caesar, with its implicit limiting of state power, has persisted in Catholic belief and action in ways that are less obvious in some other Christian communities' teaching and practice. The links between a number of the Eastern Orthodox churches and the rulers of the nations in which they dwelled remained exceptionally strong until the twentieth century – so much so that *caesaropapism* became a tendency deeply ingrained in the consciousness of some Orthodox believers. In the West, the doctrine of the Divine Right of Kings enjoyed considerable favour in Anglican communities and some Lutheran confessions, and even received some support from a number of absolutist Catholic monarchs. This doctrine, however, found very few supporters among Catholic clergy and bishops precisely because of the manner in which it diminished the Church's autonomy from the state and blurred the spiritual–temporal distinction. The sixteenth-century scholastic theologian Francisco Suárez, SJ, wrote powerfully and strongly against the idea (Suárez, 1944). Another sixteenth-century theologian, St Robert Bellarmine, later proclaimed a Doctor of the Church, specifically refuted the divine right arguments articulated by one of the theory's most famous proponents, James I of England, and also penned the famous *Tractatus de potestate Summi Pontificis in rebus temporalibus adversus Gulielmum Barclaeum* (1610) in opposition to Galician tendencies (which involved, among other things, the extension of the French state's powers over ecclesiastical affairs) in the Catholic Church in France (Brodrick, 1950: 224). Nor were divine right theories ever accepted by the Popes, primarily because of the manner in which they blurred the spiritual and temporal realms.

A great English saint, Sir Thomas More, understood this point very well. His careful but unambiguous opposition to King Henry VIII and Thomas Cromwell as they drove the Church in England into schism was motivated by several factors (Gregg, 2007). But one element was More's conviction that the Catholic Church's authority in religious matters such as the indissolubility of marriage and the Pope's dispensing power was greater than the demands of the state's laws. 'The custom of the Christian people,' More wrote, 'in matters of the sacraments and of faith has the force of a more powerful law than has any custom of any people whatsoever in civil matters, since the latter relies only on human agreement, [while] the former is procured and prospers by divine intervention' (More, 1969: 415). More considered patently absurd the claim advanced by the distinguished legal scholar Christopher St Germain that Scripture and conscience should be subject to the demands of English common law as determined by the king-in-parliament. He also recognised that these and other assertions made to legitimise the Henrican legal revolution of the 1530s would expand the state's power beyond fundamental limits long established in the Catholic Church's authoritative sources of knowledge: Scripture, tradition, magisterial teaching and the natural law.

The very nature of the Catholic Church's own self-understanding therefore means that it cannot accept a state that purports to have no theoretical or practical limits, regardless of whether the absolutist claims are made by an eighteenth-century monarch, a nineteenth-century Jacobin, a twentieth-century Bolshevik or a 21st-century radical secularist. This was dramatically underlined by Pius XI in his encyclical *Mit Brennender Sorge* (1937) protesting about the Nazi regime's treatment of the Catholic Church in Germany:

> Whoever exalts race, or the people, or the State, or a particular
> form of State, or the depositories of power, or any other
> fundamental value of the human community – however necessary

and honourable be their function in worldly things – whoever raises these notions above their standard value and divinizes them to an idolatrous level, distorts and perverts an order of the world planned and created by God; he is far from the true faith in God and from the concept of life which that faith upholds. (MBS 8).

The roots of a Catholic vision of limited state power, however, go beyond the desire to maintain the Church's own rightful autonomy and its understanding of the correct relationship between the spiritual and temporal realms. It also owes much to (a) the Catholic understanding of the human person as a free, social, sinful and responsible creature, called to choose moral greatness but capable of profound degeneracy; and (b) the Church's stress on the importance of each person pursuing human flourishing by choosing to live in the Truth definitively revealed by Christ to His Church and rejecting the path of evil.

Freedom and the call to perfection

Each human person, it appears, is designed by nature to want to be free. But what, we should ask, is so special about human freedom? Why is it *worth* being free? Responding to such questions, the Catholic Church maintains that human freedom is important because, as the Second Vatican Council taught in its Declaration on Religious Freedom, *Dignitatis humanae* (1965), 'man's response to God in faith must be free … The act of faith is of its very nature a free act. Man, redeemed by Christ the Saviour and through Christ Jesus called to be God's adopted son, cannot give his adherence to God revealing Himself unless, under the drawing of the Father, he offers to God the reasonable and free submission of faith' (DH 10).

Freedom is not only important because it allows people to respond to God's grace. Catholicism underlines human liberty as an essential prerequisite for people freely choosing and acting as they ought to act. In his encyclical on the Church's moral teaching, *Veritatis splendor* (1993), John Paul II stressed that God made man free not only so that each person can find God, but so that we might 'freely attain perfection'. The Pope immediately added, 'Attaining such perfection means *personally building up that perfection in himself.* Indeed, just as man in exercising his dominion over the world shapes it in accordance with his own intelligence and will, so too in performing morally good acts, man strengthens, develops and consolidates within himself his likeness to God' (VS 39). The perfection to which John Paul II – consistent with the entire Catholic tradition – states all people are called is one which the Swiss theologian Servais Pinckaers, OP, describes as 'freedom for excellence' (Pinckaers, 1993: 354–78). This is the 'self-command' that comes when a person, having discerned the moral goods knowable through reason and the Catholic faith, directs his will to these goods and acts freely and consistently to realise them in his life, aided by God's grace. It amounts to a freedom that Christ's call to each person to live the life of the Beatitudes is both possible and enriching, and a foretaste of the beatific vision that is God.

Liberty, then, in the sense of liberty from unreasonable coercion, is – from the Catholic standpoint – not an end in itself. It is a means for attaining the higher freedom that is called self-mastery: that is, when we discern through faith and reason what is and is not compatible with Christ's call to perfection, and then, through exercising our rational free will, we choose morally good acts and assimilate the truth about the good into our very being.

While Catholicism holds that humans need to be free to choose the higher freedom to which Christ calls everyone, it also teaches that we are social creatures who need other people and who have real concrete responsibilities to others. This much is evident from our everyday experience. From the moment of our conception, we depend upon our mother for sustenance. As babies we are helpless, utterly dependent upon others' good will, especially that of our families. As we grow, our associations become less exclusively familial. They increasingly become the outcome of human reason and choice. This reflects our condition as a social being whose capacity for self-reliance is limited. St Thomas Aquinas highlighted this truth when he wrote:

It is not possible for one man to arrive at knowledge of all these things by his own individual reason. It is therefore necessary for man to live in a multitude so that each one may assist his fellows, and different men may be occupied in seeking, by their reason, to make different discoveries – one, for example, in medicine, one in this, another in that. (Aquinas, 1948: I, 6)

Nor did Aquinas imagine that our dependence upon associational life is confined to our immediate circumstances. When we engage in shaping material, be it physical or intellectual in nature, we almost always draw upon a common stock of human knowledge. This can range from something as fundamental as language to a specific technique developed over time by particular professions.

At the same time, the Church teaches that these same free and associational human beings sometimes make sinful choices that damage themselves and others around them. As Thomas More wrote, we all possess the capacity to abuse our liberty and concoct many 'worldly fantasies' of our own making (More, 1976: 226). While Catholicism does not teach that we are somehow 'free from' the demands of truth, it acknowledges that, as creatures marked by sin, we have the capacity to rebel against the truth revealed by faith and reason. Such rebellion, however, only leads us to neglect what is reasonable and true – and therefore reality – and enter into the prison of untruth and escapism. In More's words, 'Is it not a beastly thing to see a man that has reason so rule himself that his feet may not bear him, but ... rolls and reels until he falls into the gutter?' (More, 1931: 495).

The situation is further complicated by the fact that in any given society of persons, the range of different, sometimes incompatible, possibilities for reasonable choice by individuals and associations continues to expand. It therefore becomes increasingly difficult to reconcile all choices with each other. Decisions thus need to be made concerning the rules and policies that reconcile different reasonable choices and address problems arising from unreasonable choices.

In certain areas, various procedures emerge to resolve particular problems. Though no serious Catholic would sacralise the market economy, John Paul II noted that the market economy has thus far proved to be the most efficient human means for meeting the basic material needs of entire societies (*Centesimus annus*, 32, 34). Likewise, the price mechanism's ability to reflect the supply-and-demand status of goods and services provides people with some of the information they need in order to choose what to purchase. But even here, judgements need to be made concerning what to do when, for example, a person reneges on their promise to pay the agreed-upon price.

The legal philosopher John Finnis observes that there are only two ways to resolve such conflicts: unanimity or authority (Finnis, 1980: 231–3). The voluntary undertakings agreed upon in a contract, for example, are grounded upon unanimity inasmuch as the contracting individuals adhere to the original agreement. When there is a breakdown of unanimity, the parties to the contract must either decide to dissolve the contract (unanimity), or admit to the authority of a law demanding completion of agreed undertakings, or be held to their undertakings by some organisation wielding a recognised authority (ibid.: 232).

The ongoing increase of possible reasonable and unreasonable choices in most societies decreases the possibility of achieving unanimity on a range of questions. While this may mirror increasing dissension about the proper ends of people, it also reflects an increase in the incompatible but nonetheless reasonable ways of pursuing incompatible but reasonable ends. It is true that traditions, customs and other non-governmental mechanisms often assume a role in providing resolutions to some of these issues. In other cases, however, there may be need for recourse to an authority that can bind people with the force of law – something which markets cannot do. This especially concerns deterring and prohibiting, for instance, criminal behaviour, and more particularly the administration of justice. The very nature of legal justice is such that it involves investing a particular community (the state) with authority, giving particular institutions of that community the responsibility of exercising that authority (legislatures, executives and judiciary), and defining and delimiting the powers of these institutions (constitutions, statute law and common law).

The preceding analysis makes it clear that, from a Catholic and natural law perspective, the legitimacy of the state and political life as a whole is rooted in two elements. The first is each person's natural call – whether they realise it or not – to freely pursue human flourishing and the subsequent need to resolve what might be called 'coordination problems'. The second is the administration of justice, most particularly legal justice (right relations between the individual and the community) and commutative justice (voluntary relations between individuals, especially as mediated through the form of contract). As Benedict XVI reminded his readers in his encyclical *Deus caritas est*, 'The just ordering of society and the State is a central responsibility of politics. As Augustine once said, a State which is not governed according to justice would be just a bunch of thieves: "*Remota itaque iustitia quid sunt regna nisi magna latrocinia?*"' (DCE 28).

In both theory and practice, however, the two often overlap. This becomes clear when we think of instances of legal coercion that may be legitimately exercised by state authorities. On one level, the use of state coercion against, for instance, thieves and murderers is rooted in society's need for an institution to be charged with realising restorative and retributive justice. But the deterrent effect of these powers is such that they help people to understand the moral evil involved in such acts and discourage them from choosing these actions. To this extent, the state's coercive powers help people to choose good rather than evil acts. In other words, Catholic teaching holds that even the coercive powers associated with the state are grounded in the state's responsibility to assist people to pursue perfection. Nevertheless, the Church recognises that these considerations need to be balanced against the fact that people can assimilate the good only if they can freely choose the good for themselves.

We see, then, that Christ's call to all people to choose freely the higher freedom of human perfection is central to understanding how the

Catholic Church understands the state's role as well as its limitations. This becomes clearer when we reflect upon Catholic teaching about what is described in Church teaching as the 'common good' of a political community (i.e. a sovereign nation).

The state and the common good

The phrase 'the common good' is regularly referenced by Popes, bishops and theologians when discussing the nature of the state and the purposes of politics. The expression is not, however, a paraphrase for collectivism or socialism. It does not equate with the tenets of any particular ideology, precisely because the Catholic Church grounds the political community's common good in Christ's call to all to pursue human perfection.

In its Pastoral Constitution on the Church in the Modern World, *Gaudium et spes* (1965), the Second Vatican Council defines the political community's common good as embracing the 'sum of those conditions of the social life whereby men, families and associations more adequately and readily may attain their own perfection' (GS 74). As a form of human association, the political community may thus be understood as existing to assist all its members to realise human perfection. Its ways of doing so might include interacting with other political communities, protecting its members from hostile outsiders, vindicating justice by punishing wrongdoers, and defining the responsibilities associated with particular relationships, such as contractual duties. What these activities have in common is that they are all conditions that *assist*, as distinct from directly cause, people to achieve self-mastery. It is harder, for example, to choose to pursue the good of knowledge in a situation of civil disorder. Likewise, we know that the incentives for us to work are radically diminished if there is no guarantee that our earnings will not be arbitrarily confiscated through taxation or otherwise.

These conditions thus constitute a political community's common good. A particular characteristic of this common good is that it is not the all-inclusive end of its members. Rather it is instrumental as it is directed to assisting the flourishing of persons (Aquinas, 1997: III, ch. 80 nn. 14, 15). The political community's common good thus helps both to define its legitimate authority and to limit it. For the political community's authority does not derive its power from itself. It always proceeds from the responsibility of state institutions to serve a political community's common good, which is in turn directed to a higher end – assisting rather than supplanting people as they pursue human flourishing and disdain evil.

Given the state's responsibility for the political common good, it would be easy to conclude that the state bears direct responsibility for protecting all the conditions that constitute this common good. Such assumptions are, however, unwarranted. This becomes apparent when we reflect upon a principle much articulated in Catholic Social Teaching: the concept of subsidiarity. This idea was partially formulated by Aquinas when he commented, 'it is contrary to the proper character of the state's government to impede people from acting according to their responsibilities – except in emergencies' (ibid.: III, ch. 71, n. 4). A fuller definition of subsidiarity was articulated by John Paul II, following Pius XI, in his 1991 encyclical *Centesimus annus*: 'a community of a higher order should not interfere in the internal life of a community of a lower order, depriving the latter of its functions, but rather should support it in case of need and help to co-ordinate its activity with the activities of the rest of society, always with a view to the common good' (CA 48).

The interventions of higher communities, such as the state, in the activities of lower bodies ought therefore to be made with reference to the common good: i.e. the conditions that enable all persons to fulfil themselves. Subsidiarity thus combines axioms of non-interference and assistance. It follows that when a case of assistance and coordination through law or the government proves necessary, as much respect as possible should be accorded to the rightful autonomy of the assisted person or community.

The significance of this principle thus lies not so much in the autonomy that subsidiarity confers upon people, but in the fact that this autonomy is essential if people are to choose freely basic moral goods. Subsidiarity has therefore less to do with efficiency than with people attaining perfection under their own volition. A basic requirement for realising this perfection is to act and do things for ourselves – as the fruit of our own reflection, choices and acts – rather than have others do them for us. The principle of subsidiarity also reminds us of the fact that there are a host of free associations and communities that precede the state and which establish many of the conditions that assist people to achieve perfection. They thus have a primary responsibility to give others what they are objectively owed in justice, tempered, Catholics will add, by mercy.

Provided that the political community's common good is understood in the terms stated above, we can be confident it will not become the basis for authoritarian tendencies. For one thing, the state's responsibility for the political community's common good is to help people to make choices for virtue – not to force them to do so. Second, the common good, properly understood, does not necessarily require uniformity. It actually creates room for pluralism insofar as it seeks to enable as many people as possible to pursue basic moral goods in a potentially infinite number of ways.

Prudence, sin and love

This understanding of the political community and its common good provides us with the basis for reflecting upon the principles that determine what state authorities may do in a society that values human freedom and human flourishing. Far from constituting an open-ended invitation to expanded government, it points in the direction of limited government. It indicates, for example, that the political community is only one of a number of communities and should not therefore displace or absorb the proper responsibilities of other individuals and associations. Considered in this way, the Catholic understanding of the political community's common good is incompatible with totalitarianism of any kind, precisely because the totalitarian state attempts to absorb all other groups within itself.

The state's ability to perform this assistance role is complicated by a number of factors. One is the knowledge problem. Attempting to determine the conditions that constitute a political community's common good is a difficult exercise. Though some elements are constant – such as the protection of innocent life – the totality of these conditions is never static. The state authorities cannot know everything about all the conditions that constitute a political community's common good at any one point in time. Neither legislators nor judges are, for example, in a position to know the number and particular character of obligations incumbent upon all individuals and associations.

Another significant problem is the fact that the people occupying positions of state authority, be they in the executive, legislature or judiciary, are not perfect. From a Catholic standpoint – not to mention everyday human experience and the lessons of history – state officials are also fallen creatures marked by the stain of original sin and, like the rest of us, sometime choose evil rather than good. They are just as prone as anyone else to making mistakes, to acting outside their area of competence, or even to abusing their position for personal interest. There is a tendency on some Catholics' part (though the problem is hardly confined to Catholics) to imagine that state officials, be they elected or appointed, will always act in the interests of the common good. The lesson of every study of bureaucracy from Max Weber onwards is that the real, as opposed to stated, goals of such organisations and officials often have very little to do with the common good and far more to do with the bureaucracy's self-interest and its desire to preserve and expand its powers.

We are thus faced with dilemmas. If we are to flourish as human beings, we need to act under our own volition. Yet we cannot do so if our decisions are constantly pre-empted for us by the state. On the other hand, our opportunities for free choice may be unreasonably limited if certain prerequisites such as the rule of law which rely heavily upon state authority for their efficacy are absent. At the same time, we know, given man's fallen nature, that a considerable proportion of those people in positions of political and legal power have little interest in the common good and, in some instances, have ceased to be able to distinguish between their own self-interest and a given society's common good.

On one level, the sheer difficulty of resolving these dilemmas is a good reason to ensure that the powers of state institutions are defined as unambiguously as possible and limited in their application. This may limit, to some extent, the effects of the misguided, mistaken and sometimes sinful choices of state officials. At the same time, the same dilemmas underline the importance of the Church reminding government officials that they have a special responsibility to cultivate a special type of human wisdom if they are to perform their responsibilities for a society's political common good. This wisdom consists of discerning what the political community can reasonably contribute towards the liberty and flourishing of its members, and what it cannot (Finnis, 1998: 186). Aquinas underlined this point when he specified three levels of prudential wisdom: individual *prudentia*; domestic practical reasonableness; and political practical reasonableness. 'The good of individuals, the good of families, and the good of *civitas*,' he wrote, 'are different ends; so there are necessarily different species of *prudentia* corresponding to this difference in their respective ends' (Aquinas, 1963: II, II, q. 48).

One way of prudentially discerning the role of government institutions in a given situation is to ask ourselves what the state can and cannot generally do well. This may be determined by identifying other groups' deficiencies and asking when no other community, save the state, can render the assistance that will remedy the deficiency until the ailing non-state organisation can reassume its appropriate role.

Reason and experience tell us that no family is capable of securing public order or administering justice within a political community. Nor can any private person, local association or church successfully undertake such a role. The same reason and experience suggest, however, that the state is a very inadequate child-raiser. In normal circumstances, this function is properly performed by a family that knows and loves its children. When the family experiences problems beyond its control, it should normally be the case that the extended family or neighbours are the first to render assistance. When no other group can render the appropriate form of assistance, it may then be necessary for the state to act.

Hence the fact that children are best raised by their families does not rule out, in principle, any possibility of state intervention in particular circumstances. Examples might be when the police are summoned to stop an incident of spousal abuse. The urgent need to protect the goods of life and health in such cases makes it imprudent to wait for other family members or other intermediate groups to intervene. Normally, however, direct state intervention in family matters is unwise because it involves the application of political wisdom – and power – to a sphere where domestic wisdom and authority ought to prevail. The state's responsibility to maintain an order of justice will nevertheless occasionally necessitate such intervention, precisely because failure to act coercively against spousal abuse may contribute to a deterioration of the public order essential for a political community's common good. Though it is impossible for the state to prevent all cases of, for instance, stealing and intentional killing, such actions should always be prohibited by state authority. Unless such practices face the ultimate sanction of state punishment, a fundamental condition that assists all to fulfil themselves will not prevail.

This principle is central to Catholic teaching concerning, for example, the subject of intentional abortion. The Catholic Church teaches that it is neither possible nor desirable for the state to forbid all evil acts. The Church's teaching in favour of legally prohibiting intentional abortion is, however, partly derived from its awareness that the common good is directly damaged by the removal of any protection from lethal force from innocent human beings who, though *in vitro*, enjoy – as science and reason demonstrate – the same fundamental characteristics of being human as all other members of the human species.

This suggests that, in principle, state institutions may act in ways that contribute to the moral–cultural dimension of a society's common good. Yet the same common good demands that the state should not attempt to protect or alter a society's moral ecology in ways that seek to force people to acquire virtuous dispositions. This point is well explained by the Catholic theologian Germain Grisez. Though recognising that a political community will not be well ordered unless most of its members are encouraged to freely choose acts that contribute to human flourishing, Grisez insists that it is not the state's direct responsibility to demand virtue in general:

> even though a political society cannot flourish without virtuous citizens, it plainly cannot be government's proper end *directly* to promote virtue in general ... both the limits of political society's common good and its instrumentality in relation to the good of citizens as individuals and non-political communities set analogous limits on the extent to which government can rightly concern itself with other aspects of morality, especially insofar as they concern the interior acts and affections of heart rather than the outward behaviour which directly affects other people. (Grisez, 1993: 850)[1]

The important word in Grisez's reflection is *directly*. This indicates that the state's legitimate concern for public order is not limited to upholding the law and procedurally adjudicating disputes. Rather it is a question of state institutions indirectly supporting the efforts of individuals to choose the good freely.

In his first encyclical letter, *Deus caritas est* (2005), Benedict XVI integrated many of these points into a reflection upon the role played by the Christian theological virtue of love in limiting state power. The state – and, by extension, law – is, Pope Benedict noted, primarily concerned with the realisation of legal justice. But Pope Benedict reminded his readers that 'There is no ordering of the State so just that it can eliminate the need for a service of love. ... There will always be suffering

---

1   Emphasis added.

which cries out for consolation and help. There will always be loneliness. There will always be situations of material need where help in the form of concrete love of neighbour is indispensable' (DCE 28). *Deus caritas est* also explains that a state attempting to take care of all problems would inevitably degenerate into a soulless bureaucracy that treats people as things rather than persons. 'The State which would provide everything, absorbing everything into itself, would ultimately become a mere bureaucracy incapable of guaranteeing the very thing which the suffering person – every person – needs: namely, loving personal concern' (DCE 28). This does not mean, Benedict maintained, that society does not need a state. What, the encyclical comments, '[w]e do not need [is] a State which regulates and controls everything' (DCE 28). Instead society requires 'a State which, in accordance with the principle of subsidiarity, generously acknowledges and supports initiatives arising from the different social forces and combines spontaneity with closeness to those in need' (DCE 28).

The encyclical's emphasis on the state's supporting and assisting role is thus linked by Pope Benedict to the priority that ought to be given to the spontaneous activities that emerge from the rest of society. This, the Church teaches, should shape the state's activity in the economic realm. While John Paul II's *Centesimus annus* noted that one of the state's tasks 'is that of overseeing and directing the exercise of human rights in the economic sector', the encyclical immediately added that 'primary responsibility in this area belongs not to the State but to individuals and to the various groups and associations which make up society. The State could not directly ensure the right to work for all its citizens unless it controlled every aspect of economic life and restricted the free initiative of individuals' (CA 48). Reflecting on this point, the Catholic moral theologian Joseph Boyle suggests 'there is a significant limit on the extent to which the polity can provide welfare rights' (Boyle, 2001: 218).

Conclusion

Much more could be written on the Catholic case for limited government than the preliminary analysis contained in this chapter. What is perhaps most striking, however, is the extent to which its argumentation differs from contemporary secular arguments for limited government. Though not indifferent to issues of efficiency and utility much stressed by economists, the Catholic case for limiting the state proceeds primarily from concerns for human liberty, human flourishing, the instrumental nature of the political community's common good, the demands of Christian love, and the critical moral and social importance of non-state organisations (ranging from the family to intermediate associations), as well as a deep awareness of the power of sin and its effects upon our fallen world.

At an even deeper level, Catholicism rejects the notion that the state – or any other human institution – constitutes the final horizon of human existence. The Church refuses to place its hope of each person's ultimate salvation in the state. Though Catholicism's fundamental attitude to government and law is not negative, the Catholic Church points to a hope that goes not just beyond the state but beyond political activity in general. 'Fear God and honour the Emperor,' proclaims the First Letter of Peter (2:14). And yet, as Joseph Ratzinger once preached in a sermon for Catholic German politicians, 'Christian faith has destroyed the myth of the divine state, the myth of the state as paradise' (Ratzinger, 1988: 151). Put more simply, the infinite necessarily limits the finite.

References

Acton, J. (1948), *Essays on Freedom and Power*, ed. G. Himmelfarb, Boston, MA: Crossroad.

Aquinas, T. (1948), *De Regimine principum ad regem Cypri*, Taurini: Marietti.

Aquinas, T. (1963), *Summa Theologiae*, London: Blackfriars.

Aquinas, T. (1997) *Summa Contra Gentiles*, Notre Dame, IN: University of Notre Dame Press.

Boyle, J. (2001) 'Fairness in holdings: a natural law account of property and welfare rights', *Social Philosophy and Policy*, 18(1).

Brodrick, J. (1950), *Robert Bellarmine, 1541–1621*, London: Longman.

Charles, R., SJ (1998), *Christian Social Witness and Teaching: The Catholic Tradition from Genesis to Centesimus Annus*, vol. 1: *From Biblical Times to the Late Nineteenth Century*, Leominister: Gracewing.

Finnis, J. (1980), *Natural Law and Natural Rights*, Oxford: Clarendon Press.

Finnis, J. (1998), 'Public good: the specifically political common good in Aquinas', in Robert P. George (ed.), *Natural Law and Moral Inquiry: Ethics, Metaphysics, and Politics in the Work of Germain Grisez*, Washington, DC: Georgetown University Press.

Gregg, S. (2007), 'Legal revolution: Sir Thomas More, Christopher Saint Germain, and the schism of Henry VIII', *Ave Maria Law Review*, forthcoming.

Grisez, G. (1993), *The Way of the Lord Jesus*, vol. 2: *Living a Christian Life*, Quincy, IL: Franciscan Press.

More, T. (1931), *The English Works of Sir Thomas More*, ed. W. E. Campbell et al., vol.1, London: Eyre & Spottiswoode.

More, T. (1969), *The Yale Edition of the Complete Works of St Thomas More*, vol. 5, part I: *Responsio ad Lutherum: Latin and English texts*, ed. John M. Headley, New Haven, CT: Yale University Press.

More, T. (1976), *The Yale Edition of the Complete Works of St Thomas More*, vol. 13: *A Treatise upon the Passion*, ed. Garry E. Haupt, New Haven, CT: Yale University Press.

Pinckaers, S., OP (1993), *Les Sources de la morale chrétienne*, 3rd edn, Fribourg: Université de Fribourg.

Ratzinger, J. (1988), *Church, Ecumenism and Politics: New Essays in Ecclesiology*, Middlegreen: St Paul Publications.

Ratzinger, J. (1996), *Salt of the Earth: The Church at the End of the Millennium*, San Francisco, CA: Ignatius Press.

Ratzinger, J. (2006) *Values in a Time of Upheaval*, San Francisco, CA: Ignatius Press.

Suárez, F., SJ (1944), *Selections from Three Works of Francisco Suárez, S.J.: De legibus, ac Deo legislatore, 1612. Defensio fidei catholicae, et apostolicae adversus anglicanae sectae errores, 1613. De triplici virtute theologica, fide, spe, et charitate, 1621*, Oxford: Clarendon Press.

Appendix
MAJOR CHURCH DOCUMENTS TO WHICH THE AUTHORS REFER

Author	Document	Date
John Paul II	*Centesimus annus*	1991
Benedict XVI	*Deus caritas est*	2005
Second Vatican Council	*Dignitatis humanae*	1965
John Paul II	*Dives in misericordia*	1980
John Paul II	*Ecclesia in America*	1999
John Paul II	*Ecclesia in Europa*	2003
John Paul II	*Familiaris consortio*	1982
Second Vatican Council	*Gaudium et spes*	1965
Second Vatican Council	*Gravissimum educationis*	1965
John Paul II	*Laborem exercens*	1981
Second Vatican Council	*Lumen gentium*	1965
John XXIII	*Mater et magistra*	1961
Pius XI	*Mit Brennender Sorge*	1937
Paul VI	*Octogesima adveniens*	1971
John XXIII	*Pacem in terris*	1963
Paul VI	*Populorum progressio*	1967
Pius XI	*Quadragesimo anno*	1931
John Paul II	*Redemptor hominis*	1979
Leo XIII	*Rerum novarum*	1891
John Paul II	*Sollicitudo rei socialis*	1987
John Paul II	*Veritatis splendor*	1993

These documents can be obtained from the Vatican website:
www.vatican.va/phome_en.htm, free of charge

ABOUT THE IEA

The Institute is a research and educational charity (No. CC 235 351), limited by guarantee. Its mission is to improve understanding of the fundamental institutions of a free society by analysing and expounding the role of markets in solving economic and social problems.

The IEA achieves its mission by:

- a high-quality publishing programme
- conferences, seminars, lectures and other events
- outreach to school and college students
- brokering media introductions and appearances

The IEA, which was established in 1955 by the late Sir Antony Fisher, is an educational charity, not a political organisation. It is independent of any political party or group and does not carry on activities intended to affect support for any political party or candidate in any election or referendum, or at any other time. It is financed by sales of publications, conference fees and voluntary donations.

In addition to its main series of publications the IEA also publishes a quarterly journal, *Economic Affairs*.

The IEA is aided in its work by a distinguished international Academic Advisory Council and an eminent panel of Honorary Fellows. Together with other academics, they review prospective IEA publications, their comments being passed on anonymously to authors. All IEA papers are therefore subject to the same rigorous independent refereeing process as used by leading academic journals.

IEA publications enjoy widespread classroom use and course adoptions in schools and universities. They are also sold throughout the world and often translated/reprinted.

Since 1974 the IEA has helped to create a worldwide network of 100 similar institutions in over 70 countries. They are all independent but share the IEA's mission.

Views expressed in the IEA's publications are those of the authors, not those of the Institute (which has no corporate view), its Managing Trustees, Academic Advisory Council members or senior staff.

Members of the Institute's Academic Advisory Council, Honorary Fellows, Trustees and Staff are listed on the following page.

The Institute gratefully acknowledges financial support for its publications programme and other work from a generous benefaction by the late Alec and Beryl Warren.

The Institute of Economic Affairs
2 Lord North Street, Westminster, London SW1P 3LB
Tel: 020 7799 8900
Fax: 020 7799 2137
Email: iea@iea.org.uk
Internet: iea.org.uk

Other papers recently published by the IEA include:

WHO, What and Why?
Transnational Government, Legitimacy and the World Health Organization
Roger Scruton
Occasional Paper 113; ISBN 0 255 36487 3; £8.00

The World Turned Rightside Up
A New Trading Agenda for the Age of Globalisation
John C. Hulsman
Occasional Paper 114; ISBN 0 255 36495 4; £8.00

The Representation of Business in English Literature
Introduced and edited by Arthur Pollard
Readings 53; ISBN 0 255 36491 1; £12.00

Anti-Liberalism 2000
The Rise of New Millennium Collectivism
David Henderson
Occasional Paper 115; ISBN 0 255 36497 0; £7.50

Capitalism, Morality and Markets
Brian Griffiths, Robert A. Sirico, Norman Barry & Frank Field
Readings 54; ISBN 0 255 36496 2; £7.50

A Conversation with Harris and Seldon
Ralph Harris & Arthur Seldon
Occasional Paper 116; ISBN 0 255 36498 9; £7.50

Malaria and the DDT Story
Richard Tren & Roger Bate
Occasional Paper 117; ISBN 0 255 36499 7; £10.00

A Plea to Economists Who Favour Liberty: Assist the Everyman
Daniel B. Klein
Occasional Paper 118; ISBN 0 255 36501 2; £10.00

The Changing Fortunes of Economic Liberalism
Yesterday, Today and Tomorrow
David Henderson
Occasional Paper 105 (new edition); ISBN 0 255 36520 9; £12.50

The Global Education Industry
Lessons from Private Education in Developing Countries
James Tooley
Hobart Paper 141 (new edition); ISBN 0 255 36503 9; £12.50

Saving Our Streams
The Role of the Anglers' Conservation Association in
Protecting English and Welsh Rivers
Roger Bate
Research Monograph 53; ISBN 0 255 36494 6; £10.00

Better Off Out?
The Benefits or Costs of EU Membership
Brian Hindley & Martin Howe
Occasional Paper 99 (new edition); ISBN 0 255 36502 0; £10.00

Buckingham at 25
Freeing the Universities from State Control
Edited by James Tooley
Readings 55; ISBN 0 255 36512 8; £15.00

Lectures on Regulatory and Competition Policy
Irwin M. Stelzer
Occasional Paper 120; ISBN 0 255 36511 X; £12.50

Misguided Virtue
False Notions of Corporate Social Responsibility
David Henderson
Hobart Paper 142; ISBN 0 255 36510 1; £12.50

HIV and Aids in Schools
The Political Economy of Pressure Groups and Miseducation
Barrie Craven, Pauline Dixon, Gordon Stewart & James Tooley
Occasional Paper 121; ISBN 0 255 36522 5; £10.00

The Road to Serfdom
The Reader's Digest *condensed version*
Friedrich A. Hayek
Occasional Paper 122; ISBN 0 255 36530 6; £7.50

Bastiat's *The Law*
Introduction by Norman Barry
Occasional Paper 123; ISBN 0 255 36509 8; £7.50

A Globalist Manifesto for Public Policy
Charles Calomiris
Occasional Paper 124; ISBN 0 255 36525 x; £7.50

Euthanasia for Death Duties
Putting Inheritance Tax Out of Its Misery
Barry Bracewell-Milnes
Research Monograph 54; ISBN 0 255 36513 6; £10.00

Liberating the Land
The Case for Private Land-use Planning
Mark Pennington
Hobart Paper 143; ISBN 0 255 36508 x; £10.00

IEA Yearbook of Government Performance 2002/2003
Edited by Peter Warburton
Yearbook 1; ISBN 0 255 36532 2; £15.00

Britain's Relative Economic Performance, 1870–1999
Nicholas Crafts
Research Monograph 55; ISBN 0 255 36524 1; £10.00

Should We Have Faith in Central Banks?
Otmar Issing
Occasional Paper 125; ISBN 0 255 36528 4; £7.50

The Dilemma of Democracy
Arthur Seldon
Hobart Paper 136 (reissue); ISBN 0 255 36536 5; £10.00

Capital Controls: a 'Cure' Worse Than the Problem?
Forrest Capie
Research Monograph 56; ISBN 0 255 36506 3; £10.00

The Poverty of 'Development Economics'
Deepak Lal
Hobart Paper 144 (reissue); ISBN 0 255 36519 5; £15.00

Should Britain Join the Euro?
The Chancellor's Five Tests Examined
Patrick Minford
Occasional Paper 126; ISBN 0 255 36527 6; £7.50

Post-Communist Transition: Some Lessons
Leszek Balcerowicz
Occasional Paper 127; ISBN 0 255 36533 0; £7.50

A Tribute to Peter Bauer
John Blundell et al.
Occasional Paper 128; ISBN 0 255 36531 4; £10.00

Employment Tribunals
Their Growth and the Case for Radical Reform
J. R. Shackleton
Hobart Paper 145; ISBN 0 255 36515 2; £10.00

Fifty Economic Fallacies Exposed
Geoffrey E. Wood
Occasional Paper 129; ISBN 0 255 36518 7; £12.50

A Market in Airport Slots
Keith Boyfield (editor), David Starkie, Tom Bass & Barry Humphreys
Readings 56; ISBN 0 255 36505 5; £10.00

Money, Inflation and the Constitutional Position of the Central Bank
Milton Friedman & Charles A. E. Goodhart
Readings 57; ISBN 0 255 36538 1; £10.00

railway.com
Parallels between the Early British Railways and the ICT Revolution
Robert C. B. Miller
Research Monograph 57; ISBN 0 255 36534 9; £12.50

The Regulation of Financial Markets
Edited by Philip Booth & David Currie
Readings 58; ISBN 0 255 36551 9; £12.50

Climate Alarmism Reconsidered
Robert L. Bradley Jr
Hobart Paper 146; ISBN 0 255 36541 1; £12.50

Government Failure: E. G. West on Education
Edited by James Tooley & James Stanfield
Occasional Paper 130; ISBN 0 255 36552 7; £12.50

Corporate Governance: Accountability in the Marketplace
Elaine Sternberg
Second edition
Hobart Paper 147; ISBN 0 255 36542 X; £12.50

The Land Use Planning System
Evaluating Options for Reform
John Corkindale
Hobart Paper 148; ISBN 0 255 36550 0; £10.00

Economy and Virtue
Essays on the Theme of Markets and Morality
Edited by Dennis O'Keeffe
Readings 59; ISBN 0 255 36504 7; £12.50

Free Markets Under Siege
Cartels, Politics and Social Welfare
Richard A. Epstein
Occasional Paper 132; ISBN 0 255 36553 5; £10.00

Unshackling Accountants
D. R. Myddelton
Hobart Paper 149; ISBN 0 255 36559 4; £12.50

The Euro as Politics
Pedro Schwartz
Research Monograph 58; ISBN 0 255 36535 7; £12.50

Pricing Our Roads
Vision and Reality
Stephen Glaister & Daniel J. Graham
Research Monograph 59; ISBN 0 255 36562 4; £10.00

The Role of Business in the Modern World
Progress, Pressures, and Prospects for the Market Economy
David Henderson
Hobart Paper 150; ISBN 0 255 36548 9; £12.50

Public Service Broadcasting Without the BBC?
Alan Peacock
Occasional Paper 133; ISBN 0 255 36565 9; £10.00

The ECB and the Euro: the First Five Years
Otmar Issing
Occasional Paper 134; ISBN 0 255 36555 1; £10.00

Towards a Liberal Utopia?
Edited by Philip Booth
Hobart Paperback 32; ISBN 0 255 36563 2; £15.00

The Way Out of the Pensions Quagmire
Philip Booth & Deborah Cooper
Research Monograph 60; ISBN 0 255 36517 9; £12.50

Black Wednesday
A Re-examination of Britain's Experience in the Exchange Rate Mechanism
Alan Budd
Occasional Paper 135; ISBN 0 255 36566 7; £7.50

Crime: Economic Incentives and Social Networks
Paul Ormerod
Hobart Paper 151; ISBN 0 255 36554 3; £10.00

The Road to Serfdom *with* **The Intellectuals and Socialism**
Friedrich A. Hayek
Occasional Paper 136; ISBN 0 255 36576 4; £10.00

Money and Asset Prices in Boom and Bust
Tim Congdon
Hobart Paper 152; ISBN 0 255 36570 5; £10.00

The Dangers of Bus Re-regulation
and Other Perspectives on Markets in Transport
John Hibbs et al.
Occasional Paper 137; ISBN 0 255 36572 1; £10.00

The New Rural Economy
Change, Dynamism and Government Policy
Berkeley Hill et al.
Occasional Paper 138; ISBN 0 255 36546 2; £15.00

The Benefits of Tax Competition
Richard Teather
Hobart Paper 153; ISBN 0 255 36569 1; £12.50

Wheels of Fortune
Self-funding Infrastructure and the Free Market Case for a Land Tax
Fred Harrison
Hobart Paper 154; ISBN 0 255 36589 6; £12.50

Were 364 Economists All Wrong?
Edited by Philip Booth
Readings 60
ISBN-13: 978 0 255 36588 8; £10.00

Europe After the 'No' Votes
Mapping a New Economic Path
Patrick A. Messerlin
Occasional Paper 139
ISBN-13: 978 0 255 36580 2; £10.00

The Railways, the Market and the Government
John Hibbs et al.
Readings 61
ISBN-13: 978 0 255 36567 3; £12.50

Corruption: The World's Big C
Cases, Causes, Consequences, Cures
Ian Senior
Research Monograph 61
ISBN-13: 978 0 255 36571 0; £12.50

Sir Humphrey's Legacy
Facing Up to the Cost of Public Sector Pensions
Neil Record
Hobart Paper 156
ISBN-13: 978 0 255 36578 9; £10.00

The Economics of Law
Cento Veljanovski
Second edition
Hobart Paper 157
ISBN-13: 978 0 255 36561 1; £12.50

Living with Leviathan
Public Spending, Taxes and Economic Performance
David B. Smith
Hobart Paper 158
ISBN-13: 978 0 255 36579 6; £12.50

The Vote Motive
Gordon Tullock
New edition
Hobart Paperback 33
ISBN-13: 978 0 255 36577 2; £10.00

Waging the War of Ideas
John Blundell
Third edition
Occasional Paper 131
ISBN-13: 978 0 255 36606 9; £12.50

The War Between the State and the Family
How Government Divides and Impoverishes
Patricia Morgan
Hobart Paper 159
ISBN-13: 978 0 255 36596 3; £10.00

All the listed IEA papers, including those that are out of print, can be downloaded from www.iea.org.uk. Purchases can also be made through the website. To order copies of currently available IEA papers, or to enquire about availability, please contact:

Gazelle
IEA orders
FREEPOST RLYS-EAHU-YSCZ
White Cross Mills
Hightown
Lancaster LA1 4XS

Tel: 01524 68765
Fax: 01524 63232
Email: sales@gazellebooks.co.uk

The IEA also offers a subscription service to its publications. For a single annual payment, currently £40.00 in the UK, you will receive every monograph the IEA publishes during the course of a year and discounts on our extensive back catalogue. For more information, please contact:

Adam Myers
Subscriptions
The Institute of Economic Affairs
2 Lord North Street
London SW1P 3LB

Tel: 020 7799 8920
Fax: 020 7799 2137
Website: www.iea.org.uk